WOMEN AT WORK

Women at Work

An Economic Perspective

Edited by

TITO BOERI
DANIELA DEL BOCA
CHRISTOPHER PISSARIDES

with

Rolf Aaberge, Giuseppe Bertola, Ugo Colombino, Giovanni Andrea Cornia,
John Ermisch, Gøsta Esping-Andersen, Marco Francesconi,
Pietro Garibaldi, Florence Jaumotte, Valérie Lechene, Claudia Olivetti,
Silvia Pasqua, Barbara Petrongolo, Richard Rogerson,
Steinar Strøm and Etienne Wasmer

OXFORD
UNIVERSITY PRESS

This book has been printed digitally and produced in a standard specification
in order to ensure its continuing availability

OXFORD
UNIVERSITY PRESS

Great Clarendon Street, Oxford OX2 6DP

Oxford University Press is a department of the University of Oxford.
It furthers the University's objective of excellence in research, scholarship,
and education by publishing worldwide in

Oxford New York

Auckland Cape Town Dar es Salaam Hong Kong Karachi
Kuala Lumpur Madrid Melbourne Mexico City Nairobi
New Delhi Shanghai Taipei Toronto
With offices in
Argentina Austria Brazil Chile Czech Republic France Greece
Guatemala Hungary Italy Japan South Korea Poland Portugal
Singapore Switzerland Thailand Turkey Ukraine Vietnam

ISBN 978-0-19-928188-6

Acknowledgements

The two studies that make up the Reports in this volume were originally prepared for the fifth European conference of the *Fondazione Rodolfo Debenedetti*, which was held in Alghero in June 2003. The reports draw a lot on the discussion in Alghero, which involved an audience of qualified academicians, professional economists, representatives of unions and employers' associations, industrialists, and policy makers.

Needless to say, we are very much indebted to all those who attended that conference and contributed actively to the discussion. In particular, we wish to express our gratitude to Anna Diamantopoulou, European Commissioner for Employment and Social Affairs for her insightful opening remarks; to Anna Maria Loi, Head of the Equal Opportunities Commission at Regione Sardegna, for her contribution to the discussion, and to Michaela Erbenova for her contribution on the specific issue of women's participation in formerly planned economies. We also wish to thank Marco Tedde, the Mayor of Alghero, for his warm hospitality, and Agar Brugiavini and Chiara Saraceno for having skilfully chaired the two sessions of the conference. We are very grateful to Carlo De Benedetti, who both arranged this event and opened the conference. Finanical support from the Center for Household, Labor and Demographic Economics (CHILD) is also gratefully acknowledged.

A special thank you to Giovanna Albano, Mauro Maggioni and Roberta Marcaletti, who assisted Pietro Garibaldi and myself in the organization of the conference. I am also grateful to Francesco Fasani and Domenico Tabasso who contributed to the final stages of preparation of the event.

Contents

**Part II. Women's Participation in the Labor Market
and Fertility: The Effects of Social Policies**   121

Rolf Aaberge, Ugo Colombino, Daniela Del Boca (ed.)
John Ermisch, Marco Francesconi, Silvia Pasqua and Steinar Strøm

List of Figures

List of Tables

List of Tables

List of Contributors

Rolf Aaberge, Research Department Statistics, Norway

Giuseppe Bertola, European University Institute, Fiesole and University of Turin

Tito Boeri, Bocconi University and Fondazione RDB

Ugo Colombino, University of Turin and Child

Giovanni Andrea Cornia, University of Florence and CAPORDE

Daniela Del Boca, University of Turin and Child

John Ermisch, University of Essex

Gøsta Esping-Andersen, Universitat Pompeu Fabra

Marco Francesconi, University of Essex

Pietro Garibaldi, Bocconi University and Fondazione RDB

Florence Jaumotte, OECD

Valérie Lechene, Oxford University and **Giovanni Andrea Cornia,** University of Florence and CAPORDE

Claudia Olivetti, Boston University

Silvia Pasqua, University of Turin and Child

Barbara Petrongolo, London School of Economics

Christopher Pissarides, London School of Economics

Richard Rogerson, Arizona State University

Steinar Strøm, University of Oslo and University of Turin

Etienne Wasmer, Ecares, Université Libre de Bruxelles

Introduction

More Women at Work in Europe

This volume is about gender gaps in employment and wages, participation of women in the labor market, fertility and the welfare of children. It discusses how the trend towards the greater participation of women in labor markets interacts with gender differences in pay. It dwells on the scope for further increasing the number of women in the labor force in Europe without negatively affecting the cognitive development of children and, more generally, their early childhood experience. The policy relevance of the findings in this volume is self-evident: the Heads of Governments of the EU agreed five years ago, at the Spring 2000 Lisbon meeting of the European Council, to accelerate the trend towards the greater participation of women in the labor force. But the means of achieving this target, and the trade-offs involved when more women are pushed into paid employment by policy measures were not discussed, either in Lisbon or in the subsequent Spring European Councils. Any policy of the magnitude of the Lisbon agenda must involve losers somewhere along the line and ignoring such trade-offs puts at risk the entire reform process. The aim of this volume, then, is to contribute to a better-informed policy debate about these issues, and hopefully to a more realistic set of targets and policies for Europe.

Women at Work: this is the stylized fact

If there is a stylized fact characterizing postwar OECD labor markets, it is the womenization of the labor force. Wherever you go, whatever statistics you look at, a marked decline in the gender employment gap is noticeable—the difference in employment rates between men and women. The gap has not yet been eliminated anywhere, although some countries, notably the Nordics, get very close to a one-to-one female to male employment rate.

More women at work does not necessarily imply a more egalitarian distribution of pay between men and women. In fact, wage differentials between men and women are wider in countries with the largest female employment rates. For instance, the United States displays a significantly larger gender wage gap than Europe does, but has a female employment rate up to 10 percentage points higher than the EU average. Similarly, within the European Union, countries with the greatest labor market participation of women display the greatest differentials in average pay between men and women.

How can it be that the employment gap is narrowing down just as the wage gap is expanding? Or, at least, it is not contracting, in spite of equal opportunity legislation and ongoing changes in social norms which recognize a greater role for women in the world of work. A key explanation provided in this volume is that a greater spread in wages contributes to the increase in the participation of women, by allowing more job creation in services, and enabling the startup of many low-skill self-employment activities. Thus, greater wage differentials, including relatively large *gender* pay gaps, are often the outcome of the same processes that reduce the gender *employment* gap. It is important to eliminate discrimination between men and women in the labor market, but eliminating discrimination does not necessarily mean average equal pay between men and women. On average, men have more work experience, and experience is rewarded with higher pay. At least initially, when female employment rates rise, it may be necessary to accept greater differentials in pay as unavoidable. Wage differentials between men and women should decline later on, when women move up the occupational ladder and acquire more work experience. If there is a sequencing in the closure of the gender gaps, it involves closing the employment gap first, and only later the wage gap, through the occupational promotion of women.

Lisbon and Beyond

In Lisbon in March 2000, the Heads of Governments of the European Union subscribed to the very ambitious goal of raising the employment rate of both men and women by almost 10 percentage points in less than ten years. This goal can only be achieved by the greater participation of women. Indeed, the EU leaders defined a specific, and even more ambitious, target for women: their employment rate should rise to 60 per cent from 54 per cent in less than ten years, by 2010. This involves a marked acceleration of the trend in the number of women at work when compared with previous decades.

However, accelerating job creation for the benefit of women will require some relaxation of institutional structures, which are compressing wages from below. As argued above, many women typically enter the labor market in low-skill occupations, which can survive only if they can pay low wages. The reason for the low pay is not necessarily discrimination. Women who are outside the labor force, like young workers, are often inexperienced, and sometimes have only basic education and skills. When wage structures are compressed from below, the number of jobs that can be created at the low end of the productivity spectrum are limited, restricting an important stepping stone for women into better and more rewarding jobs.

One year after Lisbon, in 2001, the Spring EU Council in Stockholm implicitly acknowledged the risk that, in fact, a fast track to Lisbon could increase the gender wage gap, when it added a strong equal opportunities content to the Lisbon strategy. But gender wage gaps do not disappear simply by stating that men and women should be treated equally, especially at a time of the acceleration of women's entry into the labor market. Also, it is necessary for women to spend longer in their jobs and acquire skills and experience.

As shown in Part I of this volume, it is possible to attain the Lisbon target in southern Europe by 2010 by freezing all jobs currently held by women until they reach the age of 65. This, however, does not appear feasible at present. Employment rates are strongly declining with age: women at work typically retire at ages 50 and 55 in these countries, driven mainly by the generous pension benefits that are available to them at this age. Evidence shows that the supply of women's labor is more responsive to changes in pension benefits than is the labor supply of men. Given that women live longer than men, more generous pension systems reward women more than men. If we are to reach the Lisbon goals, something will have to be done to reform pension systems, in order to reduce the incentives to retire early.

Because many jobs can be done by both men and women, an acceleration of the womenization of the workforce may also involve, at least temporarily, some crowding out of groups with a weak attachment to the labor market. The most likely groups to be affected are youths, who, like women, are new entrants to the labor market, with low occupational experience. This has partly occurred in countries that have experienced a relatively fast and sizeable increase in female employment rates. But over time, as women at work acquire more job-related experience, they no longer compete for jobs with young people. Female employment eventually complements male (and youth) employment, encouraging the creation of new jobs. Contrary to popular wisdom, there is no such thing as a fixed labor pool that has to be shared by men and women: women at work do not reduce job opportunities for men, although in the short run, a steep increase in women's employment rates may create some distributional tensions. More women at work sooner or later contribute to more job creation to everyone's benefit.

More women at work may also negatively affect fertility rates in a Continent where the population is rapidly ageing and therefore in desperate need of more children. 'Old Europe' may get even older, while 'New Europe' disappointingly, is not rejuvenating the European population: the new member countries of the European Union are ageing almost as rapidly as the rest of Europe, although many EU Members could learn from the experience of the Scandinavian countries. The same goes for the new members of the European Union which experienced a sharp drop in female employment rates in their transition from central planning to a market economy. The way in which the state treats women with children at work, in terms of childcare facilities or tax benefits available, are key to this concern.

The welfare of children may also be badly affected insofar as their mothers devote less time to childcare. This is more likely to happen when jobs available to mothers are full-time, the child is young and there is no second parent (father). Or, if there is one, because of social norms and career concerns, he does not substitute for the working mother when she has young children. Again, a key to avoiding such unfavorable outcomes would be a new set of policy instruments that enables more flexibility in the types of jobs that women with children can get, without putting at risk their job security and promotion prospects.

Outline of the volume

Our research suggests that a faster womenization of the workforce is desirable, but that this also involves a number of relevant trade-offs, which need to be carefully assessed with pragmatism and without prejudice. The task set out in this volume is to characterize the relevant trade-offs and propose policies reducing the opportunity costs of increasing participation.

As in previous books for the Fondazione Rodolfo Debenedetti, this volume assembles contributions from two teams of leading scholars in the field. Part I presents reports from the first team, which was co-ordinated by Christopher Pissarides and includes Pietro Garibaldi, Claudia Olivetti, Barbara Petrongolo and Etienne Wasmer. It focuses on the labor market outcomes of women and their interactions with other groups in the labor force. Part II is devoted to the contribution of the second team, led by Daniela Del Boca and includes Rolf Aaberge, Ugo Colombino, John Ermisch, Marco Francesconi, Silvia Pasqua and Steinar Strom. It dwells on the family–employment trade-offs, and on its implications for the design of taxation and social policy.

Implications for Policy

The two parts in the volume together provide important reading on the indications for policy. To give an example, the deregulation of labor markets should be accompanied by measures 'greasing the wheels' of flows from temporary to permanent employment. This is because women often tend to concentrate on the many flexible contractual types created by the partial labor market reforms carried out in Europe in the last decade. If women feel stuck in such temporary jobs, they may decide either not to have children, because they do not have the secure income required to raise a family: or, they may abandon work altogether and focus on the family if they do not have financial needs. If women are to combine family with work, it is important to make sure that labor market reforms do not increase gender segregation. For example, one might envisage tax-deductions or other incentives for the conversion of temporary into permanent contracts for women. Longer-term contractual arrangements for women should also encourage investment in job-specific human capital, reducing the likelihood of women competing for jobs with young workers.

By comparing the two parts of the volume, one gets the impression that Europe may be characterized by two equilibria: one includes the southern countries, which display low participation of women and low fertility; the other is dominated by the Nordic countries, which have very high participation rates, and fertility rates above the EU average. Within the first group of countries, those countries that have higher female participation rates have lower fertility rates, but within the second group of countries, countries with higher female participation rates also have higher fertility rates. Why? There are probably several self-fulfilling mechanisms at work. Some of these mechanisms may be tax-related: having fewer women at work means having a narrower tax base; this prevents the financing of family–friendly policies which could attenuate, or even reverse, the family-employment trade-off.

A second explanation for the presence of two equilibria is related to inertia in social norms which traditionally assign a greater role to men in the labor market. Insofar as such values change only when the children of working mothers start their own families, a vicious circle is set in motion whereby countries with few mothers at work tend to oppose policies and childcare infrastructures that might support more employment for women with children. This leads to the conclusion that cultural change is needed alongside economic incentives to increase women's participation. Otherwise, southern countries will struggle to move to the high-high equilibrium of northern Europe: it may take more than one generation reaching retirement age before norms can be changed from within.

A survey carried out by Fondazione Rodolfo Debenedetti in May 2003 confirms the impression that this type of mechanism is indeed at work in southern countries. A very small fraction of children aged 0 to 3 are in kindergartens in Italy. Asked whether this limited use of formal childcare facilities was due to a lack of affordable kindergartens, or to a preference of families for informal childcare by grandmothers and relatives, a majority of Italian families opted for the second explanation. This means that policies encouraging formal childcare, which are often carried out in the Nordic countries, may be quite ineffective in southern countries, where more neutral (with respect to the choice between formal and informal childcare) policies to encourage fertility, together with employment, should possibly be devised. This survey provides a strong case for having heterogeneous social policies in a heterogeneous Europe. It is not the first time, nor is it likely to be the last, that a book of the Fondazione Rodolfo Debenedetti reaches this conclusion.

* * *

Can we draw from this heterogeneity in social Europe some lessons as to the type of policies which are most effective in reconciling the employment of women, the welfare of children and fertility? Part II argues for a 'convex combination' of work and motherhood, along the Nordic social policy model. The model should combine part-time employment, childcare and parental leave following the birth of a child with limited effects on career prospects.

However, this requires a richer welfare state, which may not yet be affordable in countries with a narrow tax base. Moreover, as argued in Part I, relative wages of women are negatively affected by these types of arrangements. As argued by Gøsta Esping-Andersen in his insightful final remarks, the gender wage gap will perhaps be filled only when a more balanced sharing of childcare and family responsibilities between the two parents is found.

There is yet another lesson which can be drawn from the second part of the volume, where econometric evidence and simulation exercises for Italy and Norway are reported. In light of the higher wage elasticity of labor supply that characterizes women and individuals at low and average income levels, marginal tax reductions for low wage earners would have the potential to achieve two goals simultaneously. On the one hand, they would contribute to reducing gender inequalities in the distribution of income after tax. On the other hand, they would increase rewards from participation in the labor market of women, thereby accelerating the convergence of male and female employment rates. This is confirmed by the macroeconomic and the microeconomic evidence produced in the first and the second parts of this volume respectively.

Another important policy implication of this volume is that minimum guaranteed income schemes, a negative income tax or workfare systems, may contribute to increasing female labor supply. This is so because there is evidence that if a way is found to increase two incomes from work, more women will want to come into the labor market and seek employment. Therefore such policy instruments might also simultaneously contribute to a higher female employment, a lower gender gap and a more equal income distribution, partly offsetting the persistently large gender wage gaps documented in Part I of this volume.

Tito Boeri

PART I

WOMEN IN THE LABOR FORCE: HOW WELL IS EUROPE DOING?

Christopher Pissarides, Pietro Garibaldi, Claudia Olivetti,
Barbara Petrongolo and Etienne Wasmer*

* The authors would like to thank the discussants at the conference, Richard Rogerson, Florence Jaumotte, Tito Boeri and Giuseppe Bertola for their comments. We also thank Evangelia Vourvachaki of the London School of Economics for her research assistance.

1

Introduction

Women have made important advances in labor markets. The distinctions between the activities of single and married women are not as sharp as they used to be, and ambition to do well in a job is no longer restricted to men. Have European nations done enough to include women in their labor markets and take full advantage of the economic potential in them, and are our labor markets as kind towards women as they are towards men? Are women satisfied with their opportunities and outcomes in the labor market? And are other demographic groups benefitting or are they hurt from the competition for jobs from women?

In this chapter we address these and other questions from a variety of viewpoints. The focus is on the labor market: how many women have jobs, what jobs do they have, how much do they earn, and are labor markets giving them the chance to exploit their potential? We focus on Europe, but sometimes compare with the United States and other OECD countries where employment rates of women are high. We support the view that bringing about reforms that raise female employment rates will make both the women affected and society as a whole better off. To bring more women into the labor force means to increase the gross national product through the introduction of new activities and through the recording of activities that were hitherto unrecorded and protected from taxation and regulation. It thus corrects a distortion in the tax system: that market activities are taxed but home activities are not—and in the process the tax base is increased, which should make it easier for governments to manage their finances. In a longer-run perspective, when more of a country's population is trained and put into productive use, competing for jobs and for markets worldwide, improves the country's chances that it will make more discoveries and grow faster, with benefits for everyone.

Can Europe do better than it is currently doing? European leaders certainly think we can. In the *Presidency Conclusions* of the European Union Council in Lisbon, which took place in March 2000, and which set the agenda for employment in the Union for the next ten years, women featured prominently. Further elaborations took place in follow-up meetings in Barcelona and Stockholm, again emphasizing the role of women. The overall target for female employment is currently set at 57 per cent of the population of working age for the year 2005, and 60 per cent for the year 2010. The targets for total employment are 67 and 70 per cent respectively. Not every country is required to achieve the average target but the evaluation of progress is usually done by comparing each country's performance with the average.

The European employment agenda is as much about overall numbers as about the quality of jobs. The emphasis is on 'better' jobs, a term that is still awaiting proper definition from the Commission, and on a 'knowledge-based' economy dominated by jobs in services. The focus on education with modern electronic means and on the use of the Internet as a means of improving economic organization are welcome. It is still too early to make an evaluation of this objective. The focus on services is inevitable: service jobs account for the entire net job growth since the war and for the employment gap between Europe and the United States. But low-skill and low-paid jobs also need to be done and one of our objectives in this report is to look at the whole range of jobs and ask whether our labor market institutions are helping job creation everywhere. It is certainly the case that much of the employment gap between Europe and the United States is in low-wage service jobs, such as jobs in retailing and personal services, although gaps also exist in more complex service jobs, such as professional financial services.

We examine first the current situation with overall employment patterns and ask why there are such big differences in employment rates across Europe. We find that although European countries have had access to the same technologies that have helped American women leave the home and enter employment, not all European countries are taking advantage of these technologies. A lot of the employment rise in Europe over the last two decades is due to more favorable economic conditions. We identify some rigid institutional structures that inhibit job creation for women, such as rigidity in the establishment of small enterprises, which are a dominant form of employment growth in service industries. We conclude, however, that there are still big gaps in our knowledge of the reasons for the large differences in employment patterns, which are most pronounced when we compare northern European countries with the Mediterranean south.

When we ask what kind of jobs women hold, we find that in some countries large fractions of them hold part-time jobs. However, we find that women in part-time jobs derive as much job satisfaction as those in full-time jobs, in contrast to temporary jobs, which are less sought after.

Following the analysis of employment patterns, we turn to a close examination of wage earnings and the wage gap between men and women. As part of the overall employment targets of Lisbon, the European Union also requires equality of employment opportunity and wage earnings, and has set targets for the male–female gap in earnings. We find evidence that the wage gap is still present, although it has probably narrowed. A proper evaluation of relative wage gaps across Europe shows that there are no big differences across countries, and wage gaps are closely connected with overall levels of inequality and with the skill of the worker—low-skill workers being the most vulnerable to discrimination.

An examination of the competition for jobs in the labor market reveals that women probably compete more with young workers than with prime-age males. We suggest policy options to deal both with the objectives of the European Employment Strategy and with the competition for jobs between women and young workers.

Chapter 2 sets out some facts about employment and Chapters 3–5 examine, in turn, overall employment patterns, the types of jobs held by women and the earnings of women relative to the earnings of men. Section 6 looks at the consequences of female entry for other groups in the labor market and Chapter 7 brings together our evaluation of the European employment targets and our policy suggestions for improvement.

2

Women's Employment Patterns:
Some Facts

We begin with some facts about female employment rates in 15 European countries (Norway and 15 European Union members except for Luxembourg), Canada and the United States. We divide the 15 European countries into four groups: Mediterranean (Spain, Italy, Greece), Nordic (Sweden, Finland, Norway, Denmark), Anglo-Saxon (United Kingdom) and rest of Europe (Austria, Belgium, France, Germany, Ireland, Netherlands and Portugal). We show that there are substantial differences between the four groups, but fewer differences within each group. This is especially true of the Nordic and Mediterranean countries, with the rest of Europe showing more within-group differences. Our classification also reflects substantial differences in the organization of the welfare state, particularly so between the Nordic and Mediterranean countries.[1] The fact that the biggest differences in the welfare state and in female employment rates are both between the Nordic and Mediterranean countries is not likely to be coincidental, although with some important exceptions (e.g. in the provision of subsidized childcare) there are no clear-cut correlations between female employment rates and measurable features of the welfare state.

Table 2.1 records the progress made by women in the total employment rate since 1960 and the distance that needs to be covered to meet the Lisbon objectives. A glance at performance in 2000, shows the gaps that are still substantial are in the Mediterranean countries, and in Belgium, France and Ireland. Figure 2.1 shows that the employment gap is due mainly to inactivity, although some differences are also due to unemployment differentials. Nevertheless, the patterns shown in Figure 2.1 allow us to talk about successes or failures in either participation or employment without the risk of major inconsistencies.[2]

Figures 2.2 and 2.3 show that there is a correlation across countries between the employment performance of men and women. Although some of the correlation shown in Figure 2.2 is due to the business cycle, which affects both

---

[1] See for example Bertola et al. (2001) and references to the political literature mentioned there.

[2] Since the completion of this study we became aware of a study by Genre et al. (2003) which examines cross-country differences in participation rates, obtaining results that are similar to ours. We are grateful to Anna Lamo for making available to us both the data used in their study and a preliminary draft of their paper.

Table 2.1. *Female employment rates, 1960–2000 persons aged 15 to 64 years*

	1960	1980	2000	Men, 2000	Lisbon distance
Nordic	40.5	64.3	70.3	78.6	10.3
Denmark	42.7	66.2	71.2	80.4	11.2
Finland	54.9	65.0	64.3	69.7	4.3
Norway	26.1	58.4	73.4	88.1	13.4
Sweden	38.1	67.6	72.1	76.2	12.1
Anglo-Saxon	43.1	54.5	65.2	79.3	5.2
United Kingdom	43.1	54.5	65.2	79.3	5.2
Mediterranean		30.8	40.1	69.7	−19.9
Greece		30.7	40.4	70.2	−19.6
Italy	28.1	33.2	39.7	68.5	−20.3
Spain	21.0	28.4	40.3	70.3	−19.7
Rest of Europe		41.0	56.6	74.4	−3.4
Austria		52.4	59.3	78.1	−0.7
Belgium	29.6	35.0	51.1	69.8	−8.9
France	42.9	50.0	53.1	68.1	−6.9
Germany	35.0	34.8	58.1	73.5	−1.9
Ireland		32.2	52.2	74.0	−7.8
Netherlands		35.7	62.1	81.1	2.1
Portugal		47.1	60.1	75.9	0.1
North America		53.1	66.6	77.8	
United States	39.5	53.9	68.0	80.4	
Canada		52.3	65.1	75.2	
Average			58.6	75.2	

Note: Lisbon distance is the percentage difference between the female employment rate in 2000 and 60 per cent.
Source: OECD 2000.

female and male employment rates, most of it is due to the correlation between the employment rates of men over 55 and women. The European Union has a target for the overall employment rate of the over-55 year-olds ('active ageing'), which is 50 per cent by 2010. It appears that the countries that are failing the EU targets in the female labor market are also failing them in the labor market for older persons.

The gender employment gap, defined as the difference in the employment rate between men and women, is falling in all countries in our sample. On average, the gender gap nearly halved since 1980, from 30 per cent to 16.7 per cent by the year 2000. The fall in the gender gap was mainly due to the rising female employment rate, which took place in all countries in our sample, but also to a falling employment rate for men, especially for the older groups.

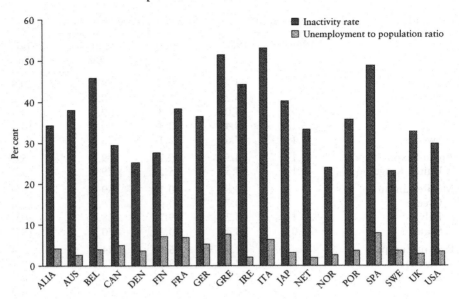

Figure 2.1. *Female inactivity and unemployment as per cent of population of working age, 2000*

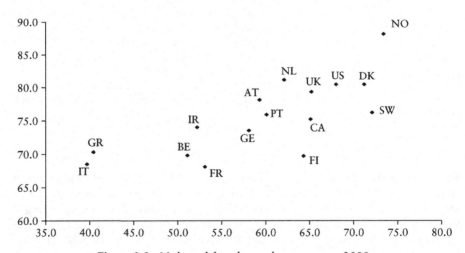

Figure 2.2. *Male and female employment rate, 2000*

Women tend to work on average fewer hours each week than men, so focusing on the gender employment gap understates the difference in the supply of hours of work from each gender. We show next some facts about part-time employment, which demonstrates this point. Whether the European Union should also have an agenda for reducing the differential in hours of work,

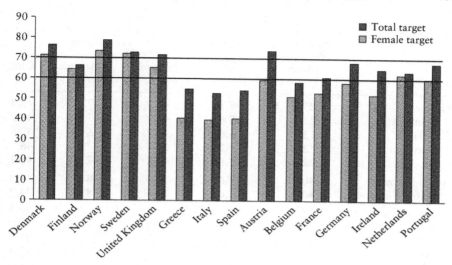

Figure 2.3. *Male and female distance from Lisbon target, 2000*

however, is a difficult question. Men and women may have different preferences about part-time and full-time jobs, given family circumstances and other
sources of family income, in which case the focus of the European Employment
Strategy on employment rather than on hours of work is the correct one.[3] We
address this question in more depth in Chapter 4.

The experience of European countries with part-time jobs is varied. Table 2.2
gives the incidence of part-time employment for men and women (the fraction of
jobs held which require on average less than 30 hours a week) and the share of
women in full-time and part-time employment. The incidence of part-time work
among women is lowest in the Nordic countries (with the exception of Norway),
where the rate is comparable to the rate in North America. The female share of
full-time and part-time work in the Nordic countries is also close to the North
American share. In the rest of Europe, however, there is generally more incidence of part-time work, with women accounting for a bigger share of part-time
employment. Whether we view the growth of part-time employment as a
transitional phase, towards the integration of women into the full-time labor
market, or as a regular occurrence that provides diversity for the women who
want it, is a moot point. We will address some of these issues later in this report.

The Netherlands has the highest incidence of part-time work, with 57 per cent
of employed women working part-time, and Norway and the United Kingdom

---

[3] Of course, one can make the same preferences argument about overall employment, namely,
that men and women may have different tastes about work and home, and the European Union
should not be imposing employment targets across the board. But it would be hard to claim that
a gender employment gap in the Mediterranean countries of 30 points is due to women's
preferences, when the gaps in other European countries are so much less.

Table 2.2. *Women and part-time work*

	Incidence of part-time		Female share		
	Women	Men	Full-time work	Part-time work	Total
Nordic	25.6	8.1	41.9	72.1	47.3
Denmark	23.9	8.6	42.4	71.2	46.9
Finland	13.5	6.6	45.7	64.9	47.6
Norway	42.5	9.7	35.7	79.1	46.7
Sweden	22.6	7.6	43.8	73.3	48.2
Anglo-Saxon	40.2	7.6	34.6	81.3	44.9
United Kingdom	40.2	7.6	34.6	81.3	44.9
Mediterranean	16.3	3.6	34.2	72.4	37.4
Greece	9.2	2.9	36.4	66.5	38.0
Italy	23.4	5.5	32.3	71.3	37.0
Spain	16.4	2.5	33.8	79.5	37.3
Rest of Europe	34.5	6.6	34.7	81.0	43.2
Austria	24.3	2.3	37.9	89.2	44.1
Belgium	34.4	6.9	35.1	79.4	42.3
France	24.8	5.3	39.2	79.2	44.9
Germany	33.7	4.4	35.2	85.8	43.9
Ireland	32.9	7.5	33.6	75.6	41.2
Netherlands	57.1	13.0	27.1	76.8	42.9
Portugal	12.6	3.0	42.7	77.9	45.3
North America	23.2	8.6	42.1	70.0	46.4
United States (1999)	19.4	7.3	43.1	69.7	46.6
Canada	27.0	9.8	41.0	70.3	46.2
Average	29.2	6.9	39.2	80.4	45.8

come next, with 40 per cent. Although these three are also countries with high overall employment rates for women, there does not appear to be a close association between the incidence of part-time work and the overall employment rate (Fig. 2.4). The correlation, however, fails because the North American and rest of Europe countries exhibit a variety of patterns. The low-employment Mediterranean countries show low incidence of part-time employment.

Tables 2.3 and 2.4 look at the role of education, focusing on men and women in the age group 25–54. Table 2.3 shows the overall employment rate for men and women for two educational groups, those with secondary school or below, and those with university or equivalent degree qualification. It is striking, but perhaps not surprising, how employment rates vary with education.

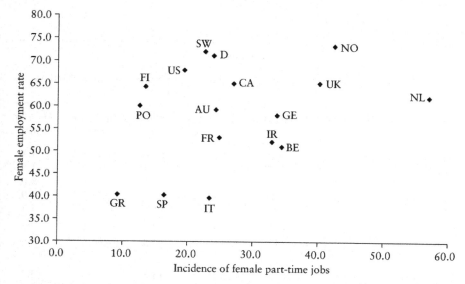

Figure 2.4. *Female employment rate and incidence of female part-time jobs*

The better-educated group experiences far higher employment rates than the less-well-educated group in all countries in our sample. The gender employment gap is also far less for the more educated group. Even in the Mediterranean countries, women with university education are characterized by an employment rate close to 70 per cent. The most striking example in this respect is Portugal, where employment among highly educated women reaches 90 per cent.

Because the gender employment gap is smaller in the population with post-secondary education, if the educational attainment of women were to increase, the gender employment gap should fall. There are encouraging developments along this dimension. Table 2.4 shows that at ages 35–54 women represent 52.1 per cent of the population with a higher educational qualification, but in the 25–34 age group they represent 54.1 per cent. This pattern is visible across country groups, and is also visible, even more emphatically, for the case of tertiary education.

The gender employment gap widens substantially when one takes into account the presence of children. Women are still the gender predominantly responsible for looking after children: the presence of children in a household increases the employment prospects of men and reduces those of women. On average, as Table 2.5 shows, the gender gap rises from 14.4 per cent for women without children, to more than 27 per cent for women with two or more children. This pattern holds both in the Nordic countries (with an increase from 3.3 per cent to 14 per cent in the gender gap) and in the Mediterranean countries (an increase from 27.8 to 48 per cent). The United Kingdom is

Table 2.3. *Women employment rate and employment gender gap by educational attainment*

| | Persons aged 25 to 54 years | | | | | |
| | Total | | Less than upper secondary | | University/tertiary | |
	Employment rate	*Gender gap*[a]	Employment rate	*Gender gap*[a]	Employment rate	*Gender gap*[a]
Nordic	80.3	6.5	66.7	11.6	87.1	5.4
Denmark	80.5	7.7	68.2	9.2	88.7	4.5
Finland	77.6	7.0	69.5	8.3	84.8	8.0
Norway	81.5	7.1	63.8	14.6	87.3	4.9
Sweden	81.7	4.1	65.4	14.5	87.8	4.3
Anglo-Saxon	73.1	14.4	49.7	17.3	86.4	8.0
United Kingdom	73.1	14.4	49.7	17.3	86.4	8.0
Mediterranean	51.3	34.9	38.7	45.8	77.0	13.2
Greece	52.6	35.9	42.1	45.5	78.4	12.4
Italy	50.7	33.9	35.8	46.8	78.7	12.4
Spain	50.6	34.8	38.1	45.1	74.0	14.8
Rest of Europe	68.5	19.6	54.2	26.6	85.6	8.8
Austria	73.5	16.2	61.6	17.6	86.5	9.2
Belgium	67.8	20.1	47.4	32.3	86.7	8.6
France	69.6	17.7	56.5	23.6	83.1	8.5
Germany	71.1	16.3	55.4	20.9	83.4	10.5
Ireland	53.1	29.0	33.7	39.5	79.9	13.3
Netherlands	70.9	21.4	53.4	32.8	86.6	8.8
Portugal	73.9	16.4	71.5	19.7	93.0	2.6
North America	74.1	13.3	50.9	23.7	80.9	10.4
United States (1999)	74.1	14.8	49.7	26.5	81.9	11.6
Canada	74.0	11.8	52.0	20.8	79.8	9.2
Average	72.2	20.2	56.0	28.3	88.5	9.7

[a] Difference between male and female employment rate

another striking example. The gender gap increases from 5.4 per cent to 28.2 per cent when a woman has two or more children. A similar pattern holds, perhaps surprisingly, for the United States. The differences in employment rates across countries appear to be bigger for women with no children than for women with two or more children. Perhaps not surprisingly, women with children are more likely to work part-time but men with children less likely to do so (see Table 2.6).

Table 2.4. *Female share in the population by educational attainment*

| | Percentage of women in the total population in each category | | | | | | | |
| | At least upper secondary education | | | | Tertiary education | | | |
	25–34	35–54	55–64	Total	25–34	35–54	55–64	Total
Nordic	50.2	49.5	47.8	49.4	55.8	52.4	45.2	52.5
Denmark	51.4	47.9	41.8	47.8	55.4	53.1	38.3	51.7
Finland	50.8	50.6	51.1	50.7	59.5	53.9	47.6	54.6
Norway	49.8	48.8	47.5	48.9	55.2	48.9	43.8	50.4
Sweden	48.9	50.9	50.7	50.2	53.1	53.8	51.3	53.2
Anglo-Saxon	49.2	47.6	34.5	46.5	46.8	47.0	36.2	45.6
United Kingdom	49.2	47.6	34.5	46.5	46.8	47.0	36.2	45.6
Mediterranean	52.4	48.5	40.9	49.3	55.2	45.3	34.5	47.9
Greece	52.2	49.3	42.6	49.5	55.2	42.9	30.3	46.0
Italy	52.0	48.3	42.2	49.1	55.3	46.9	39.9	48.7
Spain	52.9	47.9	38.0	49.2	55.0	46.2	33.4	48.9
Rest of Europe	51.2	49.1	45.0	49.3	52.4	46.7	39.6	47.5
Austria	47.9	45.3	42.7	45.7	50.3	39.0	25.1	40.2
Belgium	51.4	50.4	46.7	50.3	53.7	50.4	43.3	50.7
France	50.2	48.0	44.3	48.3	54.0	50.8	46.5	51.6
Germany	48.4	47.1	43.6	46.7	45.8	39.1	29.3	38.7
Ireland	54.1	53.7	52.8	53.7	52.0	48.1	44.9	49.4
Netherlands	50.8	46.8	40.3	47.1	50.5	41.8	37.5	43.9
Portugal	55.7	52.8	44.6	53.5	60.5	57.6	50.6	58.1
North America	51.1	50.9	50.8	51.0	52.5	49.5	46.0	49.9
United States (1999)	51.5	51.2	52.1	51.4	53.4	50.0	45.0	50.3
Canada	50.6	50.7	49.6	50.5	51.6	49.1	47.1	49.6
Average	54.1	52.1	47.4	52.3	56.6	50.8	42.6	51.7

2.1 WOMEN'S ROLE IN OVERALL EMPLOYMENT GROWTH

European countries have experienced a variety of employment dynamics since the early 1980s. Table 2.7 shows that some high-employment countries, led by Sweden, lost a substantial number of jobs in the last two decades, whereas others, led by the Netherlands and Ireland, made substantial gains. How are these changes related to the changes in female employment rates? We decompose average employment growth in each country by gender, age and part-time or full-time work, and assess how much each dimension contributed, in accounting terms, to average employment growth.

Table 2.5. *Female employment rate by presence of children*

| | Persons aged 25 to 54 years | | | | | | | |
| | Total | | No children | | One child | | Two or more children | |
	Employment rate	Gender gap	Employment rate	Gender gap	Employment rate	Gender gap	Employment rate	Gender gap
Nordic	80.3	6.5	80.6	3.3	82.6	8.4	77.6	14.0
Denmark	80.5	7.7	78.5	7.7	88.1	3.5	77.2	12.9
Finland	77.6	7.0	79.2	0.1	78.5	11.8	73.5	19.7
Norway	81.5	7.1	82.9	5.9	83.3	–	78.0	–
Sweden	81.7	4.1	81.9	-0.4	80.6	9.8	81.8	9.4
Anglo-Saxon	73.1	14.4	79.9	5.4	72.9	17.1	62.3	28.2
United Kingdom	73.1	14.4	79.9	5.4	72.9	17.1	62.3	28.2
Mediterranean	51.3	34.9	53.5	27.8	51.2	42.0	45.3	48.0
Greece	52.6	35.9	53.1	31.1	53.9	40.3	50.3	45.4
Italy	50.7	33.9	52.8	26.2	52.1	40.9	42.4	49.9
Spain	50.6	34.8	54.6	26.0	47.6	44.7	43.3	48.6
Rest of Europe	68.5	19.6	72.3	12.5	70.2	22.3	60.6	31.6
Austria	73.5	16.2	76.0	10.5	75.6	18.5	65.7	29.0
Belgium	67.8	20.1	65.6	17.4	71.8	23.5	69.3	24.7
France	69.6	17.7	73.5	9.6	74.1	18.7	58.8	32.9
Germany	71.1	16.3	77.3	7.2	70.4	21.2	56.3	35.6
Ireland	53.1	29.0	65.8	14.1	51.0	33.2	40.8	43.2
Netherlands	70.9	21.4	75.3	15.6	69.9	24.3	63.3	30.8
Portugal	73.9	16.4	72.6	13.4	78.5	16.6	70.3	24.8
North America	74.1	13.3	77.5	6.6	75.3	16.1	66.5	26.3
United States (1999)	74.1	14.8	78.6	7.2	75.6	17.4	64.7	29.0
Canada	74.0	11.8	76.5	6.0	74.9	14.9	68.2	23.6
Average	51.7	19.6	53.5	14.4	51.8	23.5	49.1	27.1

Table 2.6. *Part-time work by gender and presence of children*

	Percentage of persons working part time in total employment by category, workers aged 25 to 54 years						
	Women				Men		
	No children	One child	Two or more children	Total	No children	With children	Total
Nordic	16.3	18.0	23.3	18.8	5.1	3.4	4.2
Denmark	18.5	13.3	16.2	16.6	–	–	3.7
Finland	7.5	8.6	13.6	9.2	–	–	3.7
Norway	24.7	33.5	41.1	31.8	5.0	–	5.0
Sweden	14.6	16.7	22.2	17.9	5.2	3.4	4.3
Anglo-Saxon	23.7	46.6	62.8	38.6	4.1	3.2	3.7
United Kingdom	23.7	46.6	62.8	38.6	4.1	3.2	3.7
Mediterranean	14.0	18.1	21.4	16.2	3.6	2.7	3.2
Greece	8.4	9.7	11.2	9.2	2.8	2.5	2.7
Italy	20.0	27.2	34.4	24.1	5.5	4.5	5.1
Spain	13.7	17.4	18.6	15.3	2.6	1.2	1.9
Rest of Europe	22.4	36.8	46.1	31.0	4.5	3.1	3.9
Austria	17.4	33.6	43.7	26.7	2.1	1.7	1.9
Belgium	29.2	34.7	46.1	34.7	6.5	5.1	5.9
France	20.0	23.7	31.8	23.7	5.2	3.6	4.4
Germany	24.0	45.3	60.2	35.2	4.2	2.3	3.4
Ireland	16.6	37.2	46.4	29.7	4.3	3.6	4.0
Netherlands	38.3	72.6	82.7	55.9	6.2	4.6	5.5
Portugal	11.5	10.5	11.3	11.2	2.7	1.3	2.0
North America	13.5	19.3	27.1	18.0	4.3	2.5	3.5
United States (1999)	10.1	15.8	23.6	14.6	3.5	1.8	2.7
Canada	17.0	22.9	30.7	21.4	5.2	3.2	4.3
Average	18.5	27.6	35.1	24.4	4.4	3.0	3.8

Table 2.8 shows the decompositions of the average rate of employment growth between 1983 and 1997. Our results clearly reflect the narrowing of the gender gap. In all European Union countries, employment growth was much faster for females than males. Youths experienced below average employment growth, a fact that largely reflects changes in the schooling age and more generally the increase in education. The fall in the gender employment gap is accounted for by the growth of employment of women aged 25–49. In every country, the contribution to employment growth by prime-age women dominates that of prime-age men, even among low-employment countries such as Italy and Greece. Job creation performance among those aged 50–64 was

Table 2.7. *Employment rate and employment growth, 1980, 2000*

	Employment rate		Δ(L/P) [3]	Empl. growth [4]	Δ(WP) [5]	Lisbon distance
	1980–82 [1]	1998–00 [2]				
Nordic	74.36	73.05				
Denmark	72.14	76.06	3.91	0.58	0.36	6.06
Finland	71.97	66.03	−5.94	0.04	0.34	−3.97
Norway	74.31	78.62	4.31	0.88	0.57	8.62
Sweden	79.02	71.49	−7.53	−0.10	0.35	1.49
Anglo-Saxon	67.65	71.40				
United Kingdom	67.65	71.40	3.75	0.52	0.37	1.40
Mediterranean	55.03	53.72				
Greece	55.31	54.66	−0.65	0.80	0.76	−15.34
Italy	56.72	52.48	−4.24	0.00	0.39	−17.52
Spain	53.05	54.00	0.95	0.91	0.76	−16.00
Rest of Europe	62.02	65.03				
Austria	75.79	73.48	−2.31	0.43	0.62	3.48
Belgium	56.90	58.06	1.16	0.25	0.19	−11.94
France	63.13	60.51	−2.61	0.39	0.60	−9.49
Germany	64.87	67.92	3.05	0.30	0.47	−2.08
Ireland	56.68	64.54	7.86	1.92	1.20	−5.46
Netherlands	53.96	63.26	9.31	1.47	0.71	−6.74
Portugal	62.81	67.45	4.64	0.87	0.48	−2.55
North America	66.26	72.75				
United States (1999)	65.51	74.40	8.89	1.54	0.92	
Canada	67.01	71.11	4.10	1.49	1.15	
Average	64.5	66.2				

Key: [1] Average 1980–82.
[2] Average 1998–00.
[3] Change in employment-working age population ratio (in percentage points). Average 1998–00 minus average 1980–82.
[4] Average employment growth (in per cent).
[5] Average growth of working-age population.

more mixed, reflecting in part the tendency towards early retirement in a number of countries. Nevertheless, the fall in employment among those aged 50–64 is much more marked for men than for women.

There are substantial differences within Europe, especially in the role played by part-time jobs. The country that stands out in this respect is the Netherlands, the top European performer. The growth of employment among women aged 25 to 49 years, typically in part-time jobs, accounts for about half the growth of

Table 2.8. *Contribution to average employment growth between 1983 and 2000 by age, gender and part-time/full-time*

	Male			Female			Total[1]
	15–24[2]	25–49[2]	50–64[2]	15–24[2]	25–49[2]	50–64[2]	
Belgium							
Part-time	0.03	0.14	0.03	0.03	0.52	0.07	0.82
Full-time	−0.18	−0.12	−0.28	−0.16	0.11	−0.02	−0.65
All contracts	−0.15	0.02	−0.25	−0.13	0.63	0.05	0.17
Germany							
Part-time	0.03	0.07	0.04	0.03	0.30	0.07	0.53
Full-time	−0.26	0.00	−0.21	−0.27	0.00	−0.01	−0.75
All contracts	−0.23	0.07	−0.18	−0.24	0.29	0.06	−0.22
Denmark							
Part-time	0.07	0.05	0.01	0.14	−0.21	−0.01	0.05
Full-time	−0.09	0.17	0.20	−0.11	0.43	0.27	0.88
All contracts	−0.02	0.22	0.21	0.03	0.22	0.26	0.93
France							
Part-time	0.02	0.07	0.02	0.03	0.33	0.06	0.53
Full-time	−0.17	0.18	−0.02	−0.16	0.20	0.05	0.09
All contracts	−0.15	0.25	0.00	−0.13	0.53	0.12	0.62
Greece							
Part-time	0.00	−0.01	−0.01	−0.01	−0.13	−0.01	−0.18
Full-time	−0.05	0.23	0.03	−0.03	0.56	0.10	0.84
All contracts	−0.05	0.22	0.02	−0.04	0.43	0.09	0.65
Ireland							
Part-time	0.07	0.07	0.05	0.17	0.46	0.15	0.96
Full-time	0.01	0.75	0.15	−0.11	0.98	0.10	1.88
All contracts	0.08	0.82	0.20	0.06	1.44	0.25	2.84
Italy							
Part-time	0.00	0.06	0.00	0.01	0.18	0.01	0.26
Full-time	−0.19	0.08	−0.14	−0.14	0.21	0.05	−0.13
All contracts	−0.19	0.14	−0.14	−0.13	0.39	0.06	0.12
Netherlands							
Part-time	0.24	0.12	0.11	0.25	0.97	0.32	1.99
Full-time	−0.18	0.43	0.28	−0.20	0.27	0.06	0.66
All contracts	0.06	0.55	0.39	0.05	1.24	0.38	2.66
Portugal							
Part-time	0.00	0.01	0.03	−0.01	0.11	0.12	0.26
Full-time	−0.16	0.37	−0.08	−0.07	0.58	0.07	0.71
All contracts	−0.16	0.38	−0.05	−0.08	0.69	0.19	0.98
United Kingdom							
Part-time	0.09	0.06	0.07	0.10	0.21	0.08	0.61
Full-time	−0.20	0.38	−0.17	−0.18	0.46	0.10	0.39
All contracts	−0.11	0.44	−0.11	−0.08	0.67	0.18	0.99

Key: [1]Refers to total average employment growth by type of contract.
[2]Refers to different age groups.
Source: Garibaldi-Mauro, 2002.

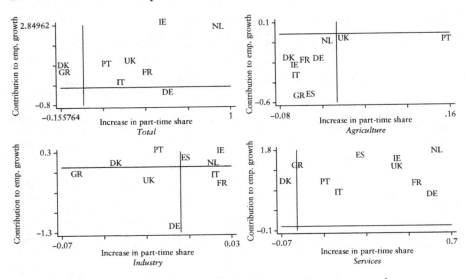

Figure 2.5. *Share of part-time jobs and employment growth*

overall employment. To a large extent the Dutch 'employment miracle' is a part-time female employment miracle. The experience of Ireland, the other employment success story of the last twenty years, is more uniform across decompositions, with substantial employment growth observed for both men and women, and both full-time and part-time jobs. In Belgium, Germany, France and Italy, we observe growth in part-time jobs alongside a decline in full-time jobs.

Figure 2.5 plots overall employment growth (averaged over 1983–1997) against the change in the share of part-time jobs, for the ten countries for which we have data, to test whether there is a positive association between employment growth and growth in the share of part-time jobs. As in the comparison of employment levels in Figure 2.4, there is no clear evidence in Figure 2.5 that countries which experienced a rise in the share of part-time jobs also experienced a rise in overall employment. The simple correlation coefficient for the ten observations in Figure 2.5 is 0.4.[4]

---

[4] See Garibaldi and Mauro (2002) for more discussion and econometric tests of the claims made in this section.

3

Explanations behind Women's Employment Patterns

There are two events that need explaining in the history of the overall female employment rate. First, what are the reasons for the big rise in the employment rate in recent decades, and secondly, why does the rate differ so much across countries? Because employment rates across countries differ by much more than unemployment rates, the same questions can be asked about the participation rate, and in our discussion we refer to both, although we do not discuss unemployment (see Fig. 2.1 (p. 14)). Both employment and participation are influenced by supply and demand factors. Employment may be low because not enough women want to enter the labor market, or participation may be low because not many jobs are being offered to attract the women into the labor market. In the first case, low participation rates are explained by women's preferences, in the second by employers' preferences and discouragement on the part of women. It is very difficult to disentangle these two effects, and it is made more difficult by the role of wages in the determination of the participation rate and the employment rate. In the world of the frictionless neoclassical economic model the participation rate drives the employment rate: according to this model the reason employment rates differ across countries is due to women's preferences, given technology and wages. But when the influence of institutions is taken into account the answer could be different and no general rules can be used to make inferences or welfare statements about participation and employment rates.

The countries in our sample enjoy similar technological structures and standards of living, so it is more likely that the explanation for the differences in the employment and participation rates originates in their institutional structures than in women's preferences for work. We review first the explanations put forward in the literature for the rise in participation and employment rates in recent decades and then use aggregate OECD data to identify macroeconomic and institutional influences on employment rates.

3.1 THE RISE OF FEMALE EMPLOYMENT: A BRIEF REVIEW OF EXPLANATIONS

Most research on the reasons for the big rise in women's participation rate has been done in the United States. Apart from the obvious advantage of the availability of good data (and many resources devoted to pure research), the United States has the advantage of large participation rates which are a fairly recent phenomenon. Since there are relatively few institutional barriers to job creation in US labor markets, the reasons for the growth in female employment rates are usually sought in the factors that shape women's preferences for work over the home ('home production') and in technological advances.

At the beginning of the twenty-first century, only 18 per cent of American women were part of the labor force. By the year 2001, this fraction had reached 61 per cent. This trend has been particularly prominent for married women. The labor force participation rate of married women rose from 5 per cent in 1900 to about 60 per cent in 2001. There are few plausible explanations for this change that have been investigated in the literature. One set of factors influences women's participation rates through their own influence on the desired supply of labor to the market: the diffusion of new household technologies allows women to decrease the time spent in home production and so releases time for market work. The improvement in working conditions in the market place, both in terms of status and in terms of hours of work, makes it more attractive for women to go out to seek work. Also, the availability of contraceptive methods allows women to plan their fertility and the timing of births, making it easier for them to plan a career. A second set of factors has influenced the demand for women's labor services. Key to these factors is the shift from manufacturing to services, which employ more women in jobs such as clerical work and sales. Other favorable developments are the introduction of new technologies that have made it possible for firms to create more 'female-friendly' jobs, and changes in the wage structure that have favored women. Finally, the rise in the female employment rate is also explained in terms of the change in society's attitudes towards the role that women should play in the home and in the market place.

In what follows, we review some of the explanations for the US experience that have been proposed in the literature. We first discuss explanations for the growth trend in women's participation since the beginning of the twentieth century. Then we review the post-World War II period and, in particular, the big increase in married women's labor force participation that occurred in the United States between 1970 and the 1990s. Some of the explanations proposed for this dramatic increase also apply to European countries, which have experienced a similar diffusion of market and domestic technologies.

The influential work by Goldin (1990) provides an extensive analysis of the change in women's role in the labor market in the twentieth century. In particular, using cross-city estimates of income and wage elasticities, Goldin studies how the relative importance of supply and demand factors in explaining women's labor market experience has changed over time. She shows that the increase in women's participation in the United States between 1890 and 1930 may be mostly due to supply factors. Over this time period, women were mostly employed in manufacturing and agriculture where working conditions were meagre. As a consequence, a social stigma was attached to a working wife: it meant that the husband was in poor financial conditions.[1] Between 1940 and 1960 this situation changed, mostly because of changes in the type of jobs available. The availability of clerical jobs and the increase in the schooling level of working women made the stigma associated with a working wife much weaker. The importance of this change was enhanced by improvements in the housework production process, and by the increase in the availability of market goods that could substitute for home-produced products.

Over the final decades of the century both demand and supply factors became important in contributing to the increase in women's participation, as women's labor market experiences became more similar to those of men. The increase in the availability of better jobs for women was interpreted by Galor and Weil (1996) as a form of female-biased technological change. In particular, they argue that there is a link between skill-biased technological change and changes in women's fertility and labor choices.

Smith and Ward (1985) explicitly measure the contribution of demand factors to the increase in female participation over the final decades of the century. They show that about 60 per cent of the increase in North American women's labor force participation between 1950 and 1980 may be attributed to the increase in real wages that took place over this time period. These calculations take into account the change in fertility that also occurred in response to the wage rise. Their breakdowns allow us to have an indicative measure of the contribution of other factors to the increase in women's participation, such as the introduction of new contraceptive methods, the increasing level of schooling, and changes in gender role attitudes. Some of these explanations have been analysed in more recent papers. For instance, Goldin and Katz (2002) argue that the introduction and diffusion of the oral contraceptive (the pill) facilitated a woman's investment in human capital by virtually eliminating the chance of a disruptive accidental pregnancy. Indeed, they show how the number of women entering professional degrees, such as Medical School, Business School, and Law School, increased substantially between the early 1970s (when the pill first started to become generally available) and the late 1990s (when there were almost as many female first-year students in Law and Medicine as male).[2]

Greenwood, Seshadri and Yorukoglu (2002) focus instead on the liberating effect of new consumer durables (such as the washing machine, and the microwave) that reduced the amount of time required in the household,

---

[1] According to a Gallup poll conducted in 1938, about 80 per cent of men and women disapproved of a married woman working if her husband was capable of supporting her.

[2] Other social trends of the early 1970s may also help to explain the rise in the number of women with professional degrees. In particular, as argued by Costa (2000), the passage of Title IX in 1972, which applied civil rights legislation to universities, may have had an impact on the admission practices of graduate and professional schools.

allowing women to allocate more time to the labor market. They find that about 10 per cent of the growth in female labor force participation between the beginning of the twentieth century and 1980 may be due to the introduction and diffusion of these domestic appliances. However, although the evidence they presented supports their hypotheses for the period 1940 to 1970, this seems not to be a convincing explanation for women's behavior over the 1980s and the 1990s. By this time such goods were widely available in every household in the country but women's participation continued to grow substantially.

Finally, some authors investigate the importance of society's views about the role of women on their work decisions. Fernandez, Fogli, and Olivetti (2002) examine the hypothesis that an increase in the proportion of men with mothers who work makes working more attractive to their wives. A working mother either influences her son's preferences for a working wife or directly makes him a better partner for a working woman by increasing his productivity in the household.[3] This mechanism implies a persistent effect on the labor force by the participation of women in subsequent generations. Neumark and Postlewaite (1998) also study the importance of social norms in women's employment decisions. They develop an augmented version of the standard neoclassical model where relative income concerns enter women's utility functions and hence their labor choices. They argue that women's employment decisions are significantly affected by the employment decisions of their reference group (including sisters and sisters-in-law).

A number of contributions gives a quantitative assessment of the importance of the observed changes in the US wage structure and labor market returns in the explanation of the increase in the labor supply of married women between the 1970s and the 1990s. Starting with the work by Katz and Murphy (1992), several researchers have documented how returns to education and experience, and within-group wage inequality, have been rising for both men and women over this time period. This evidence indicates that these changes in the wage structure can be taken, at least to some extent, as exogenous with respect to women's prior work behavior.[4] Pencavel (1998) studies the change in women's employment decisions between 1975 and 1994. He finds that the increase in women's wages account for between one-quarter to a half of the increase in

---

[3] One criticism of this assumption is that women may have been influenced by the past work experience of their own mothers. The empirical evidence, however, shows that this is not the case. The Fernández *et al.* (2002) argument does not preclude the possibility that as more women join the labor force, attitudes towards these women change in society at large.

[4] Market wages influence women's decisions to work, marry and have children, and vice versa. The studies we discuss in this section mainly focus on the first direction of causality. Pasqua in this volume looks at the opposite direction of causality. In particular, she uses data from the ECHP to analyse the impact of increased female labor force participation on family income inequality. She finds that increased female employment has an equalizing effect on the household income distribution.

women's labor supply (depending on the cohort), with the increased attractiveness of the market place relative to the household accounting for the rest. Moreover, he finds that husband's wages have a very minor role in explaining a married woman's work decisions. This is consistent with the work of Juhn and Murphy (1997), which shows that the slowdown of married men's earnings growth in the 1980s and 1990s cannot explain the increase in married women's labor force participation.[5]

Olivetti (2001) develops a life-cycle model with human capital accumulation and home production and uses it to quantitatively assess the consequences of the increase in the relative returns to labor market experience on married women's life-cycle labor supply. She finds that most of the increase in lifetime hours worked by married women between 1970 and 1990 may be attributed to the increase in the relative returns to experience, whereas the decrease in the gender wage gap can only explain about 20 per cent of the increase in hours worked. She argues that in the 1970s married women temporarily cut back on market work during childrearing years. A cost of this withdrawal is the loss in accumulated labor market experience. This cost became bigger in the 1990s so married women decreased the interruptions in market hours, increasing the number of hours they supply to the market.[6]

Jones, Manuelli and McGrattan (2003) study the effects of the decline of the gender wage gap and of technological improvements in the production of non-market goods on female labor supply over the past three decades. They find that the decline in the gender wage gap can explain a larger increase in married women's participation than the technological improvements in the production of non-market goods.[7] This is not surprising, because as we argued above, the diffusion process of such goods was completed by the 1970s whereas the largest decline in the gender wage gap occurred in the 1980s. As also shown in Mulligan and Yona (2002), the decline in the wage gap is not enough to produce the observed increase in married women's participation to the labor market. They show, however, that a simple model of household specialisation can predict the observed increase in the labor force participation of married women in response to an increase in wage inequality relative to the gender wage gap.

Finally, using a life-cycle framework, Attanasio, Low, and Sánchez-Marcos (2003) find that the shifts in the cost of children relative to lifetime earnings are

---

[5] Additional evidence that during the 1980s returns to labor market experience increased more for women than for men is provided by Blau and Kahn (1997) and O'Neill and Polachek (1993). These studies show that the increase in the returns to experience and the increase in the actual experience for women can explain a large portion of the decrease in the gender wage gap. (See chapter 5 on the gender wage gap.)

[6] Caucutt *et al.* (2002) also investigate the impact of the increased returns to experience on women's fertility decisions.

[7] Their model also predicts that hours worked by single women and married men do not change much following a small decline in the gender wage gap. This is consistent with the empirical evidence.

an important explanation for the observed change in married women's labor force participation. In their paper, the main factor affecting this cost is the depreciation of human capital that occurs as a consequence of labor market interruptions. However, this claim may be due to the particular model that they employed. In their model, the role of human capital depreciation is very similar to the role played by returns to labor market experience in a model that also includes the intensive margin of women's labor supply decisions.

The literature that studies the different unemployment experiences of Europe and the United States over the 1980s and the 1990s emphasizes the role of the interaction between labor market institutions in Europe and other macroeconomic shocks. As pointed out by Bertola *et al.* (2002), the interaction between labor market institutions and macroeconomic forces, which lies behind the rise of unemployment in some countries, in all likelihood also had a negative impact on the relative employment of some demographic groups (including women). Moreover, it is also claimed that the same macroeconomic forces may have been responsible for the observed change in the US wage structure. But this is the same change that made market work more attractive than work at home for married women in the United States. If part of the increase in US women's work hours is due to the increase in wages, the compression of the European wage structure may be one of the reasons why European women do not on average work as much as American women.

3.2 EXPLAINING CROSS-COUNTRY DIFFERENCES

Cross-country differences in participation rates existed throughout our sample but also changed over time. Even if we compare country experiences since 1980, the female employment gap between, say, the United States and Germany in 1980 was about 5 percentage points in favor of the United States but by 2000 it increased to 10 points. To take another example, in 1980 the gap between the United Kingdom and France was 5 points in favor of the United Kingdom, but by 2000 it increased to 12 points. There has been a uniform increase in female employment rates but some countries did better than others. We investigate here whether the reasons for the differences in country experiences can be attributed to the institutional structure of their labor or product markets.

We follow the methodology of Blanchard and Wolfers (2000) and try to identify differences in the responses of employment rates to an unspecified set of 'unobservable' shocks. The idea behind these tests is that the reasons for the increase in female employment rates cannot be quantified—as we argued in the first part of this section they have to do with the increased availability of consumer durables, developments in medicine and shifts in technology and social attitudes that cannot be easily measured for use in time series analysis. We assume instead that all countries in our sample had access to the same domestic and market technologies, which is a reasonable assumption given that our sample consists of the rich OECD countries since 1970. We then remove the common trends in participation rates with time dummies and the unexplained mean gaps between countries with country-fixed effects, and allow a set of institutional variables to influence the way that each country's participation rate responded to the new technologies. The estimated regression is:

$$E_{it} = c_i + d_t + d_t \sum_k b_k x_{it}^k + v_{it}$$

where E_{it} is the employment rate in country i at time t, c_i is the country-fixed effect, d_t is a time dummy for each period in our sample, x_{it}^k is a set of k institutions that takes different values in each country and some over time as well, and v_{it} is an error term. The equation was estimated with non-linear least squares for 14 of the European countries in our sample (some of the institutional variables for Greece were missing), Switzerland, Australia, New Zealand, Japan, Canada and the United States.

The results are shown in Table 3.1. The institutions included are mostly labor market institutions, employment protection legislation, unionization, unemployment insurance benefits and labor taxes. But we also include an index of product market regulation, the OECD measure of the administrative costs of setting up new companies. Although this measure refers specifically to the difficulty faced by potential entrepreneurs when setting up a company, it is correlated with other measures of product market regulation and we interpret it more generally as an index of the overall regulation of small companies. Employment protection legislation changes very little during the sample because of the absence of information on earlier years, and the company start-up costs do not vary at all. Only one observation per country is available, for the late 1990s.

The results show that the only institution that is statistically significant is the index of product market regulation, although there is also weak support for the proposition that unionization exerts a negative influence on employment. Product market regulation may be especially important for women's employment because women are mostly employed in smaller establishments in the service sector—retailing, catering etc.—and if regulation impedes the entry and expansion of such establishments, it restricts job creation. Product-market regulation also appears to be a significant, and mostly neglected, institution in the determination of overall employment rates.[8] Unionization is a more commonly tested institution, with generally negative implications for overall employment rates. Our estimates imply small effects on female employment rates. In previous research Bertola *et al.* (2002) found that countries with more widespread union membership experience less female employment relative to

---

[8] See, for example, Nicoletti *et al.* (2001), Pissarides (2003), Lopez-Garcia (2003).

Table 3.1. *Institutional influences on female employment rates (common unobservable shocks, five-year averages, 1970–1995)*

Variable	Estimates	Fixed effects, %		Common trend	Institutional influence
Const	0.48 (21.26)	Austria	47.4		
1975/79	0.02 (1.82)	Belgium	39.5		
1980/84	0.04 (3.59)	Denmark	58.3		
1985/89	0.08 (6.20)	Finland	61.7		
1990/95	0.10 (7.61)	France	45.5		
Employment protection	0.025 (0.07)	Germany	46.5	1970/74	**Union density**
Union density	−1.07 (1.35)	Ireland	28.3	to	Sample max −4.7%
Union coordination	0.11 (0.52)	Italy	34.2	1990/95	Sample min +3.5%
Replacement ratio	0.17 (0.28)	Netherlands	30.8	→	
Benefit duration	−0.30 (0.81)	Norway	47.2	+10.3%	
Tax wedge	1.06 (0.80)	Portugal	45.4		**Start-up costs**
Start-up Costs	−0.47 (2.43)	Spain	24.9		Sample max −12.8%
Fixed effects	Yes	Sweden	63.8		Sample min +6.8%
Observations	89	UK	50.0		
R²	0.95	Canada	46.7		
		US	48.5		

Note: The dependent variable is the ratio of employment to the population of working age. Estimated by non-linear least squares. The variables are all five-year averages, except for the last period, which has six years. The error terms may suffer from groupwise heteroskedasticity which might influence the efficiency of the estimates. All variables are entered as deviations from sample means. Additional countries included but not reported: Australia, Japan, New Zealand, Switzerland. The base values are the estimated constant plus the fixed effects. The common trend is the estimate of the time dummy for 1990/95, i.e. the estimated rise in employment for a country with all institutional variables at sample means. The effect of the two significant variables is reported for the country with the highest and lowest value in the sample in 1990/95.

male. The natural reconciliation of our respective findings is that although unions reduce male employment, they reduce female employment by even more. This is a surprising conclusion, in view of the fact that the unionized sectors of the economy tend to be the ones that have a higher ratio of male-to-female employment, such as manufacturing or big state enterprises.

Bertola *et al.* (2002) studied only the gap between male and female employment (not their absolute levels) and found only two other institutions influencing it, unemployment insurance and a measure of pension provision. Unemployment insurance was found to decrease the gap, which again can be reconciled with our findings if UI reduces male employment but has no impact on female employment, as one would expect given the small coverage of women in most countries. Pensions were found to increase the gap, which again can be interpreted as being driven by the male employment rate, because women are not covered by pensions to the extent that men are.

A study closer to ours, which studies participation rates only since 1980, is by Genre *et al.* (2003). The authors find that both unemployment insurance and unionization reduce female participation rates, but as in our case, employment protection and labor taxes did not have a significant influence on participation. As in the Bertola *et al.* (2002) study, product market regulation indicators were omitted from the Genre *et al.* study, although the authors found a variable for the fraction of women in part-time jobs to be significant. Although as we argue later we believe that making part-time work more widely available should increase female employment rates, we did not find a good exogenous statistical measure of this link to include in our final regressions.[9]

We quantify the effect of unionization and start-up costs on the employment rate by showing the predicted employment rate for the country that has the biggest and smallest union density, and the most stringent and least stringent start-up index. Our estimates say that if a country has all institutional variables at mean values, its employment rate between 1970/74 and 1990/95 would have increased by 10.3 per cent because of the common unobserved shocks (the consumer durables, the pill, etc.). But if this country was the most unionized in the sample, employment would have increased by 4.7 per cent less, that is, by 5.6 percentage points. The other estimates reported in the last column of Table 3.1 have a similar interpretation.

Caution should be exercised in interpreting the results with regard to unionization because the estimate is imprecise, due to a large standard error. But product market regulation is estimated to have a large and precise impact

---

[9] The fraction of female employment that is part-time is endogenous, on the assumption that a lot of the variation in participation rates is due to the participation of women with children, who have a preference for part-time jobs. Nonetheless, when we tried this variable in our employment regressions it did not work as well as it did in the participation regressions of Genre *et al.* (2003). (See also Fig. 2.5.)

on employment. The country with the most stringent regulations in the setting up of new companies (Italy) is predicted to have as much as 12.8 percentage points of employment less than the mean, and the country with the most liberal start-up requirements (Denmark) is predicted to have 6.8 percentage points more than the mean. These effects are very large and implausible, especially if our index is interpreted strictly as showing the effect of start-up costs only. They should be taken only as indicative of the important role that the excessive regulation of businesses could play in discouraging women from seeking work. This is a neglected issue in the empirical literature and more research is needed on its full impact.

The introduction of further controls in our regressions alters the details of our results but does not alter the basic findings. In the regressions reported in Table 3.1 the underlying assumption is that the shocks that drive the changes in female employment rates over time are common across countries. We tried to differentiate between country shocks by using information on output growth, terms of trade, real interest rates and cyclical indicators (the results are not reported). Given that our data are five-year averages and that our focus is on changes in employment rates in the medium-to-long run, we failed to find significant cyclical influences on employment rates. Of the other time series variables only the terms of trade effect was significant and as expected, showing that improvements in the international competitiveness of a country are beneficial for female employment.

Another influence on female employment, which one would intuitively expect to have a big role, is religion. A glance at our summary tables would seem to associate Catholicism with less female employment and Protestantism with more. We experimented with a variety of measures for religion but unfortunately the results were not robust enough to report. For example, we found that when we measured religion by the percentage of Protestants in the population we did not find significant results, but when we measured it by the fraction of Catholics and Orthodox in the population, results pointed to less female employment in those countries with a higher fraction of Catholics and Orthodox. Results, however, were not very precise. Our results contrast with those of Algan and Cahuc (2003), who argue that religions influence male 'breadwinner' values, which in turn influence female participation rates.

A question that has attracted attention in connection with female employment rates is whether state provision of family care units increases participation. At the Barcelona summit, for example, European leaders decided that by 2010 governments in the European Union should provide day care for as many as 90 per cent of children from the age of 3 to the school mandatory age, and for 33 per cent of children under the age of 3. We were not able to find data for family day care since 1970, but we found data since 1980 for the majority of our countries. The variable that we used in our regressions is total spending by the state on family day care divided by the number of women in employment. Family day care turned out to be statistically significant in both the regression without time controls other than the time dummies and in the regressions with the country-specific controls. An interesting finding in these regressions is that once day care spending is included, the level and duration of unemployment benefits become a stronger negative influence on employment. This suggests that any negative effects of unemployment compensation on female employment are offset if the welfare state also provides generous day care services for women entering employment.

The regressions with family day care are not reported, because the sample is much smaller and the estimates of the other coefficients are not altered in significant ways. We show instead, in Figure 3.1, all the observations of the family day care variable against the female employment rate. Most of the countries in our sample spend very little on family day care and this is reflected in the concentration of points to the left of the graph. But the positive correlation between the big spenders and their employment rates, essentially the Scandinavian countries, is evident. The graph also shows a time series correlation. The sequences of points moving in the north-eastern direction, evident in the graph, are points that apply to single countries since 1980. Countries that have increased family day care spending and experienced a growth in female employment rates include the four Scandinavian countries and also Austria, Germany and Ireland.

A final issue that we addressed is whether the dynamics of female employment during our sample period have been driven by convergence to some common rate of employment, which may nevertheless not be exactly the same in all countries because of institutional differences. Convergence may be justified on the basis of transfers of technology and practices (e.g. the spreading of

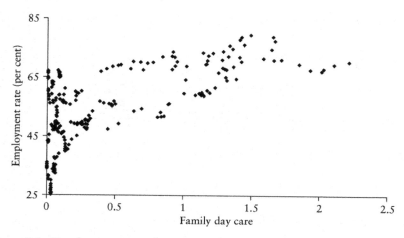

Figure 3.1. *Employment rate of women and average family day care spending per employed woman*

consumer durables or contraceptive methods) which are not picked up by our variables. At first glance, convergence does not appear to be a major force in the dynamics of female employment rates, although there is evidence of some weak forces operating in that direction. We show this with two graphs. In Figure 3.2 we show the path for the female employment rate in the 19 countries in our sample that have data going back to 1970, from 1970–75 to 1990–95. Naturally, with so many countries it is not possible to label each curve and follow through individual developments on a single graph, but the graph shows more or less parallel lines running from the 1970s to the 1990s. The highest line is for Sweden and the lowest is for Spain. Although in more recent years the Swedish line turns down and the Spanish line turns up, overall there does not seem to be a narrowing of the band.

Figure 3.3 plots the initial employment level in each country against its average rate of growth over the 1970/75 to 1990/95 period. If the employment dynamics were driven by convergence, the points in Figure 3.3 should lie along a negatively sloped curve. There is some weak evidence that this has been the case, especially, when the very low employment countries (Spain, Italy, Ireland) are omitted. But although convergence does not seem to be a major force over our entire sample period, it does seem to have been picking up in more recent years. Figure 3.4 shows the same kind of relationship as shown in Figure 3.3, but using 1980 as the base year. The negative correlation that we were looking for in Figure 3.3 is now clearer. The possibility that the dynamics of female employment rates changed around 1980 opens up exciting avenues for future work, because it coincides with the intensification of the moves for European integration and the liberalization of labor mobility.

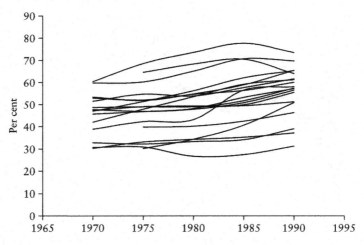

Figure 3.2. *Employment rate of women 1970–1990, 19 countries*

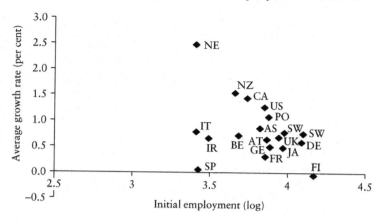

Figure 3.3. *Initial employment rate and average growth rate, 1970–1995, 19 countries*

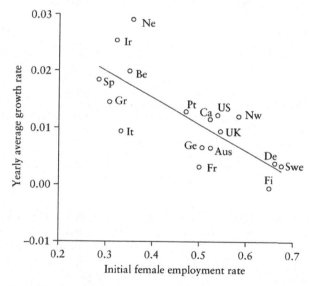

Figure 3.4. *Initial female employment rate and yearly average growth rate, 1980–2000, 17 countries*

Results with regressions intended to test for convergence were mixed, although on balance the coefficient on initial employment, when entered as an independent variable, was a negative number. Table 3.2 reports one such regression, which repeats the regression of Table 3.1, but retains only the three more significant institutional variables. The dependent variable is the rate of growth of the employment rate, and the most important institutional

Table 3.2. *Test of convergence in female employment rates (unobservable shocks, five-year averages, 1970–1995)*

Variable	Estimates
Const	0.32 (2.27)
1980/84	0.05 (0.07)
1985/89	1.10 (5.79)
1990/95	1.02 (0.42)
Initial employment	−0.074 (2.07)
Employment protection	–
Union density	−0.062 (1.31)
Union coordination	–
Replacement ratio	–
Benefit duration	–
Tax wedge	0.091 (1.20)
Start-up costs	−0.021 (2.39)
Fixed effects	No
Observations	62
R^2	0.20

Note: The dependent variable is the difference in the logs of the employment rate. The variables, including the employment rate, are all five-year averages, except for the last period, which has six years. So the dependent variable is the five-year change in (log) employment. Institutional variables are entered both interactively with time dummies and non-interactively, and estimation is possible with the unchanging institutions because of the absence of fixed effects. Estimation is by non-linear least squares. The error terms may suffer from groupwise heteroskedasticity which might influence the efficiency of the estimates.

variable is still product market regulation. The tax wedge is of the wrong sign but not significant at conventional levels, a finding that is also present in the participation regressions of Genre *et al.* (2003). The initial employment level, however, is significant and with negative sign, which shows that once institutional influences are controlled for and fixed effects not included, there is evidence of some convergence in employment rates. We note that in this regression the initial employment level is entered in logs, and the growth rate is a five-year average, so the estimated coefficient of − 0.074 implies that if two countries have an initial employment level that differs by 10 per cent, on average the employment growth rate of the lower-employment country was higher by 0.74 per cent per five-year period. So the estimated convergence is very slow, as it implies that there is catching up after approximately 60 or more years.

4

Job Segregation

What types of jobs do women hold? Is there evidence of job segregation, namely, of discrimination leading women into atypical forms of employment where their skills are not utilized to their full potential? Occupational segregation has received some attention in the economics literature,[1] but less is known on systematic differences in the types of employment contracts held by women. The OECD (2002, Ch. 2) reported some evidence of gender discrimination in the types of jobs held by women, and in this section we probe deeper into this issue by making use of the European Community Household Panel.

The recent growth in 'irregular' jobs, both in Europe and the United States, has attracted a lot of attention. Irregular, or 'atypical' jobs typically include part-time, temporary and casual jobs (see Meulders *et al.* 1994; OECD 1999, Ch. 1, and the June 2002 issue of the *Economic Journal* on 'Temporary Work' for an overview). A key factor to understanding recent labor market developments lies in our ability to understand the nature of these jobs, who has them and what rights they carry. Here we focus only on the aspects that are directly relevant to female employment.

We saw that a lot of women are in part-time jobs. Part-time jobs provide an opportunity for flexible hours of work, and for combining work with family commitments. But part-time work is sometimes criticised as a form of underemployment, paying lower wages and providing inferior fringe benefits than full-time work (see OECD 1999, Ch. 1). Similarly, temporary contracts provide firms with a useful means of worker screening, and therefore represent useful stepping-stones towards offers of permanent employment. But they may also be used as a cheaper option for adjusting employment, with lower wages and severance payments, and poor training (see Booth *et al.* 2002).

The existing studies for the United States have identified a slight wage penalty attached to part-time work (Blank 1990). Evidence on labor market transitions, however, suggests that both part-time and temporary work are often part of the transition out of unemployment, leading to regular

---

[1] The main findings in the Dolado *et al.* (2002) international study on gender occupational segregation are: (i) there is higher occupational segregation in the European Union than in the United States, mainly due to a lower share of women in managerial and professional jobs; (ii) there is strong positive correlation between occupational segregation and the share of part-time jobs; and (iii) there is a weaker positive correlation between the unexplained part of the gender pay gap and the share of women across occupations. (See also references therein.)

employment in the future (Blank 1989; Farber 1999). For the United Kingdom, Harkness (1996) shows that despite the narrowing gender wage gap in full-time jobs, women in part-time jobs have made less progress in attaining earnings parity with men, and lag behind full-timers in both skills and earnings. Bardasi and Gornick (2000) find evidence of significant part-time wage penalties in five industrialized countries, whose sources in terms of observable causes and wage discrimination vary markedly across countries.

Fixed-term contracts also seem to pay lower wages in the United Kingdom (Booth *et al.* 2002), France (Blanchard and Landier 2000), Spain (Jimeno and Toharia 1993 and De la Rica 2003), and Italy (Cipollone 2004), but they offer fairly different prospects of promotion across countries. While temporary jobs indeed seem to represent stepping-stones to permanent work in the United Kingdom (Booth *et al.* 2002), temporary employment turns out to be not so 'temporary' in southern Europe, providing workers with relatively low prospects of transition to permanent work (see Blanchard and Landier 2000 for France, Alba 1998 and Güell and Petrongolo 2003 for Spain, and Cipollone 2003 for Italy).

As the incidence of atypical forms of employment may differ across genders, systematic features of these jobs may be a potential explanation for the gender gap in wages, job satisfactions, and ultimately of gender discrimination in the labor market. In this section, we examine whether this is indeed the case.

Labor market discrimination is commonly defined as the residual difference in labor market outcomes that cannot be explained by factors such as the worker's preferences for the job, or her education and skills (Altonji and Blank 1999). Studies on gender discrimination have typically addressed the question of wage discrimination, namely, what fraction of the gender wage differential cannot be explained by differences in skills or in their labor market rate of return. Discrimination through job segregation is another form of discrimination, which may also lead to wage gaps, if the jobs to which women are segregated are lower-paying ones.

Of course, job segregation can arise for reasons other than discrimination. First, men and women may differ in their human capital and productivity in non-market activities, potentially leading to differences in comparative advantages across jobs. Secondly, their preferences for the characteristics of jobs may also differ. Discrimination refers to the unexplained residual, if any, after segregation due to such factors has been controlled for.

A major issue in decomposing the reasons for segregation is the source of differences in skills and job preferences across genders. Investment in women's human capital may be discouraged by the expectation of future labor market discrimination and by pre-labor market discrimination in the quality and quantity of schooling (Thomas 1990). Also, women's preferences for certain types of jobs—typically part-time jobs—may be driven by social norms (Akerlof and Kranton 2000), or the impossibility of finding someone to help with housework. While it would be difficult to quantify these effects, the potential endogeneity of human capital investments and preferences with respect to gender discrimination should be borne in mind. It implies that the portion of job segregation that cannot be explained by measurable differences in human capital or preferences provides a lower bound for the extent of gender discrimination in the labor market.

4.1 THE DATA

We use data drawn from the European Community Household Panel Survey (ECHPS), which is available for six annual waves (1994–1999) and currently covers all the Lisbon-15 EU member states. The ECHPS is an unbalanced household-based panel survey, containing annual information on a few thousands of households per country.[2] The Employment section of the survey contains information on the type of jobs held by members of the selected households, including working hours, type of contract and wages. Several indices of job satisfaction are also reported, either overall satisfaction or satisfaction with specific job attributes, namely the quality of jobs, working hours, job security and earnings.

For the purposes of our analysis we select all employees aged 16–64 with complete information on the type of employment contract they hold. Table 4.1 reports some summary statistics on the distribution of atypical forms of employment across genders and the associated raw wage differentials. We are not exploiting the panel dimension of the data set here, and simply compute averages of relevant variables across individuals and waves for each country. The resulting sample statistics can be interpreted as medium run averages of the relevant variables.[3]

To obtain data on part-time work, we use information on the number of hours (including paid overtime) that individuals work weekly in their main job, and we define as part-timers those working fewer than 30 hours.[4] As shown in

---

[2] The initial sample sizes are as follows. Austria: 3,380; Belgium: 3490; Denmark: 3,482; Finland: 4,139; France: 7,344; Germany: 11,175; Greece: 5,523; Ireland: 4,048; Italy: 7,115; Luxembourg: 1,011; Netherlands: 5,187; Portugal: 4,881; Spain: 7,206; Sweden: 5,891; UK: 10,905. These figures are the number of households included in the first wave for each country, which corresponds to 1994 for countries except, 1995 for Austria, 1996 for Finland and 1997 for Sweden.

[3] Note that the time covered by these data is different from the one in the data reported in Section 2, so averages may differ. There might also be some sample bias and some differences due to the different collection methods, although this is unlikely to affect the averages much because samples are big and definitions standard.

[4] Although countries may differ in their definitions of part-time work, as well as in their definitions of the length of a standard working week (see Bardasi and Gornick 2000), a common 30-hour cut-off is the criterion often used in international statistics (see for example OECD 2002, Ch. 2). The ECHPS, however, also provides a more subjective definition of part-time, directly asking workers whether they normally work 30 hours or more, or less than 30 hours per week. The two part-time indicators are strongly correlated (from 75% in Italy and Greece to 99% in the

Table 4.1. Summary statistics on male and female employment

	UK	SWE	FIN	DEN	GER	NET	BEL	LUX	AUT	IRE	FRA	ITA	SPA	POR	GRE
Males															
Part-time	3.3	3.8	3.8	2.8	1.7	4.8	2.5	1.8	2.1	7.6	4.3	4.5	2.6	1.4	6.0
Involuntary part-time|P-T	24.7	n.a.	28.9	2.4	8.9	13.5	4.9	27.3	18.5	66.0	48.3	26.8	44.6	32.8	43.8
On temporary job	7.4	6.2	12.9	12.2	8.3	8.2	7.8	4.6	7.9	13.5	8.8	12.0	34.9	19.6	22.0
Involuntary temporary job	45.4	54.8	74.1	54.3	16.9	41.8	77.3	n.a.	34.8	64.7	n.a.	51.8	74.8	42.3	74.2
Hourly earnings															
Full-time/Part-time	113.8	n.a.	105.9	128.3	94.2	115.5	82.8	97.2	69.1	81.8	66.3	64.1	101.5	48.7	61.3
Permanent/Temporary	136.4	n.a.	139.7	127.6	125.7	158.9	129.3	141.5	119.4	15.3	147.7	134.3	177.3	143.9	146.7
Females															
Part-time	30.2	18.1	9.5	17.0	22.8	45.2	26.9	21.0	24.6	29.2	21.6	21.8	15.4	8.7	15.9
Involuntary part-time|P-T	7.3	n.a.	32.5	15.5	5.5	7.8	19.3	8.1	9.8	18.4	4.9	21.0	36.0	36.5	43.6
On temporary job	9.6	7.6	18.2	11.9	9.8	14.3	13.7	7.4	1.3	22.7	10.5	14.6	40.7	22.3	23.9
Involuntary temporary job	30.2	64.8	78.6	57.1	21.3	32.8	70.7	n.a.	38.9	49.6	n.a.	46.7	74.7	41.2	74.4
Hourly earnings															
Full-time/Part-time	130.0	n.a.	105.1	103.2	91.6	105.4	98.1	105.3	91.3	90.07	85.1	67.8	115.8	63.6	56.7
Permanent/Temporary	120.4	n.a.	124.1	118.7	121.0	143.0	115.5	149.7	12.3	139.2	151.5	134.3	168.3	155.8	143.7

Notes: All figures reported are %. Definition of variables: *part-time:* normally working less than 30 hours in their main job, as a % of the total number of employees; *involuntary part-time:* whose main reason for working part-time is that they wanted but they could not find a full-time job, as a % of part-time employees; *on temporary contract:* holding a fixed-term contract or no contract at all, as a % of the total number of employees; *involuntary temporary job:* whose main reason for holding a temporary contract is that they wanted but could not find a permanent job, as a % of temporary employees; *hourly earnings:* monthly wage or salary earnings divided by the number of monthly hours worked. The information on reason for part-time work and wages is not available for Sweden. The information on reason for temporary contract is not available for Luxembourg and France.

Source and sample: ECHPS, 1994–1999, employees aged 16–64 (all rows except 4 and 10) and EUROSTAT 1999, employees aged 2.5–49 (rows 4 and 10).

Table 4.1, the incidence of part time is much higher among women than among men. Except in Ireland, part-time incidence among men is below 5 per cent everywhere, while for women it goes from about 9 per cent in Portugal and Finland to 45 per cent in the Netherlands. On average, more women work part-time in central and northern Europe than in the South, while no major geographical pattern can be detected for men.

Next we present data for involuntary part-time work, including all workers who declare that they hold a part-time job because they wanted to, but could not find a full-time one. When one takes into account the reason why men and women work part time, a negative cross-country correlation between the use of part-time work and the incidence of involuntary part-time work can be detected. In particular, in northern and central Europe part-time work is less likely to be perceived as involuntary than in the South, especially by women. Finland is an exception to this general rule, behaving more like a southern than a northern European country.

The incidence of temporary work (defined as work covered by either a fixed-term contract or no contract at all) varies more across countries than across genders. In all countries considered except Spain, Portugal and Greece, on average, slightly less than 10 per cent of employed men hold temporary jobs. This proportion however rises to 25 per cent in Portugal and Greece, and to over 30 per cent in Spain. The relevant figures for women are slightly higher, but replicate quite closely this international pattern.

The ECHPS does not provide information on the reason why individuals hold temporary jobs, although it may be argued that most cases of temporary employment are indeed involuntary, as a permanent contract would be at least as good as a temporary contract from the perspective of the worker. Aggregate data published by Eurostat however provide information on the proportion of temporary employees who wanted to, but could not find a permanent job.[5] For both men and women, the fraction of temporary jobs that are declared involuntary in Finland, Belgium, Spain and Greece is about three-quarters. For the rest of the countries this fraction is substantially lower. Germany seems to be the best performing country in this respect, with only 17 per cent and 21 per cent of involuntary temporary work among men and women, respectively.

Table 4.1 finally reports hourly wages in typical relative to atypical jobs for both men and women. Full-timers in northern Europe generally earn more than part-timers for each hour that they work, but the wage differential switches in favor of part-timers when moving South. The same unexpected finding about

UK), although the one based on subjective criteria on average predicts a slightly lower incidence of part-time, and slightly higher full-time/part-time wage differentials. We tested the robustness of the empirical results of the next sections also using the subjective definition of part-time work, and obtained very similar results to the ones reported here, unless otherwise stated.

[5] Note that the selection criteria for the Eurostat data are slightly different from the ones used for the ECHPS. In particular, the Eurostat data are for 1999 only and refer to employees aged 25–49.

wage relativities was discovered by the OECD (1999, Ch. 1), using both specific national sources and Eurostat (1995) data. Temporary workers everywhere earn less per hour than permanent workers, and this is especially true in southern Europe. Spain is the country with both the highest incidence of temporary work and the highest wage penalty attached to it—around 70 per cent for both men and women.

4.2   WHO HOLDS ATYPICAL JOBS?

We next use multivariate analysis to look at how women perform in atypical jobs relatively to men by estimating binary choice models for a number of job attributes. We estimate probit models for the probabilities of working part-time, being an involuntary part-time worker, and holding a fixed-term contract, controlling for a number of individual and job characteristics.

All estimated equations include age and education effects, occupation, sector and year dummies, and control for the family composition of workers and previous unemployment history. The effect of family characteristics is allowed to differ across genders, to pick up the features of employment that may be explained by the different family commitments of each gender. The existence of an unemployment spell just prior to the current job is also controlled for, as women may experience more frequent non-employment spells than men, and atypical contracts may be used as a first stepping stone from non-employment into regular employment. Existing evidence for the United States indeed shows that atypical employment arrangements (including part-time jobs and fixed-term contracts) tend to be held disproportionately more by those who have suffered a job loss or had spells of inactivity, presumably due to the difficulty of immediately finding regular employment (Farber 1999). Related to this, evidence for Europe suggests that the share of temporary contracts is much higher among newly created jobs than among the pre-existing employment stock (see Blanchard and Landier 2002 for France, and Dolado et al. 2002, and Güell and Petrongolo 2003 for Spain). The detailed results are presented in Tables 4.2–4.4.

One way to summarize the estimates in Tables 4.2–4.4 is to use the marginal effects from the estimated probit models to compute the difference in the predicted probabilities of alternative working arrangements for women and men. We computed these differences separately into the following groups: single individuals without small children, married individuals without small children, and married individuals with small children (at least one aged 0–2 and at least one aged 3–5). Clearly such categories do not represent the whole population of employees, but they are chosen to illustrate in a parsimonious way the effect of family ties on the incidence of different types of jobs in male and female employment.

The resulting gender differences are reported in Table 4.5. The interpretation of the figures reported is as follows. When we take as an example the top left

Table 4.2. *Probit estimates of part-time equations*

	UK	SWE	FIN	DEN	GER	NET	BEL	LUX	AUT	IRE	FRA	ITA	SPA	POR	GRE
Female	0.055***	0.061***	0.015*	0.043***	0.042***	0.091***	0.071***	0.022***	0.056***	0.056***	0.059***	0.073***	0.045***	0.032***	0.030***
	(0.006)	(0.012)	(0.009)	(0.009)	(0.010)	(0.011)	(0.013)	(0.008)	(0.009)	(0.009)	(0.008)	(0.006)	(0.005)	(0.004)	(0.007)
Married	-0.074***	-0.038**	-0.009***	–	-0.095***	-0.127***	-0.061***	-0.054***	-0.014	-0.059***	-0.052***	-0.018**	-0.027***	-0.021***	-0.018**
	(0.008)	(0.014)	(0.010)	(0.011)	(0.014)	(0.013)	(0.016)	(0.011)	(0.009)	(0.011)	(0.009)	(0.007)	(0.005)	(0.005)	(0.008)
Married* Female	0.180***	0.077***	0.019	0.109***	0.255***	0.366***	0.142***	0.219***	0.110***	0.148***	0.109***	0.057***	0.048***	0.024***	0.037***
	(0.013)	(0.021)	(0.012)	(0.019)	(0.028)	(0.021)	(0.023)	(0.035)	(0.018)	(0.017)	(0.013)	(0.009)	(0.008)	(0.006)	(0.011)
Cohabiting	-0.041***	-0.036***	-0.007	-0.009	-0.018*	-0.055***	-0.005	-0.009	0.000	-0.030	-0.021**	-0.013	-0.007	-0.006	-0.007
	(0.007)	(0.013)	(0.010)	(0.010)	(0.010)	(0.011)	(0.015)	(0.009)	(0.013)	(0.019)	(0.008)	(0.019)	(0.009)	(0.006)	(0.017)
Cohabiting* Female	0.057***	0.032	-0.007	0.006	0.036	0.142***	0.045*	0.060***	0.028	0.023	0.055***	0.008	0.003	0.000	0.004
	(0.017)	(0.024)	(0.012)	(0.014)	(0.026)	(0.027)	(0.026)	(0.029)	(0.021)	(0.036)	(0.017)	(0.028)	(0.014)	(0.010)	(0.028)
Kids 0–2	0.042***	0.037	-0.018*	-0.004	0.079***	0.070***	0.022	0.010	0.014	0.001	0.022**	0.021**	-0.004	0.009	-0.008
	(0.015)	(0.026)	(0.010)	(0.014)	(0.025)	(0.019)	(0.017)	(0.015)	(0.013)	(0.013)	(0.011)	(0.009)	(0.007)	(0.006)	(0.008)
Kids 0–2 Female	0.068***	-0.006	0.037	-0.008	-0.011	0.153***	0.027	0.020	-0.008	0.039**	-0.009	-0.006	0.014	-0.008*	0.028*
	(0.019)	(0.022)	(0.027)	(0.014)	(0.013)	(0.029)	(0.021)	(0.020)	(0.012)	(0.020)	(0.010)	(0.009)	(0.011)	(0.004)	(0.016)
Kids 3–5	-0.020*	-0.035*	-0.005	0.007	0.041*	0.026	0.060***	-0.019*	-0.014	0.037**	0.017*	0.001	-0.008	0.005	0.011
	(0.011)	(0.017)	(0.012)	(0.015)	(0.018)	(0.016)	(0.018)	(0.010)	(0.010)	(0.014)	(0.010)	(0.008)	(0.006)	(0.006)	(0.009)
Kids 3–5* Female	0.198***	0.088***	0.006	-0.008	0.028	0.184***	-0.012	0.106***	0.094***	0.038**	0.006	0.011	0.024***	-0.008*	0.000
	(0.032)	(0.042)	(0.017)	(0.013)	(0.020)	(0.032)	(0.013)	(0.046)	(0.028)	(0.018)	(0.011)	(0.011)	(0.12)	(0.004)	(0.011)

Table 4.2. (Continued)

	UK	SWE	FIN	DEN	GER	NET	BEL	LUX	AUT	IRE	FRA	ITA	SPA	POR	GRE
Kids 6-10	-0.002	0.009	-0.008	0.003	0.018	0.006	-0.004	0.018	-0.002	0.014	0.005	0.005	0.001	-0.009**	0.016**
	(0.010)	(0.019)	(0.011)	(0.013)	(0.012)	(0.012)	(0.013)	(0.013)	(0.010)	(0.011)	(0.008)	(0.007)	(0.005)	(0.004)	(0.008)
Kids 6-10 Female	0.130***	0.035	0.018	0.013	0.026	0.184***	0.064***	0.011	0.066***	0.037**	0.022**	0.017*	0.005	0.007	-0.005
	(0.020)	(0.025)	(0.017)	(0.015)	(0.016)	(0.026)	(0.021)	(0.014)	(0.019)	(0.015)	(0.011)	(0.009)	(0.007)	(0.007)	(0.009)
Kids 11-15	0.036***	0.013	0.009	0.007	0.010	0.039***	0.011	0.001	-0.022**	-0.007	0.025***	0.011*	0.002	-0.003	0.006
	(0.010)	(0.020)	(0.011)	(0.012)	(0.012)	(0.013)	(0.014)	(0.011)	(0.008)	(0.009)	(0.008)	(0.006)	(0.005)	(0.004)	(0.007)
Kids 11-15 Female	0.024**	0.018	0.003	0.004	0.024	0.090***	0.032*	0.023	0.086***	0.069***	-0.001	0.001	0.008	0.004	-0.002
	(0.011)	(0.024)	(0.012)	(0.013)	(0.016)	(0.019)	(0.018)	(0.017)	(0.020)	(0.015)	(0.009)	(0.008)	(0.007)	(0.005)	(0.009)
No. Observations	35641	8160	8599	12689	12434	23156	11526	7760	14809	16102	26616	29824	26684	24423	15051

Notes: The figures reported are marginal effects obtained from probit regressions for part-time work (1 = part-time work; 0 = full-time work). Significance at 1%, 5% and 10% is denoted by ***, **, and * respectively. The estimated equations also include: age and age squared, 2 education dummies, 9 occupation dummies, 2 sector dummies, one dummy for public sector, 3 dummies for unemployment spells (if any) before the current job (unemployed for less than 6 months, for 6–12 months, or for more than 12 months), year dummies. Exception: for Sweden: no occupation or previous unemployment dummies are included, as the relevant information is not available in the data source.

Source: ECHPS.

Table 4.3. *Probit estimates of involuntary part-time equations*

	UK	SWE	FIN	DEN	GER	NET	BEL	LUX	AUT	IRE	FRA	ITA	SPA	POR	GRE
Female	0.029***	–	0.084	-0.009	-0.044	0.018*	0.052	–	0.013	-0.081*	0.193***	0.067***	0.063	0.128**	0.132**
	(0.011)		(0.100)	(0.046)	(0.050)	(0.010)	(0.058)		(0.026)	(0.044)	(0.051)	(0.024)	(0.042)	(0.061)	(0.063)
Married	0.050***	–	0.057	-0.185*	-0.043	-0.015	0.012	–	-0.105	0.195***	-0.180**	0.076**	0.085	0.067	0.089
	(0.015)		(0.139)	(0.095)	(0.063)	(0.019)	(0.089)		(0.072)	(0.042)	(0.075)	(0.033)	(0.065)	(0.091)	(0.087)
Married Female	-0.174***	–	-0.082	0.040	-0.000	-0.086***	-0.237*	–	0.019	-0.371***	-0.054	-0.252***	-0.276***	-0.145	-0.243***
	(0.051)		(0.150)	(0.068)	(0.047)	(0.028)	(0.122)		(0.042)	(0.055)	(0.079)	(0.053)	(0.062)	(0.102)	(0.091)
Cohabiting	0.093	–	0.084	-0.068	-0.055***	0.006	-0.103	–	-0.035	0.216	0.004	0.310	0.137	-0.219***	-0.189
	(0.086)		(0.151)	(0.044)	(0.010)	(0.026)	(0.076)		(0.034)	(0.147)	(0.099)	(0.357)	(0.158)	(0.071)	(0.153)
Cohabiting Female	-0.046***	–	-0.105	0.137	0.402	-0.011	-0.046	–	0.014	-0.225***	-0.070	-0.131**	-0.194*	–	0.211
	(0.011)		(0.138)	(0.114)	(0.286)	(0.021)	(0.107)		(0.074)	(0.016)	(0.013)	(0.011)	(0.116)		(0.277)
Kids 0-2	-0.008	–	0.229	-0.072***	0.014	-0.047***	0.099	–	0.035	-0.044	0.214**	-0.031	-0.056	0.094	-0.281***
	(0.031)		(0.197)	(0.026)	(0.064)	(0.015)	(0.138)		(0.075)	(0.070)	(0.105)	(0.048)	(0.104)	(0.169)	(0.108)
Kids 0-2 Female	-0.047*	–	-0.159	–	-0.047***	0.004	-0.165***	–	-0.057**	-0.130**	-0.385***	-0.062	-0.078	-0.078	0.110
	(0.014)		(0.131)		(0.016)	(0.041)	(0.061)		(0.024)	(0.060)	(0.044)	(0.044)	(0.113)	(0.148)	(0.205)
Kids 3-5	-0.038	–	-0.197*	0.518**	0.032	0.033*	0.044	–	0.103	-0.039	0.222**	-0.112***	0.056	-0.376***	-0.059
	(0.025)		(0.119)	(0.226)	(0.074)	(0.019)	(0.108)		(0.130)	(0.062)	(0.111)	(0.028)	(0.110)	(0.040)	(0.125)
Kids 3-5 Female	-0.045*	–	0.167	-0.158***	-0.064***	-0.026	-0.090	–	-0.085***	-0.113*	-0.296***	0.179*	-0.129	0.653***	-0.072
	(0.023)		(0.237)	(0.024)	(0.013)	(0.024)	(0.084)		(0.023)	(0.058)	(0.077)	(0.106)	(0.099)	(0.135)	(0.144)

Table 4.3. (Continued)

	UK	SWE	FIN	DEN	GER	NET	BEL	LUX	AUT	IRE	FRA	ITA	SPA	POR	GRE
Kids 6–10	0.049	–	0.274	-0.107	-0.028	-0.020	0.074	–	-0.014	-0.038	0.200**	-0.035	0.033	0.609***	-0.213**
	(0.040)		(0.185)	(0.077)	(0.040)	(0.017)	(0.106)		(0.074)	(0.055)	(0.086)	(0.044)	(0.077)	(0.145)	(0.098)
Kids 6–10* Female	-0.064***	–	-0.198*	-0.008	-0.021	-0.012	-0.130	–	-0.052	-0.067	-0.328***	0.009	-0.109	-0.389***	0.097
	(0.016)		(0.112)	(0.130)	(0.044)	(0.020)	(0.083)		(0.059)	(0.058)	(0.064)	(0.057)	(0.076)	(0.050)	(0.148)
Kids 11–15	0.011	–	0.195	-0.044	-0.570***	0.006	-0.029	–	0.005	-0.038	-0.025	-0.079**	-0.023	-0.010	-0.087
	(0.026)		(0.156)	(0.069)	(0.028)	(0.019)	(0.100)		(0.067)	(0.045)	(0.073)	(0.036)	(0.066)	(0.107)	(0.092)
Kids 11–15* Female	-0.036**	–	-0.238***	0.006	0.999***	-0.012	0.007	–	-0.039	-0.020	-0.049	0.027	0.036	0.069	-0.049
	(0.018)		(0.091)	(0.089)	(0.000)	(0.017)	(0.111)		(0.057)	(0.054)	(0.078)	(0.059)	(0.077)	(0.123)	(0.117)
No. Observations	2386		544	1145	1436	4693	1350		1483	1992	2346	1966	1709	966	834

Notes: The figures reported are marginal effects obtained from probit regressions for involuntary part-time work (1 = involuntary part-time work; 0 = voluntary part-time work). Significance at 1%, 5% and 10% is denoted by ***, ** and * respectively. The estimated equations also include: age and age squared, 2 education dummies, 9 occupation dummies, 2 sector dummies, one dummy for public sector, 3 dummies for unemployment spells (if any) before the current job (unemployed for less than 6 months, for 6–12 months, or for more than 12 months), year dummies. No estimates are reported for Sweden, as no information on involuntary part-time in available in the data source, nor for Luxembourg, due to the insufficient number of observations.

Source: ECHPS.

Table 4.4. *Probit estimates of temporary work equations*

	UK	SWE	FIN	DEN	GER	NET	BEL	LUX	AUT	IRE	FRA	ITA	SPA	POR	GRE
Female	0.002	0.014*	0.048***	0.020	0.001	−0.008	0.039***	−0.002	0.017**	0.046***	0.004	0.020***	0.055***	0.024**	0.025**
	(0.005)	(0.008)	(0.016)	(0.012)	(0.014)	(0.008)	(0.013)	(0.008)	(0.008)	(0.011)	(0.006)	(0.007)	(0.013)	(0.010)	(0.013)
Married	−0.029***	−0.024**	−0.005	−0.006	−0.010	−0.068***	−0.020	−0.014*	−0.015*	−0.064***	−0.059***	−0.024**	−0.088***	−0.059***	−0.040***
	(0.006)	(0.010)	(0.016)	(0.011)	(0.013)	(0.009)	(0.013)	(0.009)	(0.008)	(0.014)	(0.007)	(0.007)	(0.012)	(0.010)	(0.014)
Married* Female	0.007	−0.013	−0.014	−0.042***	−0.004	0.063***	−0.007	0.019	−0.007	0.096***	0.040***	−0.006	0.048***	0.020	0.015
	(0.007)	(0.011)	(0.019)	(0.013)	(0.017)	(0.013)	(0.015)	(0.014)	(0.010)	(0.018)	(0.010)	(0.009)	(0.017)	(0.012)	(0.018)
Cohabiting	−0.010*	−0.012	−0.003	−0.009	−0.002	−0.035***	−0.013	0.004	−0.003	−0.061***	−0.031***	0.016	0.010	0.027	0.010
	(0.006)	(0.009)	(0.017)	(0.011)	(0.018)	(0.007)	(0.013)	(0.011)	(0.011)	(0.020)	(0.005)	(0.021)	(0.012)	(0.012)	(0.018)
Cohabiting* Female	−0.010	−0.022**	0.007	−0.015	0.005	0.043***	−0.013	0.004	−0.009	0.058	0.034***	−0.021	0.078*	−0.003	0.043
	(0.008)	(0.010)	(0.024)	(0.015)	(0.027)	(0.015)	(0.017)	(0.016)	(0.015)	(0.048)	(0.013)	(0.022)	(0.029)	(0.022)	(0.036)
Kids 0–2	−0.003	−0.017	−0.017	−0.009	0.003	0.021*	−0.011	−0.018**	0.002	−0.019	0.002	0.019*	−0.008	−0.010	−0.008
	(0.008)	(0.011)	(0.016)	(0.012)	(0.018)	(0.011)	(0.013)	(0.008)	(0.010)	(0.016)	(0.007)	(0.009)	(0.015)	(0.031)	(0.061)
Kids 0–2* Female	−0.002	−0.006	−0.030	0.013	−0.034	−0.056***	0.028	0.022	−0.002	−0.048**	−0.023***	−0.027**	−0.086***	−0.009	0.004
	(0.011)	(0.017)	(0.021)	(0.020)	(0.022)	(0.007)	(0.022)	(0.021)	(0.014)	(0.018)	(0.007)	(0.011)	(0.024)	(0.017)	(0.026)
Kids 3–5	−0.000	−0.016	−0.003	−0.022*	−0.020	−0.009	−0.026**	0.015	0.008	0.002	0.001	−0.014*	−0.002	−0.012	0.016
	(0.008)	(0.011)	(0.016)	(0.012)	(0.014)	(0.009)	(0.011)	(0.012)	(0.010)	(0.016)	(0.007)	(0.008)	(0.015)	(0.012)	(0.017)
Kids 3–5* Female	0.020	0.039	0.010	0.033	0.002	0.012	0.011	−0.014	0.013	0.008	−0.004	0.006	0.034	−0.012	−0.036
	(0.013)	(0.025)	(0.023)	(0.023)	(0.028)	(0.016)	(0.019)	(0.011)	(0.016)	(0.022)	(0.009)	(0.014)	(0.027)	(0.017)	(0.023)

Table 4.4. (*Continued*)

	UK	SWE	FIN	DEN	GER	NET	BEL	LUX	AUT	IRE	FRA	ITA	SPA	POR	GRE
Kids 6–10	0.002	0.001	0.001	−0.007	0.001	−0.014*	−0.007	0.005	0.011	−0.012	0.004	−0.009	0.017	0.014	0.018
	(0.007)**	(0.012)	(0.015)	(0.011)	(0.012)	(0.008)	(0.011)	(0.010)	(0.009)	(0.012)	(0.007)	(0.007)*	(0.012)	(0.010)	(0.014)
Kids 6–10* Female	0.022**	−0.007	−0.009	−0.009	0.025	0.079***	−0.014	0.013	0.010	−0.006	0.000	0.027**	−0.019	−0.008	0.004
	(0.011)	(0.014)	(0.019)*	(0.015)	(0.022)	(0.019)	(0.014)	(0.017)	(0.013)	(0.017)	(0.009)***	(0.013)	(0.020)	(0.014)*	(0.022)
Kids 11–15	0.010	0.013	0.029*	0.014	0.021	0.028***	−0.001	−0.016*	−0.010	0.027**	0.022***	−0.002	0.030**	0.021**	−0.007
	(0.007)**	(0.014)	(0.015)	(0.012)	(0.013)	(0.010)	(0.012)	(0.008)	(0.007)	(0.011)	(0.007)	(0.007)	(0.012)	(0.009)	(0.013)*
Kids 11–15* Female	0.026**	−0.012	−0.027	0.032	−0.006	0.029**	−0.002	0.051**	−0.001	0.041**	−0.003	0.012	−0.001	−0.019	−0.031*
	(0.010)	(0.013)	(0.017)	(0.020)	(0.017)	(0.014)	(0.016)	(0.024)	(0.011)	(0.017)	(0.008)	(0.012)	(0.019)	(0.012)	(0.018)
No. Observations	26810	8272	8487	9254	7769	19217	8861	6704	14143	11928	22395	24148	21366	20693	12056

Notes: The figures reported are marginal effects obtained from probit regressions for temporary work (1 = temporary work; 0 = permanent work). Significance at 1%, 5% and 10% is denoted by ***, ** and * respectively. The estimated equations also include: age and age squared, 2 education dummies, 9 occupation dummies, 2 sector dummies, one dummy for public sector, 3 dummies for unemployment spells (if any) before the current job (unemployed for less than 6 months, for 6–12 months, or for more than 12 months), year dummies. Exception: for Sweden: no occupation or previous unemployment dummies are included, as the relevant information is not available in the data source.

Source: ECHPS.

Table 4.5. *Female versus male employment characteristics: Differential effects*

	UK	SWE	FIN	DEN	GER	NET	BEL	LUX	AUT	IRE	FRA	ITA	SPA	POR	GRE
Incidence of part-time work															
Single no kids	0.059***	0.061***	0.015*	0.043***	0.042**	0.091***	0.071***	0.022***	0.056***	0.056***	0.059***	0.073***	0.045***	0.032***	0.030***
Married, no kids	0.235***	0.138***	0.034***	0.152**	0.297***	0.457***	0.213***	0.241***	0.166***	0.204***	0.168***	0.130***	0.093***	0.056***	0.067***
Married, with kids	0.501***	0.220***	0.077***	0.136***	0.314***	0.794***	0.228***	0.367***	0.252***	0.281***	0.165***	0.135***	0.131***	0.040***	0.095***
Incidence of involuntary part-time work															
Single, no kids	0.029**	–	0.084	−0.009	−0.044	0.018	0.052	–	0.013	−0.081**	0.193***	0.067**	0.063	0.128**	0.132**
Married, no kids	−0.145***	–	0.002	0.031	−0.044	−0.068***	−0.185**	–	0.032	−0.452***	0.139***	−0.185**	−0.213***	−0.017	−0.111
Married, with kids	−0.237***	–	0.010	−0.127**	−0.155***	−0.090	−0.44***	–	−0.110**	−0.695***	−0.542***	−0.068	−0.420**	0.558**	−0.073
Incidence of temporary work															
Single, no kids	0.002	0.014*	0.048**	0.020	0.001	−0.008	0.039**	−0.002	0.017**	0.046**	0.004	0.020**	0.055***	0.024**	0.025***
Married, no kids	0.009*	0.001	0.034**	−0.022**	−0.003	0.055***	0.032*	0.017	0.01	0.142***	0.044***	0.014**	0.103***	0.044***	0.040**
Married, with kids	0.027*	0.034	0.014	0.024	−0.035	0.011	0.071**	0.025	0.021	0.102**	0.017	−0.007	0.051	0.023	0.008

Notes: The figures reported are differences between females' and males' predicted probabilities of working part-time, being an involuntary part-timer and working on a temporary job for the demographic groups listed in the first column. The figures are based on estimates of probit model including: one gender dummy, two dummies for marital or cohabitation status (interacted with gender), the presence of kids aged 0–2, 3–5, 6–10 and 11–15 respectively (interacted with gender), age and its square, 2 education dummies, 9 occupation dummies, 2 industry dummies, one dummy for public sector, year dummies. No results are reported for Sweden and Luxembourg on involuntary part time, due to missing information and small sample size respectively. Significance at 1%, 5% and 10% is denoted by *** , ** , and * respectively.

Source: ECHPS.

corner entry, we find that in the United Kingdom, single women without children are 5.5 per cent more likely than single men without children to hold a part-time job, and this difference is statistically different from zero at the 1 per cent significance level. The gender difference rises to 23.5 per cent for those married without children, and to 50.1 per cent for those married with small children.

The first set of results presented in Table 4.5 shows that in all countries considered, women are over-represented in part-time jobs (see Table 4.2 for detailed estimates of part-time equations). Among single individuals without children, gender differences range from 1.5 per cent in Finland to 9.1 per cent in the Netherlands. Such gender differences rise substantially for those married without children (above 20 per cent in a number of northern European countries, and 45 per cent in the Netherlands), and even more for those married with children (again the Netherlands are an outlier here, with a gender difference in the predicted probability of working part-time of nearly 80 per cent). Overall, the cross-country variation of gender differences is relatively small for workers without family ties, and rises substantially when married workers are considered, especially if they have young children. The high incidence of part-time jobs among women in northern European countries, documented in Table 4.1 (p. 42), is to a large extent explained by the presence of family ties. Differences in working hours for single women without children are far smaller across Europe than the differences among married women, with or without small children.

To address this point more specifically, we can take the gender differential in the incidence of part-time work for those married with children as the total to be explained by (i) gender; (ii) marital status and (iii) presence of children. The importance of gender alone (namely, the ratio between the figure reported in the first row and the corresponding figure in the third row of Table 4.5) is 5 per cent in Luxembourg, around 10 per cent in the United Kingdom and the Netherlands, and within the 15–30 per cent range in all other countries down to Ireland. But it rises to 35 per cent in France and Italy, 54 per cent in Spain and 80 per cent in Portugal. While there is no clear international pattern in the explanatory capability of marital status, it is the presence of small children that explains more than 40 per cent of the gender difference in the incidence of part-time work in the United Kingdom, Sweden and the Netherlands, and more than one-third in other northern or central European countries, while it explains less than 30 per cent in Spain and Greece, and virtually nothing in France and Italy. In Portugal the ranking reverses, with women with children being more likely to work full time. It should be noted, however, that this figure is also particularly small for non-Mediterranean countries such as Denmark, Germany and Belgium.[6]

It is to be expected that people with family commitments who are also working part time should express less dissatisfaction with their jobs than other

---

[6] For cross-country correlations between part-time incidence and labor force participation of mothers see Section 1.3 of Part II of this volume.

individuals in such jobs. At least part of the reason why they are in part-time jobs is the desire for shorter hours rather than the absence of full-time jobs. Aggregating from this to the level of the economy as a whole, it is to be expected that in countries where family ties explain most of the part-time incidence among women, women should be less likely to classify themselves involuntary part-timers.

In the second part of Table 4.5 we compute analogous gender differentials in predicted probabilities of being an involuntary part-timer, conditional on working part time (see Table 4.3 (p. 47) for detailed estimates).[7] We find that part-time work is more likely to be classified as involuntary among single women than it is among single men in the United Kingdom, France, Italy, Portugal and Greece. There are, however, differences among these countries. While this difference is around 3 per cent in the United Kingdom, it increases to 7 per cent in Italy, 13 per cent in Portugal and Greece and nearly 20 per cent in France. Ireland is the only country in our sample in which single women in part-time jobs are less likely to call themselves involuntary part-timers than single men are.

Among married individuals with children, the gender differential in the probability of being an involuntary part-timer is more mixed. In most countries it is negative, indicating that men are more likely to be involuntary part-timers, but in Finland, the Netherlands, Italy and Greece, the differential is not significant. In Portugal the differential is positive and significant.

The picture that emerges from the estimates of the two part-time equations can be broadly summarized by saying that in northern and central Europe, part-time work among women is to a large extent explained by family ties (especially when there are very young children) and it is unlikely to be perceived as the consequence of a market constraint on the number of hours worked. On the contrary, in southern European countries (including France) the explanatory power of family ties in female part-time employment is lower, and single women are more likely to be involuntary part-timers than single men are. The results for the southern countries are much easier to reconcile with discrimination against women in regular, full-time jobs than with gender differences in preferences or comparative advantages.

In our last set of results on segregation we look at the incidence of temporary work across genders, using the same specification of the regression equation as for part-time work (detailed estimates reported in Table 4.4 (p. 49)). Temporary work is more frequent among single women than it is among single men in Sweden, Finland, Belgium, Austria, and in southern Europe. The highest differential is found in Spain, at 5.5 per cent, and it is also the country with the highest overall incidence of temporary work. Being married, reinforces the tendency for more women to be in temporary work. In part, the presence of a husband's income, and in part the greater tendency for married women to enter

---

[7] No estimates are reported for Sweden, as information on reasons for part-time work is not available for this country in the ECHPS, and for Luxembourg, due to the small sample size.

and exit the labor force, make married women more willing to accept temporary and less secure jobs. The highest gender difference is in Ireland, where married women without children are about 14 per cent more likely than married men to hold a temporary contract. In second place comes Spain, with a gender differential of 10 per cent. Among workers with children, significant gender differences in the incidence of temporary work are detected only for Belgium and Ireland.

Higher incidence of temporary employment among women bears no clear interpretation in terms of family commitments by women, unless part-time jobs are typically covered by temporary contracts. We therefore consider the possibility that individuals in part-time jobs are also more likely to hold temporary contracts. A simple cross-country probit regression of the probability of holding a temporary contract on a set of country dummies and a part-time dummy reveals that part-time workers are 12 per cent more likely than full-time workers to hold a fixed-term contract, and this effect bears a t-statistic of 55.4. This correlation is sufficiently strong that failure to take it into account may bias the coefficients of interest. For example, one may obtain a significant gender effect in the estimated probability of holding a fixed-term contract simply because women are more likely to work part time, and not because they are discriminated against in the allocation of regular contracts. In order to correct for this likely bias, we estimated the part-time and the fixed-term contract equations simultaneously using a bivariate probit model. The estimated covariance between the error terms of the two equations was positive and significant at the 5 per cent level for all countries, except Luxembourg, where it was significant at the 10 per cent level. But even after correcting for this interaction, the sign and the significance of the gender and family variables in the regressions for both part-time and temporary work remained largely unchanged.

We ran a number of other tests to check the robustness of our estimates with the probit equations for job types. First, we included interactions between gender and education variables, to account for different returns to human capital for the two genders. Secondly, we removed variables for job characteristics, which may be endogenous to the choice of contract. Thirdly, considering that female labor force participation differs widely across the countries in our sample, we ran ordered probit equations that include non-employment as an alternative to full-time and part-time work, and to permanent and temporary work, respectively. The results reported here were largely unchanged when these specifications were estimated.

4.3 PREFERENCES FOR ATYPICAL JOBS

The results reported in Section 4.2 show that even after we control for a number of individual and job characteristics, women tend to take the larger share of part-time jobs in all countries, and of temporary jobs in a substantial subset of countries. An unequal allocation of genders across jobs may result from differences in productivity and preference characteristics that we have not corrected for, or employer discrimination. The estimates of the previous section control for productivity by conditioning outcomes on human capital, and for preferences by conditioning on family characteristics. In this section we address the issue of worker preferences more generally, by studying job satisfaction indices.

If the observed job allocation meets the preferences of workers (and does not negatively affect their productivity), then one should conclude that workers sort themselves efficiently across jobs. However, we have seen in the previous section that some fraction of female part-time work is indeed involuntary, as a full-time job would have been preferred to a part-time one but was not found. Aggregate Eurostat data give an even stronger negative picture for temporary work (see Table 4.1 (p. 42)).

In this section we use job satisfaction indicators to infer how worker preferences are affected when holding an atypical job. The ECHPS contains detailed information on specific dimensions of job satisfaction (overall job satisfaction, satisfaction with earnings, job security, type of job, working hours, etc.). Each aspect of job satisfaction is measured on a scale from 1 to 5, from *very dissatisfied* to *very satisfied*, and we estimate corresponding ordered probit equations, including the usual individual and job characteristics on the right-hand side, plus a dummy variable for part-time and another one for temporary jobs, each interacted with gender. The results are reported in Table 4.6.

A clear message from the first three panels of Table 4.6 is that part-time jobs tend to reduce job satisfaction (overall and with earnings) in southern Europe only (and they actually increase it in some northern European countries); while temporary jobs reduce satisfaction everywhere (overall satisfaction and satisfaction with earnings and with the type of job), but more so in the South than in the North. If anything, the negative effect of holding an atypical job on satisfaction with earnings is mitigated for women in a few cases.

Features which are most closely related to part-time or temporary jobs, like hours of work and job security, are studied in panels 4 and 5 of Table 4.6 respectively. Concerning working hours, female part-timers in northern Europe are typically more satisfied with shorter working hours than male part-timers are, but of the southern countries only Spain and Greece conform with this pattern. As expected, holding a temporary job implies lower satisfaction with job security in all countries (and again this effect is stronger in southern Europe), and women are in this case even more negatively affected than males.

The results of this section can be very broadly summarized by saying that, as far as job satisfaction is concerned, part-time jobs are generally perceived to be as good as full-time jobs in central and northern Europe, and even better than full-time jobs by women in a few cases. On the contrary, in southern Europe they tend to be perceived as inferior. Temporary jobs reduce job satisfaction everywhere, if anything more in the South than in the North. This result is

Table 4.6. *Job satisfaction on part-time and temporary contracts*

	UK	FIN	DEN	GER	NET	BEL	LUX	AUT	IRE	FRA	ITA	SPA	POR	GRE
(1) Overall job satisfaction														
Part-time	0.154***	-0.178*	0.191*	-0.093	-0.065	-0.159*	0.412	-0.058	-0.128**	0.026	-0.114**	-0.167***	-0.161*	-0.204***
Part-time* F	0.038	0.032	-0.094	0.111	0.123**	0.220**	-0.388	0.144	0.045	-0.057	0.009	0.064	-0.233***	0.136**
Temp.	-0.217***	0.000	-0.147***	-0.220***	-0.125***	-0.099*	-0.038	-0.217***	-0.301***	-0.106***	-0.449***	-0.257***	-0.353***	-0.715***
Temp.* F	0.028	0.079	0.196***	0.071	0.055	0.111	-0.039	0.014	0.140**	0.015	0.078*	0.015	0.006	0.040
No. Obs.	24013	7819	9092	7561	19491	8734	1770	14095	10017	20781	23785	21208	20621	12030
(2) Satisfaction with earnings														
Part-time	-0.054	-0.152*	0.220**	-0.061	-0.061	0.005	-0.399	0.017	-0.016	-0.131***	-0.357***	-0.369***	-0.415***	-0.383***
Part-time* F	0.234***	-0.016	0.001	0.055	0.090*	0.044	0.439	0.006	-0.050	0.093*	0.151***	0.253***	0.000	0.129*
Temp.	-0.305***	-0.171***	-0.232***	-0.206***	-0.202***	-0.145***	-0.022	-0.109**	-0.160***	0.007	-0.333***	-0.213***	-0.124**	-0.446***
Temp.* F	-0.007	0.064	0.206***	0.177***	0.106**	0.083	0.036	-0.065	0.106*	-0.149***	0.085*	0.059*	-0.044	0.037
No. Obs.	16259	7818	9175	7559	19448	8792	1770	14079	10011	20797	23781	21250	20614	12037
(3) Satisfaction with type of job														
Part-time	0.005	-0.129	0.249**	-0.069	-0.135***	-0.028	-0.040	-0.003	-0.098	0.041	-0.007	-0.053	0.065	0.078
Part-time* F	0.017	-0.053	-0.167	-0.007	0.056	0.079	0.139	0.042	-0.019	-0.034	0.017	-0.032	-0.345***	0.039
Temp.	-0.181***	-0.025	-0.129*	-0.112***	-0.122***	-0.032	0.031	-0.154***	-0.321***	0.000	-0.350***	-0.194**	-0.250***	-0.590***
Temp.* F	0.028	0.016	0.177**	0.060	0.000	0.117	0.153	-0.021	0.091	0.031	0.077*	-0.069**	0.008	0.150***
No. Obs.	26353	7812	9174	7548	19486	8781	1766	14077	9996	20801	23777	21254	20617	12037

(4) Satisfaction with working hours

Part-time	0.040	−0.299***	−0.057	0.026	0.069	0.082	−0.149	0.403***	−0.100	0.150**	0.177***	−0.095	−0.185**	0.326***
Part-time* F	0.407***	−0.40	0.529***	0.299**	0.229***	0.307***	0.591	−0.137	0.343***	−0.011	0.072	0.154**	−0.107	0.124*
Temp.	−0.037	0.036	−0.041	−0.143***	−0.006	−0.001	0.113	−0.127***	−0.226***	−0.001	−0.336***	−0.190***	−0.104***	−0.537***
Temp.* F	−0.083*	−0.098	−0.143*	0.145*	−0.122**	0.010	−0.078	−0.094	−0.081	−0.144**	0.063	−0.032	−0.004	0.086*
No. Obs.	26354	7818	9166	7550	19486	8773	1766	14077	9972	20801	23741	21240	20617	12037

(5) Satisfaction with job security

Part-time	0.133**	−0.139	−0.102	−0.054	−0.109**	−0.036	−0.08	−0.058	−0.072	−0.037	−0.175***	−0.305***	−0.253**	−0.118**
Part-time* F	−0.017	0.091	0.040	0.209	0.066	0.047	0.174	−0.036	−0.029	−0.012	0.035	0.232**	0.084	0.167**
Temp.	−0.845***	−1.033***	−0.985***	−0.523***	−1.095***	−0.730***	−0.819***	−0.535***	−1.208***	−1.106***	−1.122***	−1.206***	−0.934***	−1.337***
Temp.* F	−0.068	−0.326***	−0.265	−0.185**	−0.127**	−0.065	0.404*	−0.322***	−0.155***	−0.369***	0.069	−0.104***	−0.136***	−0.099***
No. Obs.	26226	7806	9169	7558	19440	8782	1769	14080	9995	20789	23782	21255	20613	12037

Notes: The figures reported are the coefficients obtained from ordered probit regressions for levels of subjective job satisfaction. The estimated equations also include: one gender dummy, two dummies for marital or cohabitation status (interacted with gender), the presence of kids aged 0–2, 3–5, 6–10 and 11–15 respectively (interacted with gender), age and its square, 2 education dummies, 9 occupation dummies, 2 industry dummies, one dummy for public sector, year dummies. No results are reported for Sweden as information on job satisfaction is not available. Significance at 1%, 5% and 10% is denoted by ***, ** and * respectively.

Source: ECHPS.

interesting in the light of the recent experiments of flexibility at the margin, implemented in a number of European countries through the introduction of temporary contracts.[8] Increased labor market flexibility does not seem to have come without a cost in terms of job satisfaction, especially as far as job security is concerned.

Moreover, in a few cases women's job satisfaction is less affected by atypical contracts (when it comes to earnings and working hours, and mostly in northern Europe), and in some others more affected (typically when it comes to job security). Overall, there is no convincing evidence that women are particularly happier or unhappier than men in temporary jobs, which means that different gender preferences for work cannot be relied upon to explain women's over-representation in these jobs. In some countries, women are not reported to be happier in part-time jobs either, which is more serious in view of the bigger representation of women in part-time jobs.

4.4 WAGES IN ATYPICAL JOBS

There are several reasons why similar workers may receive different wages across different types of jobs. First, labor legislation or employment agreements may be such that an important fraction of labor costs may not grow in the same proportion as the number of hours worked. Fixed labor costs include hiring, training and firing costs, administrative costs and in some cases payroll taxes. The presence of fixed labor costs implies a wage penalty to part-time jobs, because the hourly equivalent cost for them is higher than it is for full-time jobs. Secondly, labor productivity may be affected by working hours and, depending on the relationship between productivity and working hours, one can either expect a premium or a penalty associated with part-time work. Thirdly, unobserved job heterogeneity may result in wage differentials across types of contracts if part-time and full-time contracts tend to be used for systematically different jobs types. Finally, part-time jobs should pay a compensating wage differential if their non-wage characteristics are undesirable to workers, and vice versa if workers tend to like the non-wage attributes of part-time jobs. Such characteristics include, among other things, job security, working conditions, job quality and commuting costs per hour worked. Existing research has not yet provided a definitive answer to the question of the relationship between the number of working hours and hourly wages (see Wolf 2003, Ch. 2, and references therein for an overview).

Turning next to temporary jobs, it can be argued that their relatively shorter job duration reduces both firm and worker incentives to acquire job-specific

---

[8] During the 1990s, temporary employment growth accounted for around a half of total employment growth in Finland, France, Spain and Portugal, and was actually higher than total employment growth in Germany and Italy (see OECD 2002, Ch. 3)—all countries with relatively strict employment protection on permanent contracts (see OECD 1999, Ch. 2).

human capital, resulting in relatively lower wages. Apart from this, the arguments mentioned above for unobserved heterogeneity and compensating differentials in part-time jobs can be extended to temporary jobs as well (see Booth *et al.* 2002 for an overview).

This section assesses any wage penalties associated with atypical jobs by estimating wage equations for the two genders, including controls for part-time and temporary work. We use (log) hourly wages as our dependent variable, and include controls for part-time and temporary work, as well as controls for other characteristics. Our specification is:

$$\ln\left(\frac{W_{it}}{H_{it}}\right) = \alpha_1 PT_{it} + \alpha_2 TC_{ti} + x_{it}\beta + e_{it} \qquad (4.1)$$

where W_{it} denotes gross monthly earnings, H_{it} denotes normal weekly hours worked, PT_{it} and TC_{it} are controls for part-time and temporary work, respectively, x_{it} is a vector of individual and job characteristics, β is a vector of coefficients, including a constant, and e_{it} is an error term.

Equation (4.1) has weekly hours of work at the denominator of the dependent variable whereas the part-time indicator, constructed on the basis of weekly hours worked, is among the right-hand side variables. Potential measurement error in weekly hours can induce a spurious negative correlation between H_{it} and PT_{it}, and so bias upwards the estimate of the coefficient α_1. For example, an underestimate of weekly hours artificially increases hourly wages and may push the individual below the threshold for temporary work, associating temporary work with the higher hourly wages. In order to correct for this bias we ideally need an instrument for PT_{it}, which is unaffected by the measurement error in hours worked. For this purpose, we use the subjective indicator for part-time work included in the ECHPS, which is not directly constructed from the hours variable. The subjective part-time indicator is very highly correlated with PT_{it}, which was constructed on the basis of a homo-geneous 30-hours cut-off. The correlation coefficient ranges from 0.75 in Italy and Greece to 0.99 in the United Kingdom, although the part-time incidence based on the subjective measure is for all countries slightly lower than that predicted by the 30-hours cut-off (see also fn. 18 for the exact definition of the two variables).

The wage equation (4.1) was estimated separately for men and women, controlling for education, experience, marital status and family composition, previous unemployment spells, firm size, occupation and industry. Although it is feasible to compute job tenure from a retrospective question at the start of the current job, we do not control for tenure in the reported wage equations, due to the high number of missing values for this variable, especially for Germany. But the estimates of our parameters of interest α_1 and α_2 remained virtually unchanged when we controlled for job tenure (estimates not reported here).

OLS and IV estimates of equation (4.1) are reported in Tables 4.7 and 4.8 respectively. The OLS estimate of α_1 is generally higher than its IV estimate for both men and women. In particular, the difference between the OLS and the IV estimate is negligible for some northern European countries, and becomes greater as one moves South. This implies that the bias due to measurement error is greater in countries with lower incidence of part-time work, indicating that short reported working hours are more likely to be the result of measurement error in the Mediterranean countries than elsewhere.

IV estimates of equation (4.1) suggest a penalty for part-time work in the range 10–20 per cent for men in the United Kingdom, Finland, Denmark, the Netherlands, Austria and Ireland, but no effect at all in Germany, Belgium, France and Portugal, and a premium between 5 and 15 per cent in Italy, Spain and Greece. While the presence of bias due to measurement error cannot in principle be ruled out, it is likely that, at least in the southern European countries, some of the part-time wage premium is a compensating differential for inferior non-wage job attributes. This picture is confirmed by the estimates of Table 4.6 (p. 56), which suggest that workers in Mediterranean countries are less happy with the non-wage attributes of part-time jobs than workers in the rest of Europe are.

The wage differential between full-time and part-time jobs is higher everywhere for women than it is for men (except in Portugal). This is consistent with a situation in which women are more strongly discriminated against in full-time than in part-time jobs (see also Johnson and Stafford 1998).

Temporary work is everywhere associated with lower hourly wages for both men and women, and the highest differentials are found in the Netherlands and Spain. With the exception of the United Kingdom, the Scandinavian countries and Belgium, the wage penalty associated with temporary work is higher everywhere for women than for men. In several countries, gender allocation across temporary and permanent jobs is therefore a potential source of gender wage inequality. Women are over-represented in temporary jobs in several countries (namely Sweden, Finland, Belgium, Austria, Ireland and southern Europe), and given that there is a significant penalty attached to temporary work, women suffer from it on average more than men do.

We ran two robustness checks on the estimated wage equations. First, a non-random selection of individuals into our sample of wage earners may bias the estimates, especially for women, who participate in smaller numbers and might be more selective. Female labor market participation varies widely across countries and a non-random selection of women into the labor force implies that the composition of the female labor force also varies across countries. For example, assume that more educated women are more likely to participate in market work than the less educated. In a country with relatively low female participation (perhaps as a result of social norms or family commitments) the educational cut-off level above which women participate is higher, and consequently the female labor force is on average more educated, than in a country

Table 4.7. Wages on non-standard contracts, OLS estimates

	UK	FIN	DEN	GER	NET	BEL	LUX	AUT	IRE	FRA	ITA	SPA	POR	GRE
Males														
Part-time	-0.086***	-0.021	-0.148***	0.074	-0.121***	0.084**	–	0.083***	0.043*	0.085**	0.243***	0.099***	0.103***	0.256***
	(0.021)	(0.030)	(0.031)	(0.051)	(0.020)	(0.033)	–	(0.030)	(0.026)	(0.034)	(0.015)	(0.020)	(0.030)	(0.023)
On temp. contract	-0.166***	-0.185***	-0.104***	-0.128***	-0.221***	-0.118***	–	-0.098***	-0.127***	-0.175***	-0.127***	-0.203***	-0.070***	-0.142***
	(0.014)	(0.017)	(0.014)	(0.021)	(0.016)	(0.018)	–	(0.016)	(0.015)	(0.020)	(0.008)	(0.008)	(0.009)	(0.011)
No. Observations	11251	4036	3744	3225	9962	3850	770	7867	5709	3424	11844	12008	10643	6090
R^2	0.50	0.43	0.49	0.37	0.33	0.45	–	0.32	0.57	0.41	0.51	0.57	0.57	0.56
Females														
Part-time	-0.093***	-0.001	-0.061***	0.108***	-0.047***	0.046***	–	0.091***	-0.004	0.050**	0.212***	0.103***	0.050***	0.266***
	(0.009)	(0.016)	(0.014)	(0.020)	(0.010)	(0.013)	–	(0.013)	(0.013)	(0.020)	(0.008)	(0.012)	(0.016)	(0.017)
On temp. contract	-0.102***	-0.162***	-0.059***	-0.144***	-0.259***	-0.066***	–	-0.129***	-0.182***	-0.181***	-0.122***	-0.211***	-0.145***	-0.174***
	(0.013)	(0.012)	(0.015)	(0.025)	(0.012)	(0.016)	–	(0.018)	(0.013)	(0.021)	(0.010)	(0.010)	(0.011)	(0.013)
No. Observations	10680	4140	2838	2028	6927	3046	468	5574	4463	2382	7591	6598	7813	3877
R^2	0.47	0.44	0.43	0.29	0.37	0.41	–	0.34	0.63	0.35	0.57	0.63	0.67	0.66

Notes: The figures reported are the coefficients obtained from wage regressions. Dependent variable: (log) gross hourly earnings. Estimation method: OLS. Standard errors reported in brackets. Significance at 1%, 5% and 10% is denoted by ***, **, and * respectively. The estimated equations also include: 2 education dummies, potential experience and its square, one dummy for married or cohabiting, any children in the age brackets 0–2, 3–5, 6–10, and 11–15 respectively, one dummy for previously unemployed, 5 dummies for employer size, one dummy for public sector, 9 occupation dummies, 13 industry dummies and year dummies. Sweden is excluded from the sample as no information on earnings is available. No estimates are reported for Luxembourg, due to small sample size.

Source: ECHPS.

Table 4.8. *Wages on non-standard contracts, IV estimates*

	UK	FIN	DEN	GER	NET	BEL	LUX	AUT	IRE	FRA	ITA	SPA	POR	GRE
Males														
Part-time	-0.202***	-0.092***	-0.155***	0.001	-0.111***	-0.060	–	-0.122***	-0.124***	-0.004	0.153***	0.064***	0.027	0.115***
	(0.043)	(0.032)	(0.032)	(0.058)	(0.021)	(0.041)	–	(0.037)	(0.032)	(0.037)	(0.022)	(0.022)	(0.033)	(0.032)
On temp. contract	-0.166***	-0.182***	-0.104***	-0.128***	-0.217***	-0.111***	–	-0.092***	-0.109***	-0.160***	-0.118***	-0.202***	-0.068***	-0.136***
	(0.015)	(0.017)	(0.014)	(0.021)	(0.016)	(0.018)	–	(0.016)	(0.015)	(0.020)	(0.009)	(0.008)	(0.009)	(0.011)
No. Observations	10986	4036	3724	3224	9942	3836	770	7861	5688	3421	11823	11992	10643	6083
R^2	0.49	0.43	0.49	0.37	0.32	0.45	–	0.32	0.57	0.41	0.51	0.58	0.57	0.56
Females														
Part-time	-0.123***	-0.018	-0.062***	0.102***	-0.045***	0.033**	–	0.058***	-0.076***	0.036*	0.161***	0.091***	-0.035**	0.138***
	(0.018)	(0.016)	(0.014)	(0.021)	(0.010)	(0.013)	–	(0.014)	(0.015)	(0.020)	(0.011)	(0.012)	(0.018)	(0.024)
On temp. contract	-0.119***	-0.160***	-0.058***	-0.143***	-0.263***	-0.063***	–	-0.126***	-0.173***	-0.179***	-0.119***	-0.211***	-0.139***	-0.161***
	(0.015)	(0.012)	(0.015)	(0.025)	(0.012)	(0.016)	–	(0.018)	(0.013)	(0.021)	(0.010)	(0.010)	(0.011)	(0.013)
No. Observations	8207	4140	2838	2012	6891	3004	464	5565	4358	2374	7560	6573	7810	3868
R^2	0.47	0.44	0.43	0.29	0.37	0.41	–	0.34	0.63	0.35	0.57	0.63	0.67	0.66

Notes: The figures reported are the coefficients obtained from wage regressions. Dependent variable: (log) gross hourly earnings. Estimation method: IV (the part-time indicator based on a 30-hours cutoff is instrumented using the subjective part-time indicator). Standard errors reported in brackets. Significance at 1%, 5% and 10% is denoted by ***, ** and * respectively. The estimated equations also include: 2 education dummies, potential experience and its square, one dummy for married or cohabiting, any children in the age brackets 0–2, 3–5, 6–10 and 11–15 respectively, one dummy for previously unemployed, 5 dummies for employer size, one dummy for public sector, 9 occupation dummies, 13 industry dummies and year dummies. Sweden is excluded from the sample as no information on earnings is available. No estimates are reported for Luxembourg, due to small sample size.

Source: ECHPS.

with relatively high female participation. This has clear implications for international comparisons of gender wage gaps. Its implications for the gender-specific penalty to atypical jobs are unexplored, although, in principle, a higher participation cut-off along the educational distribution may affect the skill composition of typical and atypical employment and the related wage differentials.

To explore this issue we correct our estimates for sample selection using Heckman's (1979) two-step estimator. We first estimate a probit model for selection into employment, controlling for marital status, presence of children of different ages, age and education. The resulting inverse Mills' ratio is then used as an extra regressor in the wage equation (4.1). But our correction for selectivity did not alter the results from the IV regressions, so we do not report here the estimates.

Secondly, as part of the estimated wage differentials on atypical jobs may stem from the sorting of workers across jobs according to unobservable characteristics, we also obtained fixed-effect estimates, which exploit the observed wage variation for job movers. Fixed-effect estimates of wage differentials (first-difference estimates, in which the part-time status is instrumented) turned out to be quantitatively very similar to the simple IV estimates and are therefore not reported. Overall, fixed-effect estimates suggest that the wage differentials reported in Table 4.8 (p. 62) cannot be explained by unobserved worker heterogeneity.

4.5 CONCLUSIONS

Two main results have emerged from our analysis of job segregation across Europe. First, part-time and temporary jobs display systematic features that make them significantly different from 'typical' jobs. In particular, part-time jobs in southern Europe do not yield as much job satisfaction as full-time jobs, and permanent jobs are virtually everywhere regarded as superior to otherwise similar regular jobs, although differences are again more marked in southern European countries.

Secondly, given that women are over-represented in such atypical jobs in most European countries, systematic features of these jobs may be an important factor of gender differentials. Given that atypical jobs are not regarded as good as typical jobs in southern Europe, the over-representation of women in these jobs may be evidence of gender discrimination. In contrast, in central and northern Europe, atypical jobs are either less widespread (as in the case of temporary work), or seem to better mirror women's preferences for shorter working hours (as in the case of part-time work).

An interesting related question is how do women in southern Europe respond to the desire for more flexibility in hours of work, given the job segregation and discrimination against atypical jobs? Given that on average only 15 per cent of women employees hold part-time jobs in Italy, Spain, Portugal and Greece, as against an average of 25 per cent in the rest of the European Union, the obvious answer is that they tend to stay out of the labor force. But there is also some evidence of other forms of employment that offer the more flexible hours. The first of these is self-employment, a career that attracts 18.3 per cent of employed women in southern Europe, but only 7.2 per cent of employed women in other countries. The second one is unpaid work in the family business, which again attracts 7.3 per cent of employed women in southern Europe and only 1 per cent of women in the other countries. The employment of these women needs to be formalized if their rights are to be protected and the Lisbon objectives achieved. But to do this, a first step is the reduction of discrimination in atypical forms of employment.

5

Wage Gaps

We turn now to the gender wage gap which, together with the employment gap discussed in the previous section, is also an important indicator of the relative performance of women in the labor market. The gender wage gap gained added importance in Europe when it was included in a revised list of 'structural indicators' for employment, following the Stockholm European Council in 2002.

The study of the gender wage gap has attracted considerable attention, especially in the United States. Studies of its evolution emphasize the importance of gender differences in human capital (education and experience), and in the occupational structure by gender. The residual wage gap, which is left unexplained after accounting for differences in observed characteristics for men and women, is attributed to discrimination in the labor market. In addition, a number of authors have discussed the link between the gender wage gap and aggregate changes in wage inequality and in industry composition during the 1980s and 1990s.[1]

Despite the richness of this literature, there is only a small number of cross-country studies of the gender wage gap. Up to the early 1990s the reason for this was, in part, because there were no fully comparable cross-sectional data set on the employment and earnings of men and women available. However, recent studies by Blau and Kahn (1996, 2002) and the OECD (2002) use comparable cross-country data (the International Social Survey Program (ISSP) data and the European Community Household Panel respectively) to study the effects of differences in the wage structure on the relative gender wage gap. Both Blau and Kahn (1996) and OECD (2002) use the decomposition method developed by Juhn, Murphy and Pierce (1993) in order to obtain 'adjusted' measures of the wage gap that control for between-country variations in female–male differences in observed characteristics (age, education, experience) and in jobs held, and in the extent of 'equal pay' for similar (observed) characteristics. According to this decomposition technique, the comparability problem is solved by choosing one country as a benchmark, and by using the

---

[1] See Goldin (1990) for an influential historical analysis of the gender wage gap in the United States, and Altonji and Blank (1999) for an extensive review of the theoretical and empirical literature that examines the determinants of differences in pay across demographic groups (in particular the black–white and female–male wage differentials).

entire wage structure as a reference group (typically men) within the reference country in order to evaluate any 'gaps' in observed and unobserved characteristics, by gender, across different countries.[2] The application of such methodology to the analysis of the gender pay gap may be problematic since it is assumed that the estimated 'prices' of observed characteristics do not differ by gender. Blau and Kahn (2002) try to deal with this issue by estimating gender-specific wage equations for each country and by using the observed characteristics of a reference state to evaluate cross-country differences in the wage gap. These studies suggest a link between wage inequality and the gender pay gap.

Here, we use data from the 1998 wave of the ECHP to investigate the importance of adjusting for cross-country differences in patterns of female participation in cross-country studies of the gender wage gap. To explain differences in the gender wage gap across countries, we examine the role of country-specific institutions such as employment protection policies, parental leave policies, and product market regulation.

Our discussion of the gender wage gap is organized in three parts. In the first part we briefly address the US experience. We then turn to a first analysis of cross-country differences in the gender wage gap for the countries in our sample. For a subset of countries we also study how the gender wage gap has evolved between the mid-1980s and the late 1990s. In the second part, we turn to the decomposition analysis of cross-country gender differences in pay and we discuss how the issue of sample selection may be affecting cross-country comparisons, even of the adjusted wage gap. Finally, in the third part, we study the effect of country-specific institutions on cross-country differences in the gender wage gap.

5.1   THE EVOLUTION OF THE GENDER WAGE GAP IN THE US

In the United States the ratio of mean female earnings to mean male earnings among full-time workers has been hovering around 60 per cent from the mid-1950s to the late 1970s and early 1980s. Starting in the 1980s, we observe a steady and rapid increase in the relative earnings of women. By 2001, women's earnings were about 80 per cent of men's earnings.

Traditionally, women were more likely to withdraw from the labor market after marriage or after giving birth. The consensus estimate was that about half of the traditional 40 per cent differential in wages could be explained by the difference in experience (Goldin and Polachek, 1987). The major explanation for the stability of the female–male wage differential through the 1970s was that the new groups of women that started entering the labor force during that

---

[2] The same framework has also been used to compare the gender wage gap in Australia and Canada (Kidd and Shannon (1996)), and to compare Sweden and the US (Edin and Richardson (2002)).

period typically had lower education levels and lower labor market experience than those already in the market (Goldin 1990, Smith and Ward 1985). However, during the 1980s and the 1990s, women's labor market characteristics, in particular their job experience and their education, became more similar to that of men. In addition, over these two decades women also shifted to higher-paying occupations. This relative improvement in the characteristics of the female labor force contributed to the narrowing of the gap during the late 1980s. Studies by Blau and Kahn (1997) and O'Neill and Polachek (1993) show that both the increase in the rate of return to labor market experience and the increase in the actual experience of women can explain between one-third and a half of the drop in the gender gap. They also find a decline in the residual (unexplained) differential, which they interpret as evidence of a decline in discrimination. Part of the argument is that the effects of the 1964 Civil Rights Act, and of the Equal Employment Opportunities Commission which it set up, were delayed, and resulted in increased earning power for women in the 1980s and 1990s.

5.2   CROSS-COUNTRY EVIDENCE ON THE GENDER WAGE GAP

There are substantial differences in the gender wage gap across countries. Table 5.1 presents 1998 data on the female–male earnings ratio for both full-time wage and salaried employees, and for all the wage and salaried workers (including part-time workers).[3] The table shows that, for both measures, women's hourly earnings are lower than men's in all countries. On average, women are paid an hourly wage equal to 84 per cent of men's wages. The gender gap is smallest (less than 10 per cent) in the Mediterranean countries, in the Nordic countries and in Belgium and France. Conversely, the gender gap is largest (around 20 per cent) in the United States, Canada, and the United Kingdom. For the United Kingdom, Spain and Ireland the gender gap for all workers is about five percentage points higher than for full-time workers. This reflects the fact that a large fraction of women work in part-time jobs in these countries, and (consistent with our earlier econometric results for these countries) part-time workers receive lower hourly wages. However, this is not the case for the rest of the countries, particularly for the Netherlands, where the incidence of part-time jobs is high and where we also found a part-time penalty in our econometric work.

In order to investigate this issue further, we report the female–male wage ratio in hourly wages broken down by age in Table 5.2. We ask whether more

---

[3] Source: OECD, Employment Outlook (2002). We only present results for the ratio of median hourly earnings since this measure is less sensitive to the presence of outliers. See the OECD report for data on the female–male ratios of mean hourly earnings and the 20th and 80th percentiles of the hourly wage distribution.

Table 5.1. *Gender–wage ratio in 1998*

	Hourly earnings full-time wage and salary workers	Hourly earnings all wage and salary workers
Mediterranean		
Spain	93	88
Italy	91	93
Greece	80	82
Nordic		
Sweden	90	88
Finland	87	87
Denmark	93	92
Anglo-Saxon		
UK	85	79
Rest of Europe		
Austria	80	79
Belgium	94	93
France	93	93
Germany	83	83
Ireland	81	76
Netherlands	86	87
Portugal	85	85
Non-European Countries		
Canada	81	78
USA	79	76

Note: Ratio of median female to male hourly earnings.
Source: OECD, *Employment Outlook*, 2002.

recent generations of women face a smaller pay penalty on the labor market than older generations. The table shows that, with the exception of Italy, Denmark and Germany, the hourly female–male wage ratio is around 10 percentage points higher for younger women than for older women. Both age and cohort effects are at work here. First, young women tend to show a greater similarity to young men in terms of accumulated labor market experience. Secondly, for recent generations, the education gap has narrowed substantially.[4]

Finally, we turn to the analysis of how the gender wage gap has evolved between the mid-1980s and the late-1990s. Table 5.3 presents data on the growth of the female–male (median) earnings ratio for a subset of countries.[5] The gender wage gap has been declining in most of the countries in our sample

[4] See Section 1 of this report and Dolado, Felgueroso and Jimeno (2002).
[5] Source: OECD, Labor Force Statistics (online).

Table 5.2. *The gender–wage ratio by age (median hourly wages), 1998*

	25–34	35–44	45–54
Mediterranean			
Spain	94.76	95.07	82.77
Italy	98.54	97.31	92.40
Greece	100.00	88.33	79.65
Nordic			
Finland	91.13	81.98	76.00
Denmark	91.80	92.50	90.48
Anglo-Saxon			
UK	92.07	70.49	67.13
Rest of Europe			
Austria	84.12	84.78	72.61
Belgium	96.11	96.13	88.09
France	95.15	86.03	86.11
Germany	85.92	82.90	80.59
Ireland	91.07	79.49	71.29
Netherlands	98.63	84.58	76.93
Portugal	86.79	83.88	81.56
Non-European Countries			
USA	83.33	74.67	70.36

Source: Author's calculations based on ECHP data for European countries and on CPS, Demographic. File for the USA. The gap is computed as the percentage ratio of female to male wages. The sample is restricted to those who work 15+ hours per week, and excludes individuals working as apprentices and students.

since the late 1970s and early 1980s. The largest decline occurred in the United States, the United Kingdom, France, Germany and Canada. Over this time period, the wage gap was essentially constant in the Nordic countries (Finland, Sweden) and in Italy—the only country in the Mediterranean group for which we have time series data. This is an interesting result because both the strong decline in the gender wage gap in the United States, and the stagnation in the Nordic countries, occurred at a time of rising wage inequality in the United States, which alone would tend to increase the gender wage gap. It follows that while US women improved their position in the earnings distribution relative to men, so as to offset the effects of the general increase inequality, women in the Nordic countries did not.[6]

But despite the increase in the female–male earnings ratio during the 1980s and the 1990s, the North American gender ratio in the late 1990s was still below its level in Italy, Spain (where the gender gap in employment is almost

[6] See Blau and Kahn (2000), Gupta, Oaxaca and Smith (2002) and OECD, *Employment Outlook* (2002).

Table 5.3. Evolution of the gender–wage ratio

	1985	1998	Change 1998 to 1985 (%)
Mediterranean			
Italy	0.813	0.829	1.61
Nordic			
Sweden	0.832	0.810	− 2.26
Finland	0.775	0.776	0.13
Anglo-Saxon			
UK	0.665	0.734	6.95
Rest of Europe			
France	0.838	0.897	5.86
Germany	0.710	0.769	5.89
Netherlands	0.744	0.769	2.56
Non-European Countries			
Canada	0.652	0.711	5.80
USA	0.680	0.754	7.40

Note: Authors' calculation using available data from OECD, Labor Force Statistics. Female–male median earnings ratio for full-time, year-round workers.

three times as large as in the United States), and the Nordic countries (where the job segregation index is much larger than in the United States). The next section reconciles these facts in discussion of work by Blau and Kahn (1996, 2003) and the OECD (2002).

Before we move to understanding the cross-country evidence on the gender wage gap, it is interesting to briefly summarize the cross-country evidence on the existence of a labor market penalty of motherhood in terms of wages. The family gap in wages is defined as the average hourly wage difference between women with no children and mothers.[7] The theoretical justifications for the existence of a family pay gap that have been put forward in the literature include differences in human capital accumulation, differences in unobserved characteristics such as motivation and commitment to paid work, and discrimination. For example, women with children tend to have lower actual experience, job tenure and on-the-job training than women without children. Also, mothers may select into jobs that do not require overtime work or high work intensity, or else for part-time jobs. Finally, there might be instances of employers' discrimination towards mothers that are not justified by a woman's motivation or work attachment.

Although the presence of children has a negative impact on female employment in most industrialized countries, the effect on hourly wages is

[7] See Waldfogel (1998) for a survey of the theoretical and empirical literature on the family pay gap.

ambiguous and varies considerably across countries. For the US, researchers find a 10 to 15 per cent family penalty for women with children, even after controlling for differences in characteristics such as education, and work experience (see, for example, Waldfogel (1997) and Korenman and Neumark (1992)). A similar pattern holds for the United Kingdom where Harkness and Waldfogel (1999) compare the family gap in pay across seven industrialized countries, Australia, Canada, United States, Germany, Finland and Sweden. They find that the United Kingdom and the United States display a large gap in hourly wages between mothers and women without children. However, this is not true for other countries. Women with children in Finland and Sweden are paid about the same as women without children. In Australia and Canada they are paid even more than women without children. When the sample is restricted to full-time workers, the pattern begins to share similarities across all countries, with the wages of women without children exceeding those of mothers. This difference is attributed to the fact that in the United Kingdom (and to a lesser extent in the US), wages of part-time workers are much lower than those of full-time workers. This is not the case in the other countries in the sample.[8] As we argue in this section, the gender wage gap can be partially explained by cross-country differences in the selection of women into employment. Harkness and Waldfogel (1999) show, however, that the variation in family pay gaps across countries cannot be explained by differential selection into employment. They also show that differences in the wage structure do not contribute to it either.

The recent OECD (2002) employment outlook presents cross-country evidence on the family wage gap using data from the European Community Household Panel (ECHP) that is consistent with the above findings. In particular, the report shows that although there is a family wage gap in countries such as the United Kingdom, Austria, Belgium, Germany, Ireland, and the Netherlands, hourly wages for mothers are actually more than 10 per cent higher for women with children than for women without children in Mediterranean countries (Greece, Italy and Spain), in Ireland, and in the Netherlands. Moreover, once differences in observed characteristics are taken into account, a considerable family wage gap is only found in Austria and in the United Kingdom.

Overall, the cross-country evidence on the family pay gap does not show that women with children are unambiguously worse off than women without children in terms of their pay. However, in some countries this gap is quite large. These are countries where maternity leave legislation is less protective of mothers and childcare provision is dismal. Some of the studies discussed in this volume (see Del Boca and Pasqua) seem to suggest that family policies such as maternity leave and childcare policies should help close the family pay gap.

---

[8] See Section 4 in this chapter.

Maternity leave in particular, may raise women's subsequent pay by raising the likelihood that women stay with the same employer after childbirth.

5.3 EXPLAINING THE CROSS-COUNTRY EVIDENCE ON THE GENDER WAGE GAP

The evidence presented in this section shows that although US women perform quite well in terms of human capital and occupational structure in relation to their European counterparts, they face a much larger wage penalty relative to men than European women do. Blau and Kahn (1996) highlight the importance of country differences in wage structure in accounting for cross-country differences in the gender wage gap. According to their argument, since women tend to be more concentrated at the bottom of the wage distribution relative to men, institutions that compress the wage distribution, such as minimum wage legislation and highly centralized wage-setting, will also tend to decrease the gender wage gap.

In their 1996 study, Blau and Kahn use 1985–1989 International Social Survey Program (ISSP) data for 10 countries, supplemented by country-specific micro data sets for Italy, Sweden, and the United States, to analyze the importance of the overall wage structure in explaining cross-country differences in the gender wage gap. In particular, they study the reasons underlying the lower ranking of US women relative to their European counterparts on this dimension.[9]

Blau and Kahn adapt the decomposition analysis that Juhn, Murphy and Pierce (1991) used in their study of wage differentials by demographic groups. The procedure may be summarized as follows. First, the wage equation for men is estimated in each country. These regressions provide benchmark estimates of the price of observed characteristics and the level of residual wage inequality for each country.[10] The difference in the gender wage gap between two countries is then decomposed into four terms. The first term measures the contribution of cross-country differences in observed characteristics (mainly education, and experience). The second term measures the contribution of differences in the 'price' of observed characteristics, namely the return they command in the market. The third term measures the effects of cross-country differences in the relative ranking of women within the male residual wage distribution, obtained after controlling for observed characteristics (given the assumption that the male residual wage inequality is the same across countries).

---

[9] The data set was compiled from the Bank of Italy's Survey of Household Income Wealth, the Michigan Panel Study of Income Dynamics (PSID) and the Swedish Household Market and Non-Market Activities Survey (HUS). The other countries included in the analysis were Australia, Austria, Germany, Hungary, Norway, Switzerland and the United Kingdom.

[10] Men are chosen as a reference group within each country in order to minimize the sample selection bias.

Finally, the fourth term measures the cross-country difference in the gender wage gap that is explained by differences in residual inequality (if the two countries were characterized by the same relative ranking of women in the male residual wage distribution). The sum of the second and fourth terms represents the total effect of the wage structure (the sum of both observed and unobserved 'price' effects). The sum of the first and third term represents the total effect of gaps in gender differences in observed characteristics, and of differences in the 'treatment' of women in the labor market.

The estimation results obtained for this subset of countries show that US women perform better than their counterparts along this latter dimension (except for Australia and Sweden). However, the US level of inequality in the wage structure makes their relative position worse. The effect of wage inequality accounts for almost all the wage gap between the United States and other countries, except for Sweden, where it accounts for 74 per cent of the gap. The authors interpret this evidence as suggestive of the fact that differences in wage structure can account for a large part of the cross-country gender wage gap. Moreover, they analyze the relationship between cross-country differences in wage-setting institutions, male wage inequality, and cross-country differences in the wage gap, and find some suggestive evidence (albeit weak) that supports their conjecture.

In a more recent paper, Blau and Kahn (2003) test their hypothesis for a larger set of 22 countries, from the ISSP for the years 1984–1994. They use a slightly different methodology to compare gaps across countries, and allow for the prices of observed characteristics to differ across countries and across gender groups but use the observed characteristics of men and women in the United States as the benchmark. Moreover, they also include in the analysis measures of the net supply of labor by women across countries. In this case, they find stronger evidence that the variation in the gender wage gap across countries may be attributed to differences in the degree of inequality in the earnings distribution. They also show that, controlling for differences in the wage structure, the wage differential tends to be lower when the female supply of labor is lower with respect to its demand. This result is robust to the inclusion of institutional variables, collective bargaining, parental leave policies, unemployment insurance and employment protection. This evidence confirms that to the extent that labor market institutions are an important component in explaining the degree of overall wage inequality, differences in the labor market institutions can account for differences in the gender wage gap.[11]

A similar analysis is conducted for the 12 countries in the ECHP in the 2002 OECD *Employment Outlook*. The OECD study uses the same decomposition

---

[11] For example, it is found that if collective bargaining coverage were to increase from 47 per cent to 82 per cent the gender wage gap would fall by about 10 per cent. Higher collective bargaining is known to compress the overall wage structure and so reduce inequality along all dimensions.

method used by Blau and Kahn (1996) and considers an average of the
12 ECHP countries as the benchmark economy. The results of the analysis are
summarized in Table 5.4. Entries in the first column of the table represent
percentage point differences of the unadjusted wage gap in each country from
the wage gap in the benchmark economy. The second column shows the total
contribution as a result of differences in the gender gap in observed and
unobserved characteristics. Entries in the third column of the table show the
sum of the contributions as a result of cross-country differences in market
prices for observed and unobserved characteristics.

The results of this decomposition analysis show that the unadjusted wage
gap would substantially change in each country if its wage structure were
similar to that of the average benchmark country. In particular, the gender
wage gap in the United Kingdom would be reduced by between 2 and
4 percentage points under the benchmark (more compressed) wage structure.
In contrast, the adjusted wage gap would increase in the Netherlands as a
consequence of women's higher concentration in lower-paid occupational

Table 5.4. *Decomposition of cross-country differences in the gender wage gap*

	Hourly wage gap	Hourly gap adjusted	Wage structure
Mediterranean			
Spain	−4.1	−4.7	0.6
Italy	−8.5	−5.7	−2.8
Greece	−1.3	0.1	2.4
Nordic			
Finland	2.8	1.8	0.9
Denmark	−2.3	−0.8	−1.6
Anglo-Saxon			
UK	6.5	2.3	4.2
Rest of Europe			
Austria	7	8.5	−1.5
Belgium	−4.1	−3.6	−0.4
France	3.9	3.4	0.5
Germany	4.3	3.6	0.7
Ireland	2	0.1	1.9
Netherlands	3.9	9.3	−5.4
Portugal	−3.8	2.7	−6.5

Notes: Entries in the table represent percentage point differences from the gender wage gap in
the benchmark economy that are explained by each component. The hourly wage gap
represents the sum of the contributions due to cross-country differences in the gender gap in
observed and unobserved characteristics. The wage structure represents the sum of the contributions due to cross-country differences in market prices for observed and unobserved
characteristics.

Source: Table 2.B.2, OECD: *Employment Outlook*, 2002, Chapter 2.

groups. There is also evidence that less-dispersed wage structures are not necessarily beneficial to women in relation to men. For example, women tend to have a strong presence in the public sector where wages tend to be higher than in the private sector (at least for those with lower educational levels). Hence, countries such as Belgium, Denmark, Finland and the Netherlands, where the public–private wage differential is lower, tend to display higher adjusted wage gaps with respect to the benchmark economy.

The analysis also shows that this adjusted measure of the gender wage gap confirms the evidence presented in the previous section for unadjusted measures of the female–male earning ratio: the gender wage gap tends to be smaller for the Mediterranean countries (Greece, Italy and Spain) than for the Nordic and Anglo-Saxon countries (including the United States).

5.4 THE IMPORTANCE OF SAMPLE SELECTION

The analysis described above shows that both the raw gender wage gap and the adjusted wage gap are smaller in Mediterranean countries, where women's participation rate is particularly low. We argue that part of the reason why this may occur is that this type of analysis does not take into account cross-country differences in how women select (positively or negatively) into employment.

In what follows we compare the gender wage gap estimates, obtained both with and without the sample-selection correction, for the same subset of European countries analysed in the OECD study. The wage gap is computed as the difference between the male and female average log hourly earnings, which is obtained by estimating gender and country-specific equations. In such equations, the dependent variable is the logarithm of gross hourly wages,[12] and the independent variables include education (two dummies), potential experience, and potential experience squared, occupation (fifteen dummies), tenure (four dummies) public–private sector, type of contract, full time/part time, and interaction terms between part time, full time and weekly hours worked. We exclude individuals working as apprentices and students as well as the self-employed. The estimates corrected for sample selection are based on Heckman's two-step consistent estimator. The participation equation includes age, marital status, education (two dummies) and weekly hours spent in childcare.

The results of the estimation are reported in Table 5.5. The estimated 'raw' gender gap is reported in the first column. Estimates for the gender wage gap corrected for sample selection are in the second column. Once we account for sample selection the estimated gender wage gap increases by as much as a factor of two in the low-participation Mediterranean countries. In contrast, it falls

---

[12] Following the OECD report, we compute hourly earnings by dividing gross monthly earnings in the main job by 52/12 and then dividing the corresponding weekly wage by the actual hours worked per week. The 'selected' sample is restricted to individuals working 15+ hours per week.

Table 5.5. *Estimated gender wage gap, the importance of sample selection*

	'Raw' estimates	'Corrected' estimates
Mediterranean		
Spain	14.1	31.3
Italy	8.5	15.9
Greece	11.7	31.6
Nordic		
Finland	16.8	9.6
Denmark	11.4	8.0
Anglo-Saxon		
UK	24.5	26.1
Rest of Europe		
Austria	21.7	15.2
Belgium	9.4	7.4
France	12.3	7.9
Germany	19.8	14.1
Ireland	16.2	25.2
Netherlands	18.0	18.7
Portugal	10.0	9.5

Notes: The estimated gender wage gap is computed as the difference of the male and female average log hourly earnings obtained by estimating gender specific equations where the dependent variable is the logarithm of gross hourly wages. Independent variables include education (two dummies), potential experience, and potential experience squared, occupation (fifteen dummies), tenure (four dummies), public–private sector, type of contract, full time/part time, and interaction terms between part time, full time and weekly hours worked. We exclude individuals working as apprentices and students as well as self-employed. The estimates corrected for sample selections are based on the Heckman's two-step consistent estimator.

The participation equation includes age, marital status, education (two dummies) and weekly hours spent in childcare.

Source: ECHP, 1998.

substantially in the Nordic countries and is unchanged in the United Kingdom, Netherlands and Portugal.[13] Intuitively, the sample correction takes care of the fact that the wage gap differs across skill groups. With the large differences in the participation rate in the Mediterranean and (say) Nordic countries, the average gap could be distorted if the calculation did not correct for the different composition of the female labor force in each case. Evidently, since the fraction of skilled women who participate in the Mediterranean countries is relatively

---

[13] One may argue that this result depends on the fact that we are controlling for occupation, type of contract, etc. in the wage regression. For example, including occupation could alter the analysis since the estimated parameter for the returns to education would be net of the effect of occupation (and women are more likely to be in less prestigious jobs). A similar logic could be at work for the other variables. We perform our regression by including only wage and education in the wage regression and we find similar results to the one reported in Table 5.5.

larger than in the Nordic countries, our results say that the gender gap is bigger in the unskilled occupations. A simple average in the Mediterranean countries shows a small gap because there are not enough unskilled women to make the gap larger. Our results suggest that in cross-country analyses of the gender wage gap (as well as in the analysis of the gender wage gap across demographic groups), it is important to adjust for cross-country differences in patterns of female participation.[14]

5.5 CROSS-COUNTRY INSTITUTIONAL DIFFERENCES AND THE GENDER WAGE GAP

In line with our earlier work on the institutional influences on the overall employment rate across countries, in this section we investigate whether institutional differences across countries, such as employment protection policies, parental leave policies, and product market regulation, can explain any of the cross-country differences in the gender wage gap. We use a variety of data sources to build the set of institutional variables for the 1990s. The index of bargaining coverage is from Blanchflower (1996). Parental leave entitlements (weeks of leave), employment protection policy (EPL), and union density are from Nickell and Layard (1999). The information on parental leave entitlements for Greece is obtained from Table 5.8 in the OECD *Employment Outlook* (1990). The index of product market regulation, and the index of employment protection legislation for both temporary and regular contracts are taken from Nicoletti, Scarpetta, and Boylaud (1999). The maximum unemployment insurance (UI) replacement rates are from Blanchard and Wolfers (2000) where they construct this (time varying) measure of the generosity of the UI as an average of the replacement rate, the number of years over which unemployment benefits are paid, and a measure of active labor market policy. The segregation index is from Table 9.1 in Anker (1998), and it is based on a set of 75 non-agricultural two-digit occupations. Finally, the Equal Employment Opportunity indicator (EEO) is based on Table 5.11 in the 1988 OECD *Employment Outlook*. The table provides information about the year in which the equal employment opportunity legislation was introduced in each country. We use the indicator to measure the time lag since this legislation was passed in each country. Unfortunately we do not have cross-country measures of the degree of enforcement of this legislation.

We perform a cross-country regression of the estimated 'raw' gender gap presented in Table 5.4 (p. 74) on this set of institutional variables. Our measure of the gender gap is derived from the estimates of wage equations that control for gender- and country-specific differences in education, potential experience

---

[14] This is consistent with the work by Derek Neal (2002) which emphasizes the importance of adjusting measures of the black–white wage gap among women for racial differences in selection patterns.

and its square, occupation, tenure, public–private sector, type of contract, full time/part time, and interaction terms between part time, full time and weekly hours worked. The correction is for both men and women and for all the countries in our sample. For this analysis we exclude individuals working as apprentices and students and we restrict our attention to individuals working 15+ hours per week.

Table 5.6 describes the results obtained for two different specifications. We report the results for three different age categories: 25–34, 35–44 and 45–54. These results should be interpreted with caution because the sample size is very small. We have data on all the institutions for a subset of only 11 countries. We show the results for two different specifications. In the first one we include parental leave, bargaining coverage, maximum replacement ratio, the EEO indicator and the two measures of employment protection (for temporary, and regular jobs). In the second, we also control for the index of product market regulation. We find that both more generous measures of the unemployment insurance system, and measures of employment protection for temporary jobs, tend to decrease the gender wage gap. However, these effects disappear once we control for the degree of product market regulation.

It is interesting to study how the results vary by age groups. For women between 35 and 44 years old we find that, consistent with Blau and Kahn (2002), larger bargaining coverage decreases the gender gap in wages. However, this is not the case for younger women (ages 25 to 34). In this case, a greater degree of bargaining coverage tends to increase the gap. Stricter EPL for regular contracts have the same effect. This is consistent with the story that these institutions, designed to protect the 'insiders' in the labor market, have a larger negative impact on the employment and pay opportunities of the young. The results suggest that the negative effect is greater for young women than for young men. Also, for this age group, we find that both stricter EPL for temporary contracts, and a larger UI benefit replacement ratio, tend to decrease the gap.[15]

Finally, we find that for 35- to 44-year-old women, more generous parental leave entitlements tend to significantly increase the gender wage gap. This finding is consistent with the evidence provided by Ruhm (1998) who shows that parental leave is associated with higher overall female employment (consistent with our findings in respect to family day care in S. 3), but with reductions in their relative (female–male) wage.

Given the small number of observations, these results should be interpreted as suggestive evidence of these associations rather than firm conclusions. In order to overcome the data constraint somewhat, we use a variety of data sources to construct a data set of repeated cross-country observations.

---

[15] Results for specifications that include union density and benefit duration are not reported, since these two variables are never significant, and they do not add predictive power.

Table 5.6. *Cross-sectional regression, ECHP 1998*

| | Dependent variable: Estimated gender wage gap | | | | | | | |
	All		25–34		35–44		45–54	
Parental leave	0.026 (0.025)	0.025* (0.009)	0.006 (0.023)	0.006 (0.008)	0.071** (0.022)	0.0712 (0.03)	0.028 (0.035)	0.027 (0.018)
Barg. coverage	0.038 (0.032)	−0.022 (0.060)	0.294** (0.078)	0.248** (0.078)	−0.293* (0.122)	−0.276 (0.196)	0.018 (0.063)	−0.055 (0.123)
Max Rep. rate	−0.212* (0.079)	−0.113 (0.088)	−0.33** (0.058)	−0.25** (0.048)	−0.153 (0.158)	−0.182 (0.302)	−0.254 (0.113)	−0.132 (0.148)
EEO lag	0.181 (0.282)	−0.623 (0.38)	0.977* (0.398)	0.366 (0.309)	−0.442 (0.564)	−0.212 (1.4)	0.260 (0.450)	−0.725 (0.644)
EPL-regular	1.43 (1.307)	0.09 (1.04)	7.17*** (0.864)	6.15*** (0.47)	−1.82 (2.41)	−1.44 (3.80)	1.60 (1.77)	−0.045 (1.47)
EPL-temporary	−2.6*** (0.42)	0.174 (1.17)	−4.1** (0.73)	−2.0* (0.673)	−1.73 (1.07)	−2.52 (4.1.7)	−3.80* (0.715)	−0.415 (1.87)
Product market	−9.85 (4.08)		−7.49* (2.43)		2.81 (14.4)		−12.73 (6.56)	
R^2	0.88	0.9	0.89	0.9	0.84	0.844	0.88	0.95
Number of obs.	11	11	11	11	11	11	11	11

Note: The estimated gender wage gap is computed as the difference of the male and female average log hourly earnings obtained by estimating gender specific equations where the dependent variable is the logarithm of gross hourly wages. Independent variables include education (two dummies), potential experience, and potential experience squared, occupation (fifteen dummies), tenure (four dummies) public/private sector, type of contract, full time/part time, and interaction terms between part time, full time and weekly hours worked. We exclude individuals working as apprentices and students.

Key: *Significant at the 10% level. Robust standard errors in parentheses, ** Significance at the 5% level, ***Significance at the 1% level.

Sources for Institutions: The index of Bargaining Coverage is from Blanchflower (1996). Parental Leave (weeks), EPL, and Union Density are from Nickel and Layard (1999). The Equal Employment Opportunity indicator is based on Table 5.1, OECD, *Employment Outlook*, 1988. It measures the time lag since the equal employment opportunity legislation was passed in each country. The index of Product Market Regulation, and of EPL for temporary and regular contracts are from Nicoletti, Scarpetta and Boylaud (1999); The maximum UI Replacement Rates are taken from Blanchard and Wolfers (2000). The Segregation Index is from Anker (1998), Table 9.1.

Unfortunately, in this case we cannot estimate the gender wage gap so we use aggregate information on the male–female wage ratio obtained by using median earnings for full-time workers as the dependent variable in our analysis. The subset of countries for which we have information includes: Australia, Austria, Belgium, Canada, Denmark, Finland, France, Germany, Greece, Italy, Japan, Portugal, Spain, Sweden, United Kingdom and the United States of America. We consider three time periods: 1980, 1990 and 1998.[16] We estimate the following regression:

$$WG_{jt} = f_j + g_t + g_t^* X_j' b_j + e_{jt}$$

where j is a country index, and t is a period index. The dependent variable is the gender wage gap for country j at time t, and it is measured as the log of the male–female wage ratio (median earnings for full-time year-round workers). f_j is the country fixed effect, g_t is the year dummy and X_j is a vector of country-specific time-invariant institutions, with the exception of the maximum replacement ratio, and the indicators of EPL for temporary and regular contract that have a time dimension.

Table 5.7 summarizes the results obtained for this cross sectional, time series regression for 15 countries. The number of observations now increases to 36. The coefficients in the table should be interpreted as the marginal effect of each institution on the difference in the gender wage gap between 1980 and 1998. We consider three different specifications. In the first one we control for the degree of bargaining coverage, parental leave entitlements, EPL, union density and the EEO lag index. In the second specification, we add the index of product market regulation to the above list. Finally, in the third specification, we introduce the measure of gender segregation. For each specification we run the regression both with and without country fixed effects.

We find that union bargaining coverage tends to decrease the gender wage gap both in the first and in the second specification (with and without fixed effects). Once again, this is consistent with the argument put forth by Blau and Kahn (2003) that since women tend to be more concentrated at the bottom of the wage distribution in relation to men, institutions that compress the wage distribution will also tend to decrease the gender wage gap.

We also find that more generous parental leave policies tend to significantly increase the wage gap (although this effect disappears once we include country fixed effects in the regression). In the first specification, we find that higher union density tends to increase the gap. Finally, we control for sex segregation by occupation, but none of these institutions has a significant impact on cross-country differences in the gender wage gap.

[16] Sources: 1980 and 1990: Blau and Kahn (2000), data for Denmark, Greece, Portugal and Spain refer to 1994, Source: ECHP. Data for 1998 are from OECD, *Employment Outlook* (2002).

Table 5.7. *Cross-section, time series regression results*

	(1)		(2)		(3)	
Dependent variable: Gender wage gap						
Barg. coverage	−0.025*** (0.007)	−0.0148** (0.0061)	−0.025** (0.007)	−0.016* (0.007)	−0.008 (0.017)	−0.002 (0.025)
Parental leave	0.0073** (0.0028)	0.0014 (0.0032)	0.0068** (0.002)	0.003 (0.004)	0.005 (0.005)	−0.001 (0.007)
EPL	0.0149 (0.017)	0.0270 (0.0302)	0.032 (0.029)	0.033 (0.035)	−0.010 (0.042)	−0.034 (0.045)
Union density	0.0099* (0.005)	0.0104* (0.0052)	0.009 (0.006)	0.009 (0.006)	0.009 (0.012)	0.011 (0.012)
Max rep. rate	−0.0052 (0.0035)	0.0037 (0.0128)	−0.004 (0.003)	0.005 (0.015)	0.0015 (0.01)	0.001 (0.018)
EEO lag	−0.0056 (0.063)	0.0587 (0.0540)	0.018 (0.059)	0.041 (0.069)	−0.033 (0.133)	−0.008 (0.15)
Product market	–	–	−0.419 (0.413)	−0.298 (0.524)	−0.014 (0.050)	−0.045 (0.153)
Sex segregation	–	–	–	–	–	–
Year dummies	Yes	Yes	Yes	Yes	Yes	Yes
Country effects	No	Yes	No	Yes	No	Yes
R^2	0.745	0.159	0.777	0.2945	0.695	0.15
Number of obs.	40	40	40	40	31	31

Note: The coefficients in the table represent the marginal effect of each institution on the gender wage gap growth between 1980 and 1998. The gender wage gap is computed as the log of the male/female wage ratio, median earnings for full time—full year workers for the periods 1980, 1990 and 1998.

Sources: 1980 and 1990: Blau and Kahn (2000), data for Denmark, Greece, Portugal and Spain refer to 1994, ECHP. Data for 1998 are from OECD, *Employment Outlook* (2002).

Key: *Significant at the 10% level. Robust standard errors in parentheses, ** Significance at the 5% level, *** Significance at the 1% level.

Countries: Australia, Austria, Belgium, Canada, Denmark, Finland, France, Germany, Italy, Japan, Portugal, Spain, Sweden, UK, USA.

Sources for Institutions: The index of Bargaining Coverage is from Blanchflower (1996). Parental Leave (weeks), EPL, and Union Density are from Nickel and Layard (1999). The Equal Employment Opportunity indicator is based on Table 5.1, OECD, Employment Outlook 1988. It measures the time lag since the equal employment opportunity legislation was passed in each country.

The index of Product Market Regulation, and of EPL for temporary and regular contracts are from Nicoletti, Scarpetta and Boylaud (1999); The maximum UI Replacement Rates are taken from Blanchard and Wolfers (2000). The Segregation Index is from Anker (1998), Table 9.1.

5.6 CONCLUSIONS

Our analysis of the gender wage gap has shown that significant differentials in the pay of men and women remain in Europe. Although the wage gap is not as large as in America, the reasons are probably not as a result of less discrimination against women in Europe, but because wage inequality is bigger in the United States, the mean earnings of men and women are also further apart. Unions appear to close some of the wage gap—though our analysis is not able to distinguish between this as an objective of union policy or as an outcome of the fact that unions tend to compress the wage structure. We also found that although Mediterranean countries appear at first sight to be characterized by lower wage gaps than the rest of Europe, this result is not robust when account is taken of the fact that in the Mediterranean countries female participation rates are lower and concentrated among more skilled women. Gender gaps are bigger at the lower skills level, and when we correct for the small number of unskilled women who participate in southern Europe, the wage gap widens to meet that of other European countries.

6

Rising Female Participation: The Consequences for Other Workers

In the world of neoclassical macroeconomic growth, with each country characterized by constant returns to scale, a rise in female participation induced by factors that are exogenous to the labor market (such as the more general availability of consumer durables and other factors discussed in chapter 3) might in the short run reduce the wages of all labor. But in the medium-to-long run, the capital stock rises to catch up with the higher labor supply. Even if we ignore the possibility of more research and innovation induced by the presence of more women in universities and research laboratories, the higher female supply is neutral. But there is a lot of heterogeneity in the labor market, and it is unlikely that the rise in female labor will affect all demographic and skill groups equally. We saw that women segregate into some sectors of the economy and their skills are different from those of men. It is likely that women complement some types of labor and compete with others. To give two rather obvious examples, the entry of women into the labor force creates demand for child care units, thus complementing the labor used to run those units but thereby creating competition for retail assistants, because retailing is one of the popular destinations for women.

In this chapter, we consider the consequences of an exogenous rise in the female participation rate, perhaps induced by social norms or developments outside the labor market, for the employment and wages of other demographic groups. As in previous chapters, we first review the evidence, which comes mostly from the United States, and then present some original work of our own as it applies to Europe.

6.1 WHAT DO WE KNOW?

An increase in the supply of female workers is not a homogenous increase in labor supply. In the United States, the median hourly wage of women is around the 32nd percentile of the distribution of hourly wages of men, while the median male hourly wage is at the 75th percentile of women's wages (source Current Population Survey (CPS) 1991, and author's calculations). In this sense, the average woman tends to crowd out the labor market for low-wage workers, who are likely to be unskilled men and younger workers. If wages are a good proxy for productivity, women appear to be less skilled than the average worker. We saw that there is evidence of some wage discrimination against women. But even if we account for this, the relative rank of the median woman will not rise to the rank of the median man. Is this a valid inference and are women therefore competing only with unskilled men and youths?

Some early estimates of production functions with different labor inputs were carried out in the United States and surveyed by Hamermesh and Grant (1979). Some authors disaggregated by gender allowing for an estimate of any congestion effects caused by women. Freeman (1979) introduced female workers as an explicit factor of production, but he did not find significant substitutability between younger male workers and women. This conclusion was challenged by Grant and Hamermesh (1982) who estimated a trans-log production function across industries with gender and race groups as well as physical capital. They found a strong substitutability between adult white women and younger workers. Their estimates suggest that the consequence of a 10 per cent exogenous increase in the supply of female workers reduces the wage rate of younger workers by 1.5 per cent and would reduce their employment rate by as much as 50 per cent if their wage were totally rigid. Not surprisingly, they find this number 'unbelievably large'. Berger (1983) also investigates the impact of changes in the composition of the labor force by differentiating by education, in addition and also introducing capital. He treats women as a single, homogenous group and finds that female workers are strong substitutes for both young male workers with a high school degree and young male college-educated workers.[1] He also finds some evidence of significant but weaker substitutability between older men with a high school certificate and women. Topel (1994a, b) relaxes the assumption of homogeneity for women and also finds substitutability between low-skill women (first half of their wage distribution) and low-skill men (first 33rd percentile of their wage distribution). He also found substitutability between higher-skill women (perhaps half of the skilled distribution) and two groups of men (1–33rd percentiles and 34th–66th percentiles). Topel (1997), surveying these results, claims that had women's participation remained constant, wages of the less-skilled men would not have declined, although he points out some drawbacks in this conclusion, notably in terms of the timing of the changes that occurred in supply, and the return to skills not coinciding accurately.

There are very few studies of this type for Europe. Given wage rigidities at the lower end of the wage distribution, the main effects of more female labor supply on unskilled workers and youths is likely to be primarily on their unemployment rates. In Wasmer (2001b), the share of women in the labor force is found to have a significant positive impact on the unemployment rate

[1] Young workers are defined as those with less than 15 years of experience.

of young workers in a cross-section of countries. Further, there is evidence of an inverted U-shaped interaction term with respect to the degree of decentralization of wage bargaining: flexible labor markets and highly centralized ones (Austria, Sweden) seem to have better accommodated rising female participation in terms of youth employment.

In terms of human capital, women tend to be better educated on average and tend to have higher returns to education. Given that generally women earn less than men in all occupations, the latter fact is another way of saying that the ratio of the wages of low-skill women to the wages of low-skill men is less than the corresponding ratio for high-skill workers.[2]

Rising female participation also has some implications for the supply of skills and experience in the labor market. In Wasmer (2003), a measure of the supply of experience based on French and US individual data is computed: it is the average contribution of experience to individual wages across the active population. A measure of the supply of education can be computed in the same way, as the contribution of education to wages. The outcome is that, in both countries, the supply of education increased fast in the last 30 years, while the supply of experience declined up to the mid-1980s, and then recovered in the late 1980s and the 1990s, thus exhibiting a U-shaped pattern. It is shown that the supply of experience is closely and negatively correlated with the returns to experience in the United States, indicating that labor supply factors dominate over labor demand factors.

In Wasmer (2003), the supply of experience is not only as a result of rising female participation, but is also driven by the baby-boom cohorts, changing the age composition of the labor force in the late 1970s. To focus only on the rise in female participation rates, however, leads to the same U-shape pattern, namely, women have both lower experience and lower returns to experience than men (the difference in earnings is about 30 to 50 per cent per year worked), and so a rise in female participation reduces their average experience, because new entrants have no experience. In the late 1980s and in the 1990s, the evolution of experience was different because women started having longer and more stable careers, which led to an inversion of the trend.

As an additional check of the U-shaped pattern of experience, Wasmer (2001a) calculated the supply of experience based on a 'perpetual inventory method': experience is seen as a sum of past participation rates, possibly discounted in order to account for human capital depreciation. This method is applied to eight OECD countries with sufficiently long time series, and in almost all of them, a similar pattern emerges from the data. Further, this measure of experience correlates positively with the relative employment rates of workers less than 29 years old—a reflection of the congestion effects described below, namely, the absence of experience reduces the demand for

---

[2] Of course, this finding is consistent with our finding in chapter 5, that there is more wage discrimination against women in unskilled occupations than in more skilled ones.

younger workers if they are a complement in the production process with older, more experienced workers.

In the short run, when physical capital is fixed, an exogenous increase in female participation tends to reduce aggregate wages. It is striking to notice that in countries where the labor force rose faster, such as the United States, average wages have not increased much, nor even declined, over the same time period (see Card, Kramarz and Lemieux 1999). Gottschalk (1997) shows that although male wages declined over the period 1979–1994, wages and employment of women increased significantly. This suggests either that the demand for female labor has greatly increased, or that societies now accept more easily the idea of female employment as a result of changes in social norms. In countries where the share of women in the labor force is low, such as Italy, France or Spain, average wages have increased faster over the last few decades (Bertola 1999). In the short run, growth in the participation rate matters for wages because physical capital cannot adjust, and wages need to fall to create more demand for labor. If wages do not fall, unemployment has to increase. In Europe there is clear evidence of a positive and significant impact of the growth rate of the female labor force on the unemployment rates of women and young workers (Wasmer 2001b).

6.2   MEASURING EXPERIENCE IN THE LABOR MARKET

We now attempt to derive estimates of the consequences of changes in female participation by focusing on the supply of experience, as defined in this section. Because of interruptions to labor market activity, which are more frequent for women than for men, women necessarily accumulate less labor market experience than men do. But the measures of labor market experience found in individual surveys are usually of low quality, because the exact number of years worked is typically not known. Experience is often approximated by potential experience, which is simply the respondents' ages minus their years of education. But the measurement error for this proxy is rather large. O'Neill and Polacheck (1993) estimate that the actual experience of women is about two-thirds of their potential experience, with an increase in this fraction over time and cohorts. For this reason, we prefer to use a different method that uses aggregate data to measure the experience of men and women.

Our approach is as follows: let p_{at} be the participation rate of a cohort of age a at time t. For simplicity, we ignore the gender dimension in the notation. At time $t-1$, the cohort had a participation rate of $p_{a-1,t-1}$, and at the age of entry to the labor market, say 15, that cohort had a participation rate of $p_{15,t-(a-15)}$. It follows that the average experience of the cohort of age a at time t can be written:

$$E_{a,t} = \sum_{a'=15}^{a} p_{a',t-(a-a')}\delta^{a-a'}$$

where $\delta < 1$ is a discount factor characterizing the yearly depreciation rate of the accumulated experience at rate $1 - \delta$. Since we use participation rates and not employment rates, this measure of experience is experience of the labor market, not of employment.[3] By rewriting the above formula, changing the index, and defining the potential experience of the labor market by $e = a - a'$ we obtain:

$$E_{a,t} = \sum_{e=0}^{a-15} p_{a-e,t-e}\delta^e$$

This formula is equivalent to the usual formula defining the capital stock of a plant of age a, which is the sum of depreciated past investments in physical capital. There is one difference though: unlike the initial capital stock of a plant, the initial stock of experience is known as it is simply zero at the age of 15.

The total stock of experience of men and of women is the sum across all cohorts, with weights the share of the cohorts in the male (or female) active population (denoted by $\alpha_{a,t}^K$ with $K = m, f$ for male and female). We thus obtain:

$$E_t^K = \sum_{a=15}^{64} E_{a,t}\alpha_{a,t}^K, \quad K = m, f$$

This formula also gives the average experience of labor market participants as:

$$E_t = (1 - \alpha_t^f)E_t^m + \alpha_t^f E_t^f$$

where α_t^f is the share of women in the labor force.

The OECD and the ILO provide participation data and population by gender and age intervals for several countries for the period 1960 to 1998. A logistic function of participation rates by age, gender and country is regressed on lagged values, a trend and its square. The series are then dynamically forecasted on the basis of each model to obtain retrospective data. Series of forecast errors are computed to provide confidence intervals. This method ignores the break due to the war period, with the implication that forecasts (in the present case, a more accurate word would be 'backcasts') of participation before 1945 have a systematic error. The weight of those years in the average experience

---

[3] This measure of experience is less accurate than employment experience if the issue in hand is to measure human capital (although young graduates may learn a lot when looking for jobs). Labor market experience however captures better the idea of attachment to the labor market: unemployment spells then should be included because the unemployed remain attached to the labor market. In any case, there were not enough employment data for each age and gender to enable estimation of employment experience. We argue later on that labor market experience is a good instrument for employment experience in an unemployment model.

across cohorts is however rather small between 1970 and 1998, which is the period considered in this paper (see Wasmer, 2001a, for more details on this method). We set δ equal to 1, which implies that there is no human capital depreciation.

Figures 6.1–6.4 show the calculated time series of experience by gender in the United States, the United Kingdom, Germany (western Länder), Spain, France, the Netherlands, Finland and Sweden. In all countries, the average experience level of men is between 18 and 20 years, with a decline in the 1970s as the size of the cohorts of new entrants in the labor market peaks 16 years after the baby boom. In contrast, the average experience of women differs much more across countries. In the early 1970s, it was about 5 years in the Netherlands, 6 years in Spain, 8 years in

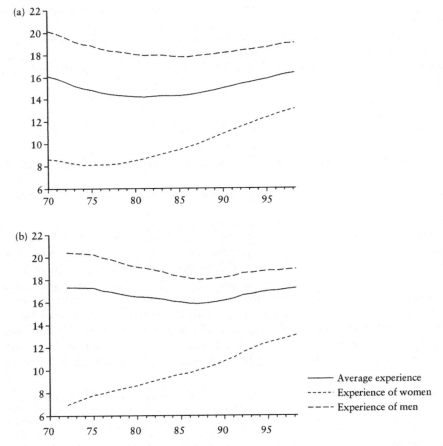

Figure 6.1. *Experience of the labor force (in years) by gender and 95% confidence interval (a) in USA; (b) in UK*

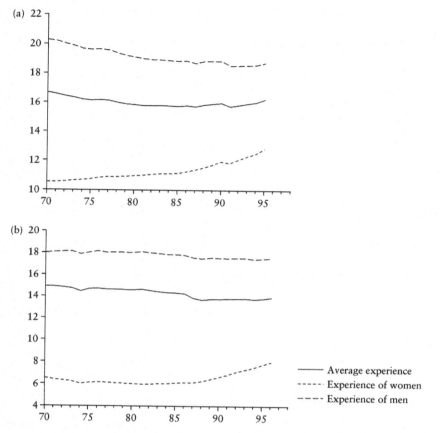

Figure 6.2. *Experience of the labor force (in years) by gender and 95% confidence interval (a) in (West) Germany; (b) in Spain*

the United Kingdom, 10 years in France, the United States and Germany, and 12 or more in Sweden and Finland. There is, however, a general trend towards gender convergence, although it is especially slow in Spain, Germany and the Netherlands.

The level of average experience is by definition a weighted average of the two series shown in the graphs, so it is closer to male experience in low participation countries than elsewhere. In most countries, average experience declined in the late 1970s, especially in countries where female participation was low and grew fast.

Women's low experience levels in the 1970s can be explained by both the low participation, or the short-term periods in the labor market, of older cohorts of women, and also, by the over-representation of young women in the

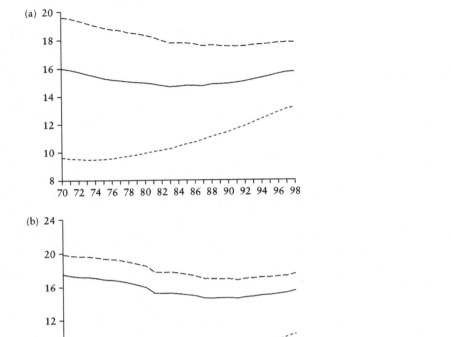

Figure 6.3. *Experience of the labor force (in years) by gender and 95% confidence interval (a) in France; (b) in the Netherlands*

female labor force. The latter is a pure cohort effect, presumably a transitory one given gender convergence. This indicates that countries with historically low levels of female participation that were affected both by the baby boom and by a rise in their female participation rates were initially also characterized by a strong reduction in their average experience. Subsequently, however, in the late 1980s, the new cohorts of the 1970s gained more experience and the average experience level in the labor market increased. Both factors, the ageing of the cohorts of the 1970s and the higher propensity of women to participate in the labor market, contributed to a U-shape experience pattern in the labor market. It is possible to go further and isolate formally the effect of female participation on the U-shape: for $E_t^f < E_t^m$, an increase in female participation raises α_t^f and initially contributes to a decline in E_t, but since E_t^f is an increasing function of past values of α_t^f the implication is that eventually both E_t and E_t^f will increase.

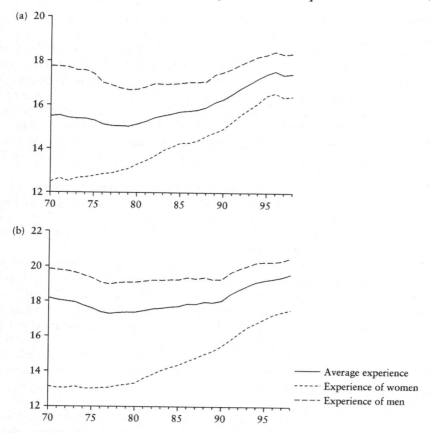

Figure 6.4. *Experience of the labor force (in years) by gender and 95% confidence interval (a) in Finland; (b) in Sweden*

6.3 MEASURING CROWDING-OUT IN THE YOUTH LABOR MARKET

A test of the substitutability between women and young workers in the labor market can be constructed by evaluating the impact of lower experience on the unemployment rate of youths. We estimate the following regression in the panel of eight countries in Figures 6.1–6.4:

$$\log(u_{i,t}^{25-34,m}) = C_i + \phi_i \cdot E_t + \varphi \cdot cycle_{i,t} + \varepsilon_{i,t}$$

$$\log(u_{i,t}^{25-34,f}) = C_i' + \phi_i' \cdot E_t + \varphi' \cdot cycle_{i,t} + \varepsilon_{i,t}'$$

where i is the country and t is time. The business cycle is controlled for by the log of unemployment of men aged 45–54. One expects a negative sign of ϕ_i and ϕ'_i if the decline in experience raises unemployment. To see this, think first of a world with perfect wage adjustment to labor supply and imagine a production function with experience as an input and decreasing returns to this input. A decrease in the supply of experience should raise the returns to experience and so weaken the relative position of youths in the labor market. If relative wages cannot adjust fully, the decline in experience results in higher youth unemployment. The coefficients ϕ_i indicate the percentage increase in the unemployment rate of the 25–34 year-old group when there is an increase of one year in average experience.[4]

A lag of the dependent variable is added to control for autocorrelation of the residuals. One might argue that experience is an endogenous variable because during unemployment the worker does not accumulate experience. This is not the case here, however, because our measure of experience is the sum of past participation rates, not of employment rates.[5]

The results are given in Table 6.1. Column (I) shows that the unemployment rate of young men is reduced by a higher level of average experience (each additional year reducing the rate of unemployment by 4 per cent). This suggests that young male workers compete with low-experience workers. Given that in all countries, women have a lower level of experience than the average (even in the 1990s), this is evidence of substitutability between young workers and women. Young female workers do not appear to be affected by overall experience, as shown in column (II). This is a priori surprising for one would expect some competition between young women and other low experience workers.

To clarify this, columns (II) and (IV) re-estimate the model by separating experience for men and women. The drawback of this specification is that, implicitly, it is assumed that the supply of experience is not aggregate, but rather segmented: one market for men, and one market for women. The outcome is reassuring for men: there is a larger impact of female experience (− 11% for each additional year), meaning that, the more experienced women are, the less competition with them occurs, while the experience of men is not significant. For women, the result is slightly more difficult to appreciate, that is

---

[4] One could alternatively think of a specification where unemployment is replaced by the employment rate. This specification is subject to endogeneity problems that do not arise with unemployment. Indeed, experience, being constructed as the sum of past participation rates, is correlated with the employment rates of young workers, both in time and across countries, which was not the case with unemployment rates. Further, the natural instrument for experience, its lagged value, is still correlated with employment rates, again as a consequence of the construction method of the experience series.

[5] It might however be the case that current participation is reduced when unemployment is higher, but this would affect only current participation, not past participation rates. This implies that experience is only marginally affected by current unemployment and can thus be considered as exogenous.

Table 6.1. *Youth unemployment and female experience*

Dependent variable	$\log(u_{i,t}^{25-34,m})$		$\log(u_{i,t}^{25-34,f})$	
	(I)	(II)	(III)	(IV)
$E_{i,t}$	-0.04^{**}	–	-0.01	–
	(2.5)		(0.65)	
$E_{i,t}^M$	–	0.04	–	0.09^*
		(1.3)		(2.5)
$E_{i,t}^F$	–	-0.11^{**}	–	-0.08^*
		(3.4)		(2.3)
$\log(u_{i,t}^{45-54,m})$	0.86^{**}	0.86^{**}	0.44^{**}	0.44^{**}
	(21.8)	(22.6)	(12.4)	(13.4)
Lagged dep. var.	0.19^{**}	0.16^{**}	0.56^{**}	0.52^{**}
	(5.4)	(4.7)	(15.9)	(13.9)
Fixed Effects	yes	yes	yes	yes
Specific Trend	yes	yes	yes	yes
Cross-section weights	yes	yes	yes	yes
#obs.	204	204	204	204
R^2	0.99	0.99	0.99	0.99
DW	0.98	0.96	1.36	1.36

Key: t-stat in parentheses. $^* =$ signif. at the 5% level, $^{**} =$ signif. at the 1% level.

to say, their unemployment rate is raised by the experience accumulation of men (with a semi-elasticity of 9 per cent), and reduced by the experience accumulation of women. One interpretation is that, as women's experience increases, the cohorts of new female entrants to the labor market are perceived as having higher labor market attachment and thus face a higher relative demand from employers. An alternative interpretation, less favorable to the econometric specification, is that the cyclical indicator used (male log unemployment rate for the 45–54 year old group) is not capturing well the cyclicality in women's labor demand. As a check, we replaced this indicator by its female counterpart and obtained insignificant results on the coefficients ϕ_i with or without breaking up experience by gender. Overall, the results of columns (I) and (II), consistent with the results of Grant and Hamermesh (1982), suggest net substitutability of young men with women, especially with low experience women, and no particular substitutability between young men and older men.

Although the institutional factors are already controlled for by country fixed effects and country specific trends, it is of interest to interact the coefficient of experience with institutional variables or with country fixed effects. Table 6.2 shows the results. For male workers, youth unemployment is reduced by an increase in average experience of the labor market participants in countries with a high level of employment protection (see column II). Interacting with country effects (column I) also shows a significant coefficient of experience

Table 6.2. *Youth unemployment and country effects*

Dependent variable	$\log(u_{i,t}^{25-34,m})$		$\log(u_{i,t}^{25-34,f})$	
	(I)	(II)	(III)	(IV)
$E_{i,t} \times$ FIN	0.37**	–	0.11	–
	(4.0)		(1.0)	
$E_{i,t} \times$ SWE	–0.31**	–	–0.02	–
	(4.2)		(0.5)	
$E_{i,t} \times$ NET	–0.75*	–	–0.30	–
	(2.3)		(1.4)	
$E_{i,t} \times$ GER	–0.60**	–	–0.44**	–
	(4.5)		(4.0)	
$E_{i,t} \times$ FRA	–0.14**	–	–0.09	–
	(3.0)		(1.7)	
$E_{i,t} \times$ SPA	0.12	–	–0.23	–
	(1.4)		(1.7)	
$E_{i,t} \times$ UK	–0.02	–	–0.46**	–
	(0.50)		(6.6)	
$E_{i,t} \times$ USA	–0.04*	–	0.04	–
	(2.0)		(2.2)	
$E_{i,t} \times$ Emp. Protection	–	–0.0057**	–	–0.0061**
		(2.6)		(2.7)
$\log(u_{i,t}^{45-54,m})$	0.91**	0.89**	0.54**	0.47**
	(24.7)	(22.9)	(16.1)	(13.5)
Lagged dep. var.	0.13**	0.18**	0.37**	0.51**
	(3.9)	(5.5)	(9.7)	(14.3)
Fixed-effects	yes	yes	yes	yes
Specific trend	yes	yes	yes	yes
Cross-section weights	yes	yes	yes	yes
#obs.	204	204	204	204
R^2	0.99	0.99	0.99	0.99
DW	1.20	1.00	1.43	1.33

Key: t-stat in parentheses. * = signif. at the 5% level, ** = signif. at the 1% level.

for Sweden, Germany, France and less so for the Netherlands and the United States, but the coefficient for Finland has the wrong sign. The fit of the model for female workers is less good (column III), although the interaction term between experience and employment protection remains negative and significant (column IV). Other regressions, specifying interaction terms between experience and benefit duration or with the replacement rate, did not exhibit significant interactions and are not reported. This is probably due to the fact that young workers are frequently not covered by unemployment insurance because of seniority rules.

6.4 CONCLUSIONS

In the US literature, the consensus is that the rise in female participation rates has adversely affected the wages of unskilled workers, and youths in particular. In Europe, where wages at the lower end or the distribution are less flexible, no such effect can be detected—but there is an effect on youth unemployment rates. We suggested a new way of measuring mean labor market experience in the labor market, by making use of an inventory method conventionally used to measure the capital stock. We found that a rise in the mean labor-market experience of women decreases the unemployment rates of both male and female young workers. To the extent that mean experience picks up the effects of female labor on youth unemployment, the negative impact is consistent with substitutability between youths and inexperienced women but complementarity between youths and experienced women.

7

What Policy Should Do

Our main objective in this section is to return to the main policy issues that we began with: the European Union's objectives of raising employment rates in the EU for women to at least 60 per cent by the year 2010 (the Lisbon target); and to achieving equality of employment opportunity and pay for men and women. Are these objectives realistic and how well have EU countries been doing in their pursuit of those targets?

Legislation aiming to end discrimination with regard to employment opportunities and wages pre-existed the Lisbon agenda. The European literature evaluating the success of such legislation is sparse but there is a rich literature on the effects of civil rights legislation on wage differentials in the United States. This legislation came into force mainly in the late 1960s and early 1970s. The first substantial legislation referring to women (again, in the US) is the Equal Pay Act of 1963, which requires equal pay for substantially equal work among men and women (but it does not include any provision for hiring, layoffs or promotions). The Title VII of the Civil Rights Act of 1964 prohibited discrimination both in employment opportunities and in wages (including hiring, layoffs or promotions). In the same year the Equal Employment Opportunity Commission (EEOC) was instituted to enforce Title VII. The 1972 Equal Employment Opportunity Act authorized the EEOC to initiate lawsuits on behalf of workers.[1] Most of the US literature, surveyed for example by Blau and Kahn (1992), and Altonji and Blank (1999), focuses on differentials by race and finds that civil rights policies helped blacks and women over the 1970s and 1980s. In particular, Beller (1982) provides some indicative evidence that Title VII led to a reduction of the gender wage gap and of occupational segregation by sex in the US between 1967 and 1974.

In Europe, there is a basic legislative framework relating to equal pay and equal treatment in the workplace that is common across EU countries. The principle of equal pay for men and women is contained in Article 119 of the EEC Treaty. Since 1975, this basic principle has been developed through a series of directives. In particular, the Council Directive 76/207/EEC also adds

---

[1] The first female discrimination case brought before the Supreme Court was '*Phillips v. Martin Marietta Corp*', in 1971. Phillips, a white woman, was not hired because she had children of pre-school age, yet men in the same situation were hired (source: EEOC, annual report 1972). The court ruled in her favor. Several similar cases were brought to the attention of the court by the mid-1980s (Olivetti 2001).

the principle of equal treatment of men and women with regards to: access to employment, vocational training and promotions and working conditions (that is, Equal Employment Opportunities). Each country is expected to determine the procedure by which these rights may be asserted. In extreme cases, national matters may be referred to the Court of Justice of the European Community.[2]

Countries in the EU, however, may differ in terms of the degree of law enforcement and in terms of the timing of introduction of country-specific Equal Pay and Equal Employment Opportunities legislation. Although Equal Pay laws have been in place in most European countries since the 1970s, legislation on Equal Employment Opportunities was introduced as late as the mid-1980s in many countries including: Austria, Finland, France, Germany, Greece, Ireland, Italy, Spain and Sweden. This legislation was introduced in 1978 in Belgium, Denmark and Norway. The United Kingdom constitutes an exception. The Equal Pay Act was introduced in 1970 and the Sex Discrimination Act in 1975 in response to national demands.

As discussed by Rice (1999), European countries substantially differ in the degree of awareness of equality issues and in the level of litigations arising from equal opportunities legislation. In particular, the United Kingdom and Ireland rank high in this dimension, whereas France and Belgium rank very low. This may be due to historical differences in the reasons why equal opportunities legislation was introduced, in response to domestic pressure as in the United Kingdom, or because of pressure from the European Union?[3]

The explanations of the rise in female employment and the closing of the wage gap that we reviewed made no reference to legislation as a cause of these changes. Although there is no decisive evidence of such causal links in the literature, Equal Employment Opportunity legislation has probably had an effect on women's choice of education and career. Women choosing to embark on long-term educational and career paths at least know that the courts can protect them from discrimination that does not allow them to reap the full rewards. The fact that discrimination occurs less in more skilled occupations may also be indirect evidence that legislation has helped, because it is easier to identify discrimination in professional occupations than in low-level routine jobs.

Legislation can also have a big impact on social norms, which as we have seen have been cited as reasons for the increased participation of women. The United Kingdom, where legislation was introduced early on, has had one of the fastest rises in female employment and wage rates. In contrast, two of the

---

[2] For a summary of the timing of the introduction of Equal Pay and Equal Employment Opportunity legislation across countries see Table 5.11 in the OECD, *Employment Outlook* (1988).

[3] Blau and Kahn (2000, 2003) briefly describe the differences in Equal Pay and Equal Employment Opportunity legislation in Europe and in the US.

countries with large participation rates and the most segregated labor markets (Sweden and Finland) were among the last European countries to introduce equal employment opportunity legislation (1984 and 1987 respectively).

We return now more explicitly to the Lisbon targets and first take a closer look at the feasibility of the overall employment target. Table 2.1 (p. 13) and Figure 2.3 (p. 15) show that several countries have achieved the quantitative target but some, the Mediterranean countries in particular, are a long way behind. However, women's education levels have been improving and social norms have been changing in favor of more women entering the labor force. There is an independent momentum that pushes up the participation rate of women and even if there is no policy change, participation rates are likely to increase. We calculate roughly the likely rise in participation rates that might be expected by the year 2010 given current trends.

The age–employment profile of women is characterized by a similar hump shape in all countries in our sample (see Figs. 7.1 and 7.2 for Sweden and Italy). The employment rates for women in their early twenties tend to be the lowest, but they increase substantially as women enter their early thirties. In most countries, the highest employment rate is observed for women in their early forties. Conversely, as women are close to the retirement age, the employment rate drops significantly. It is clear from Figures 7.1 and 7.2 that the main difference between these two extreme examples is not in the shape of the employment–age profile, but rather in the level of the employment rate within each age group.

The age–employment profiles reported in Figures 7.1 and 7.2 do not represent the average employment history of an average Swedish or Italian woman but are based on the actual employment rates of women who entered the labor market at very different points in time. In other words, the employment rates refer to women of different cohorts. For example, women in the age group

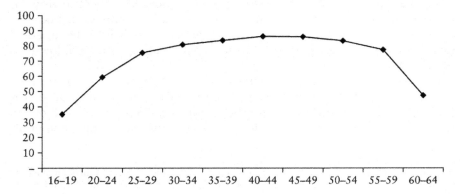

Figure 7.1. *Female employment rates by different age groups: Sweden 2001*

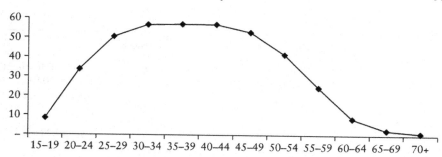

Figure 7.2. *Female employment rates by different age groups: Italy 2001*

55–60 were born in the early 1940s, while women in the age group 30–35 were born in the early 1970s. Women belonging to the first group had very low employment rates throughout their working life, since in their cohorts female participation was generally low. The typical labor market history of a woman in her prime age in the early 2000s is rather different and much more labor intensive, than that of the generation of her mother.

In the year 2010, the oldest cohort of women in the working age population will be that of women born in the late 1940s, who entered the labor force in the late 1960s or early 1970s, when participation rates were rising fast. In addition, the women in their fifties will be those who, in the early 2000s, experienced the greatest employment rates. One can argue that the latter group will have employment rates much greater than the employment rates of women currently in their fifties. Such cohort effects can be substantial, and can have sizeable effects at the macro level.

Table 7.1 calculates the female employment rate of women in 2010, based on the cohort effects mentioned above. The estimates of the working age population by different age groups and gender are obtained from the ILO population estimates. The level of employment in 2010 for different age groups is obtained in the following way. For women in the age groups 45–64, we assume that total employment in 2010 will be the same as the current total employment of those identical (albeit younger) women. For women in the age groups 15–45, we assume that the employment rate in 2010 will be as high as it is today. The results show that these cohort effects are substantial. In the case of Italy, the employment rate in the year 2010 will be 49 per cent, up from a level of 41.3 per cent in 2001. For the Mediterranean countries as a whole, the exercise suggests that cohort effects can result in an increase in the female employment rate by some 6–7 percentage points. Figure 7.3 shows in detail the shift in the age–employment profile in Italy that such effects may induce.

Finally, in Table 7.1, we also present the estimate of the employment rate in the year 2010, assuming that cohorts 14–45 will increase their employment rate by two percentage points. The aggregate effects of such an exercise are less

Table 7.1. *Cohort effects and female employment rate in 2010*

	Estimate of the female employment rate in the year 2010		
	Female employment rate 2001*	Female employment rate 2010 (hypothesis 1)	Female employment rate 2010 (hypothesis 2)
Mediterranean			
Italy	41.11	49.33	50.21
Spain	43.75	49.63	50.59
Greece	41.14	48.34	49.37
Average	42	49.1	50.06
Nordic			
Denmark	70.44	77.83	78.75
Sweden	73.48	76.22	77.17
Norway	73.75	76.5	77.46
Average	72.56	76.85	77.79
Continental			
Austria	47.12	53.85	54.54
Belgium	51.45	60.68	61.61
France	42.20	50.9	51.63
Finland	65.40	72.05	72.96
Germany	58.76	69.17	70.05
Ireland	53.99	60.34	61.44
Netherlands	63.86	71.61	72.52
Portugal	61.13	69.21	70.20
Average	55.49	63.48	64.37

Key: * Employment rates 15 + for France, Austria, 15–64 for the others.

Hypothesis 1:	Age 15–44	Employment Rate 2010 = Employment rate 2001
	Age 45–64	Employment Rate 2010 = Employment level 2001/Population 2010 * 100
Hypothesis 2:	Age 15–39	Employment Rate 2010 = Employment rate 2001 + 2%
	Age 40–44	Employment Rate 2010 = Employment rate 2001
	Age 40–44	Employment Rate 2010 = Employment level 2001/Population 2010 * 100

dramatic, for two reasons. First, employment rates of the young workers are very low, and an increase of two percentage points has little macro impact. Secondly, population ageing shifts most of the working age population to the older class, and further reduces the marginal effect of the increase in the employment rate of the younger workers.

So something like a third of the distance to the achievement of the Lisbon target will probably close even in the Mediterranean countries because of the internal dynamics of female employment rates now in place. These calculations, however, depend on women maintaining their high employment

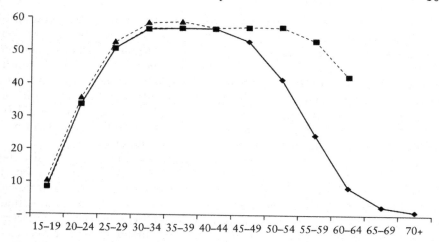

Figure 7.3. *Age employment profile in 2001 and 2010 in Italy with cohort effects*

rates into middle age. This assumes that their accumulated pension rights do not give them incentives to retire early. Currently, the pensions system in some countries gives strong incentives for early retirement. In this event, the high employment rates computed will not be achieved. So success in narrowing the gap vis-à-vis the Lisbon targets also requires reform of the pensions system—at least in some countries—to remove strong incentives to retire early.[4] Even if the internal dynamics narrow the Lisbon gap, there is still some distance to be traveled before the target is reached. And what about the other objectives of the European employment strategy, equal employment opportunity and equal pay?

Women would enter jobs in the United States in big numbers, partly because of technological and sectoral shifts, and partly because of improvements in working conditions at home. The main shift in the market place that helped women is the one from manufacturing and agriculture to services, and the main innovation at home is the availability of durables and the possibility of family planning. European women have access to the same technologies and some countries, the Nordic and the United Kingdom in particular, have for all practical purposes achieved what the United States has achieved. Our examination of the data has revealed some things that can be done to help the other countries converge with the Anglo-Saxon and Scandinavian countries.

Primary among these appears to be market deregulation, notably in the market for final output. If the service sector is to create the jobs that will

---

[4] This is obviously even more relevant to the European Union objective of 'active ageing' but it has implications for women's employment too, given that older women will have to stay in employment if the female target is to be reached.

attract the women, entrepreneurship in the service sector has to be encouraged through easy access to company creation, an operation free of intervention from the state, and easy recruitment of workers. Product market regulation takes a variety of different forms and formal econometric work is only just beginning. But indications are that heavily regulated markets have adverse effects for women's employment. We would include here high taxation for small enterprises, restrictions on the firing of employees which makes it very expensive for a small company to recruit workers, either full time or part time, and high minimum wages and social security contributions.

The creation of part-time and flexible temporary jobs should also be encouraged by policy. There is a European Union directive for the creation of more part-time jobs, as part of the overall Employment Strategy, and this is especially important for women. Although the evidence that countries that create more part-time jobs also create more overall employment is not very strong, there is some evidence pointing in this direction, and it becomes stronger and more convincing when countries at the extremes of the distribution are compared. The Mediterranean countries have not created many part-time jobs, almost certainly because their labor markets are too rigid to enable firms to create them. If they liberalize their markets to make it easier for firms to create such jobs their aggregate employment rates will almost certainly rise.

A large number of the jobs that will be created in the service sector will be in small companies or will be for people working on their own account. Successful countries, like the United Kingdom, Denmark and the Netherlands, have low product–market regulation, give incentives to new entrepreneurs, and have opened large numbers of part-time jobs. Temporary jobs may be another source of employment for women, especially in countries where regular jobs are protected by strict legislation with vested interests that do not allow change. Although we found some evidence that women do not consider temporary jobs satisfactory, their existence may be a necessary second-best solution to a more serious problem, the existence of entrenched rigidities in the labor market. But we found no evidence among women against part-time jobs. Those who have them seem to have them because they want them. At least as a start to a labor market career for women with children, part-time jobs may offer a useful first step to other forms of employment.

If the liberalization reforms that we are suggesting (most of which have been mentioned in several European Commission documents since Lisbon) are pursued, the employment of single women will almost certainly rise to the desired targets everywhere. But married women need the extra provision for family care. The European Union wants governments to provide state-subsidised care for 90 per cent of children in school-going age. Although the evidence is that the countries currently providing subsidised family care for working wives have higher employment rates of married women, the provision of such care by the state can be expensive, and we see no overwhelming economic reason for such massive support. The same objectives can be achieved if private initiative is encouraged to set up small family-care units run by a small number of individuals likely to be women with children working on their own account. Encouragement of this kind can take the form of tax incentives and long-term low-interest start-up loans or grants. Support can also take the form of state vouchers given to parents of small children, although again there is no reason why the vouchers should do more than offer a small subsidy. Unsubsidized private initiative appears to be the driving force behind family care in the United States and the United Kingdom, two high-employment countries. But it should be noted that the participation rates of women with two or more children in these two countries is not as high as it is in the Nordic countries, where state family provision is common.

What about employment equality? There is certainly evidence of some job segregation—women working in some sectors of the economy and men in others. Such segregation, however, is not necessarily a bad thing and might reflect either preferences or comparative advantage. We did not find strong evidence of discrimination in this respect. But women are also heavily represented in part-time and temporary jobs. Although as we pointed out we believe that the allocation to part-time jobs is voluntary, the over-representation in temporary jobs may not be. Legislation that is designed to ensure that men and women are given equal opportunities in all types of jobs should be enforced with the same level of strictness everywhere.

The same can be said about wages. There is evidence that although the gender wage gap has been narrowing, there is still wage discrimination against women, both in temporary jobs and in regular full-time jobs. European countries do not actually suffer as much from large wage gaps as the United States does, but the reasons are unrelated to discrimination. In the United States, there is more inequality in general, and a larger gender wage gap is one of its symptoms. In Europe stronger unions and other institutions compress the wage structure and so move women's pay closer to men's. Unions have another effect on female employment rates. There is some evidence that they affect them adversely. The adverse effect appears to be larger than any adverse effect on male employment. Generally, the effect of unions is one that works against larger participation rates but in favor of those who are already in the market.

At first glance, the Mediterranean countries appear to be doing better in achieving wage equality between men and women. This is partly because of the higher overall wage compression effects of labor market institutions—already discussed. But there is also another factor, namely, the nature of female employment rates in southern Europe. The reason why the women participating in southern Europe are on average more skilled is because there are not as many unskilled women participating as in northern Europe. The gender wage gap is smaller for higher skills and as more unskilled women come into the market and their participation rates increase, the average gap should increase.

What can governments do to reduce the difference between men's and women's rates of pay? There is already legislation in place across the European

Union making it an offence to pay different wages for similar types of work. Enforcement is not uniform, and increasing monitoring should contribute to the narrowing of the gap. The closing of the gap, however, will come only if market developments are favorable to it. In consequence, therefore, as women pursue more stable careers and advance further up the occupational ladder, the gap should be narrowing. For example, in the United States, this development has been a major force behind the narrowing of the gap. Policy can help here through education and training, and more directly through the provision of family-care units, and of other incentives to reduce the interruptions of women's careers. But where the incentive given is longer mandatory parental leave, as is the case in most countries, we found evidence that the gap widens. This is probably because with the prospect of an extended interruption on full pay, employers tend to offer lower wages to compensate.

There are of course big advantages from the increased participation of women but some groups of the population will feel the pressure of increased competition for jobs. On average the capital stock should eventually adjust to compensate the median worker for any loss of earnings, but because women are not competing directly with the median, some long-term negative consequences for some groups might remain. We identified young workers, especially men, as the ones most vulnerable to competition from newly arriving women. Governments need to provide for these workers, because the cause of the deterioration of their prospects is itself a government-initiated change. We found that in Europe, where youth wages are not as flexible as in the United States, the entry of more women raises the unemployment of young workers. This is a critical time in a worker's life and the loss of earnings, experience and the self-esteem that come with the first job can have long-term consequences for the young person's employment prospects and welfare.

For this reason welfare policies that deal with youth unemployment should be given priority by governments in countries facing a fast rise in female employment rates. Tax incentives for firms to take on youths should accompany any similar measures designed to encourage the employment of women. But whereas women do not experience much long-term unemployment, youths are an especially vulnerable group. Measures such as the ones implemented in the Nordic countries and the United Kingdom that target unemployed youths, and give them active support to speed up their transition to work, are especially effective in offsetting the adverse effects of job competition.

These measures, however, should be temporary: crowding-out effects should disappear progressively as women accumulate more experience.

Comments

FLORENCE JAUMOTTE[1]

Part I makes significant contributions on multiple topics: the 'institutional' determinants of female employment and in particular the role of product market regulation; the (possible) job segregation of women in part-time and temporary employment; and the macroeconomic effects of increased female participation, in particular for youth employment. My comments will focus mostly on the issues of part-time female employment, the role of childcare support, and the institutional determinants of female employment.

This book provides a very interesting study of whether the over-representation of women in part-time jobs is the result of segregation and discrimination against women or whether it reflects a preference of women for this more flexible form of employment. The conclusion is that in most countries, female part time is not the reflection of job segregation against women but is actually appreciated by women as a way to reconcile work and family life. The exceptions are the Southern European countries, where part time is not viewed as a desirable employment opportunity for women. This finding is confirmed by the results of a European survey on the preferences of couples with young children regarding the work pattern of women (Table C.1.1.). There, it is shown that preferences for female part time are actually low in Southern European countries (with Italy being somewhat of an exception) and in Finland. These low preferences for part-time also translate into low actual rates of part-time work in these countries. As the study on job segregation suggests, women in Southern European countries may prefer not to participate at all in the labour market or to participate through other forms of employment (self-employment or family employment) than to take on a part-time job. In other countries, the actual part-time participation is higher and there is room (sometimes significant room) to increase the part-time employment. The low preferences for female part time in Southern Europe raise the question of what are the characteristics of part-time work in Southern Europe that make it less desirable than part-time work in other countries (mostly Northern Europe). One plausible explanation for the dissatisfaction with part time could be that part-time participation of the mother is not financially viable for the family (OECD, 2002). Women in part-time jobs indeed seem to express dissatisfaction with their earnings levels. Other possible sources of dissatisfaction with part-time jobs could include job insecurity (there is some evidence of this in the study), a lack of training and career

[1] Florence Jaumotte is an economist at the Economics Department of the Organization for Economic Cooperation and Development (OECD). The views expressed in the present discussion are those of the author and do not necessarily reflect those of the OECD or of its member countries.

Table C.1.1. *Actual and preferred employment patterns among couple families with child under 6, 1998*

	Total employment			Full-time employment			Part-time employment		
	Actual	Preferred	Preferred–Actual	Actual	Preferred	Preferred–Actual	Actual	Preferred	Preferred–Actual
Scandinavia									
Sweden	64	89	25	51	67	16	13	22	9
Finland	56	89	33	49	80	31	6	9	2
Northern Europe									
Belgium	65	84	18	46	55	9	19	29	9
Austria	47	76	28	19	36	17	28	40	12
Netherlands	60	76	16	5	6	1	55	70	15
Germany	39	75	36	16	32	16	23	43	20
France	53	74	21	39	52	14	14	22	8
Ireland	50	73	24	31	31	0	19	42	24
United Kingdom	57	63	6	25	21	–4	32	42	10
Luxembourg	51	57	7	24	28	4	27	30	3
Southern Europe									
Portugal	79	92	13	75	84	10	5	8	3
Italy	47	78	31	35	50	16	12	28	16
Greece	50	76	26	42	66	23	8	11	3
Spain	32	71	39	26	60	34	6	12	5
Unweighted average	54	77	23	34	48	13	19	29	10

Source: Secretariat calculations on the basis of microdata from the *Employment Options of the Future survey* (European Foundation for the Improvement of Living and Working Conditions).

prospects, and excessive flexibility in working hours (involving for example asocial working hours). In my view, this issue should be further investigated in future research to help the formulation of policy in Southern European countries.

Although preferences for part time are relatively high in Northern European countries (excluding the Nordics), these may have been expressed to some extent taking the current policy environment as given. The latter includes among other factors the availability of affordable childcare and paid parental leaves. Thus, for example, if affordable childcare is not widely available, women may express a strong preference for part time (over full time) because this is the only possibility for them to combine market work with family life. This caveat is particularly important for Northern European countries which are generally characterised by lower levels of public support for childcare than, say, Nordic countries where full-time female participation is more common. In Nordic countries, women switched from part-time to full-time jobs as more childcare support became available, although it can not be ascertained that the latter caused the former.[2] Powell (1998) and Jaumotte (2003) also find that childcare support tends to increase full-time female participation more than part-time participation. Investigating the issue of whether women's preferences are conditioned by the policy environment or reflect intrinsic preferences is beyond the scope of this study but I believe this is an important caveat to keep in mind when evaluating preferences of women for part time.

Another source of concern regarding female part time in Northern Europe is that it may increase the precariousness of mother and child, particularly in periods of marital instability. Indeed, the study finds evidence that part-time jobs suffer from a wage penalty in some Northern European countries. This is interpreted as women accepting lower (hourly) wages because of their preferences for this type of jobs. It should also be noted that in several of these countries, the social security coverage of part-time jobs is low (OECD, 1998). This is for example the case in the United Kingdom, where short part times (which are very common) do not benefit from social security coverage and Germany which has among the highest thresholds for social security coverage of part-timers. Both the wage penalty and the low social security coverage contribute to increase the precariousness of women and their children. The fact that women are willing to accept part-time jobs with lower (hourly) wages may reflect an excess supply of part-time work by women relative to the demand for such employees by firms. There are several ways in which this imbalance may be addressed. First, increasing the availability of part-time work opportunities would require identifying and removing policy distortions (if any) against the creation of part-time work, but it may also require a change of mentality on behalf of employers. Second, it is important to ensure that women can revert to full-time jobs if they wish so after spending some time in part-time employment

---

[2] It is indeed possible that rising female education levels and the growing attachment of women to the labour force (made possible by first part-time jobs) may have pushed women to ask for more public childcare support in order to enable them to work full time.

to take care of their children.[3] For example, in the Netherlands parents were given greater rights to switch from full-time to part-time work schedules and vice-versa. Finally, another solution would be to increase childcare support as a way to give women the choice to work full time if they choose to do so, and to secure their financial independence. Childcare subsidies may be particularly desirable to help women work full time, when part-time jobs offer little prospects for training and career prospects or, more generally, are not the preferred working arrangement of women.

Public childcare support receives little attention in Part I as a potential determinant of female labour force participation. The paper emphasises mostly the potential to increase the labour supply of childless women in Europe relative to Nordic countries, North America, and the United Kingdom. However, the potential to increase the labour supply of mothers is also large (perhaps even larger), including in North America and the United Kingdom (see Table 2.5 in chapter 2). And mothers actually want to work more. Table C.1.1. shows that the gap between preferred and actual employment rates of women with a child under 6 is 23 per cent on average in the European countries. There is evidence that childcare subsidies indeed raise the labour supply of mothers (see for example chapter 3 and Jaumotte, 2003). From an economic point of view, several arguments justify the provision of childcare subsidies. First, the optimal taxation theory recommends taxing women (in particular married women and mothers) less, because their labour supply is more elastic to the wage than that of men. Low-skilled mothers are expected to be particularly responsive to the subsidies. De facto married women face a higher tax rate, due to the loss of dependent spouse's allowance and the introduction in some countries of a number of family-based tax measures. Childcare subsidies, if conditioned on the mother working, provide a way to reduce the taxation of working mothers. Second, the subsidization of childcare may help liquidity-constrained mothers to get off welfare and reach economic self-sufficiency, through the accumulation of human capital and work experience. Third, there is some evidence that childcare, in particular high-quality childcare may have potential benefits for the child's development and his integration into society (OECD, 2001).

Finally, Part I makes an interesting contribution on the effect of some institutional factors and policies on female employment. The empirical study identifies the degree of product market regulation as a (possibly) important determinant of female employment though, as the study suggests, its estimated negative impact seems extremely large. The interpretation of this effect is that a high degree of product market regulation hinders the development of the service sector which is a major employer of women. It is plausible that the large estimated coefficient on product market regulation in part captures the omission of some other variables, the more so that the product market

---

[3] For exmaple, O'Reilly and Bothfeld (2002) find that in the United Kingdom and Germany, only a small number of women are able to use part-time work as a bridge back into a full-time job. Instead, a substantial percentage drops out of employment, especially mothers of more than one child.

regulation measure used in the specification is not time-varying and most of the variation comes from the interaction of its value at the end of the 1990s with time dummies for the previous 20 years. In line with the evidence in chapter 1 that the variation in employment rates mostly reflects a variation in activity rates (supply side) and not in unemployment rates, the model could be extended to include policies such as the taxation of second earners, public expenditures on childcare, and parental leave policies, as well as control variables such as the marriage rate, fertility, education, and religious beliefs (imperfectly controlled for by country fixed effects and time dummies). Jaumotte (2003) looks at the relationship between female participation rates (as opposed to employment rates) and a number of these variables including a broader but time-varying measure of product market regulation. She finds a more moderate effect of product market regulation on female participation rates. The increase in participation between the lowest and highest sample values of product market regulation in 1999 is just below two percentage points. A somewhat surprising result of the chapter 3's empirical study is the absence of an effect of labour taxes on female employment. The measure of labour taxes used in the study may not capture the potentially important distortions imposed by the tax system on the decision of second earners (usually the wives) to participate in the labour force. More specific taxation measures, focused on the relative taxation of second earners have been shown to have strong effects on female participation (Jaumotte, 2003).

In conclusion, the paper makes some very important contributions to our understanding of the determinants of female participation, and of the extent to which women are (or are not) segregated in the labour market. It also opens further lines of research in particular on the question of how to make part time economically "fair" to women (not only in immediate financial returns, but also in terms of social security coverage and career prospects) without introducing distortions against the creation of part-time work opportunities by firms. Another related issue which in my view deserves further investigation is how to provide a policy environment which is neutral with respect to the choice of women regarding their participation in the labour market and its extent (full time versus part time).

RICHARD ROGERSON

Part I of this volume is motivated by a very simple observation: labor market outcomes for men and women differ substantially in all countries. Our ultimate objective is to understand what gives rise to these differences. However, to list some of the potential sources of these differences is basically to realize just how difficult a challenge this ultimate objective poses. Having made this claim, let me list at least a few of what I believe must be considered as candidates in our search for the factors that can account for these differences. Let me stress at the outset that I do not think there is any reason to believe that there is a single factor at work; rather, our task is more likely to try and assess the relative importance of a variety of factors.

The first candidate I think should be considered is one that I will label as heterogeneity in 'economic fundamentals'. If we leave aside for the issue of what constitutes an economic fundamental, the idea of this factor is that to the extent that there are differences in men and women either in terms of preferences and/or abilities, standard economics would tell us to potentially expect these differences to manifest themselves in terms of different economic outcomes, and specifically in different labor market outcomes. It remains a difficult question to determine what differences among men and women might be regarded as 'fundamental', and to understand what these differences should imply about labor market outcomes, but the basic point is that unless one is willing to assume a position of there being no 'fundamental' differences between men and women, identical outcomes is not the natural benchmark.

The questions begged by this first candidate lead quite naturally into the second candidate. In the context of gender differences in preferences and abilities, it is not entirely clear what constitutes an economic fundamental. Economists typically take preferences as one of the fundamentals, but one of the factors that may be very relevant for understanding women's labor market outcomes is social norms and how they evolve over time. Quantifying social norms is not easy, but there is a substantial volume of work suggesting that over time in the United States there have been fairly large changes in attitudes toward working mothers. Attitudes toward daycare have also changed. A difficulty that arises in this situation is to disentangle changes in social norms from changes in economic fundamentals. For example, is it the case that social norms toward daycare changed, or is it the case that individuals had certain priorities about daycare but updated their priors through expanded use and learned that daycare was not so bad.

A third factor that needs to be included in any analysis of the economic status of women is discrimination toward women. Discrimination has proved to be a difficult concept for economists to quantify. Standard practice has been to simply identify discrimination with the residual that cannot be explained by the factors for which economists have good measures.

The final factor that needs to be considered as a candidate for influencing the labor market outcomes of women is policy and/or institutions. This would include any policy or institutional factors that may differentially affect labor market outcomes for men and women. Policies regarding maternity leave and childcare are obvious examples of policies that may impact differently on male and female labor market outcomes, and laws (and the enforcement thereof) which make it illegal to discriminate on the basis of gender are an obvious example of an institution that may impact on men and women differently in terms of labor market outcomes. But there are also many more subtle examples. If there are differences between men and women such that women are more desirous of part-time work, then a policy or institution that makes it more difficult for firms to create part-time jobs will also impact differentially on men and women.

Having gone through this list I think it is clear that sorting out the relative importance of all of these factors is likely to be very difficult. We are dealing with many factors that are notoriously difficult to define, let alone measure. However, as difficult as the issue is, if we are to make headway, it is important to begin with a careful cataloguing and assessment of the data. And without a doubt one of the accomplishments of the reports in the first part of this volume is to bring together a great deal of data for a large set of countries over a relatively long-time period. Many interesting findings are uncovered. In some cases robust patterns in the data are presented, and in others our awareness is increased of the difficulty in drawing simple conclusions based on cross-country comparisons.

It would be possible to fill many pages simply summarizing all the interesting findings that emerge. However, rather than go into the specifics of the findings, I would like to utilize the scarce space left to me here to address two issues. The first concerns the authors' attempts to uncover the effect of various institutions on the labor market outcomes of women, and the second concerns the role of one particular factor in shaping the trend in female employment rates.

First, the methodology that the authors use is a variation on that used by Blanchard and Wolfers (2002) in their analysis of shocks and institutions in the rise of European unemployment. Part of the appeal of this methodology is that it is relatively simple and seems to impose relatively little structure; one may say that it is letting the data speak freely. Unfortunately, I think that in general the methodology is quite limiting and hence one must use it with a great deal of caution.

To illustrate this, the issue that I would like to look at more closely concerns that of dynamics. Table C2.2. shows the trend employment to population ratio of women relative to that of men for a sample of 20 OECD countries between 1970 and 2000.

As already mentioned, the statistic that I focus on here is the relative employment to population ratio of women. This is in contrast to the reported statistic the authors tend to focus on, which is simply the employment to population ratio of women. I do not intend to argue that there is any correct or incorrect measure to look at. Two countries may look very similar based on one measure, and very different based on the other, so the most important message to note is that the two measures are distinct. The reason that I have chosen to focus on the *relative* employment level of women as opposed to the *absolute* is because of a desire to disentangle the performance of women in the labor market relative to men from that of the overall performance of the labor market. That is to say, I want to distinguish between a labor market that leads to a low employment level for both men and women, from one which leads to the same low employment rate for women but a much higher employment rate for men.

Having said this, there are several items that I want to draw attention to in this table. First, in every single country there is an upward trend in the relative employment level of women between 1970 and 2000. Secondly, there is substantial dispersion in the relative employment level across countries in each of the cross-sections. Thirdly, the amount of dispersion has been decreasing over

Table C2.2. *Trend in relative employment/population rate of women*

	1970	1975	1980	1985	1990	1995	2000
Australia	0.48	0.53	0.58	0.64	0.71	0.76	0.79
Austria	0.57	0.58	0.59	0.63	0.69	0.74	0.78
Belgium	0.47	0.50	0.54	0.60	0.66	0.72	0.77
Canada	0.50	0.58	0.66	0.74	0.80	0.84	0.86
Denmark	0.63	0.70	0.77	0.83	0.86	0.87	0.88
Finland	0.76	0.81	0.86	0.90	0.92	0.92	0.91
France	0.55	0.59	0.64	0.69	0.73	0.77	0.80
Germany	0.53	0.57	0.61	0.64	0.69	0.75	0.79
Ireland	0.37	0.38	0.41	0.46	0.53	0.62	0.69
Italy	0.36	0.39	0.43	0.47	0.50	0.53	0.57
Japan	0.61	0.60	0.62	0.65	0.68	0.69	0.70
Netherlands	0.31	0.37	0.44	0.53	0.63	0.71	0.77
New Zealand	0.41	0.46	0.52	0.62	0.73	0.79	0.81
Norway	0.48	0.60	0.70	0.78	0.84	0.88	0.90
Portugal	0.50	0.54	0.57	0.63	0.69	0.75	0.79
Spain	0.32	0.35	0.37	0.40	0.44	0.51	0.57
Sweden	0.67	0.75	0.84	0.91	0.96	0.97	0.95
Switzerland	0.51	0.54	0.57	0.60	0.65	0.69	0.74
UK	0.55	0.61	0.66	0.72	0.78	0.82	0.84
US	0.55	0.61	0.69	0.75	0.80	0.83	0.85
Mean	0.51	0.55	0.60	0.66	0.71	0.76	0.79
St. Dev.	0.12	0.12	0.13	0.14	0.13	0.12	0.10
80:20 ratio	1.39	1.33	1.33	1.25	1.23	1.22	1.16

time. Based on the 80:20 ratio the dispersion has been decreasing since 1970, and based on the standard deviation it has been decreasing since 1985. Fourthly, there is a lot of persistence in the distribution. In particular, the correlation of values in 1970 and 2000 is 0.68. This is a remarkably high value for a thirty-year time horizon. Fifthly, there are several countries, notably the Scandinavian countries, for which the relative employment rate seems to have leveled off. The data would seem to suggest that countries like Canada and the United States are near to leveling off. Sixthly, the values at which the relative employment levels off seems to vary across countries. For some, this value seems to be at 0.90 or slightly above, while for others it seems closer to 0.85. It is noticeable that as an empirical matter, based on the evidence to date, the relative employment rate of women seems to be bounded away from one.

Different people may see different things when confronted with this data. Let me describe the picture that it paints for me. I think the first issue to address in thinking about these cross-country evolutions is what is responsible for the upward trend observed in all countries. The fact that it is observed in all countries tells us that it is something very pervasive. Unfortunately I do not think that we really know what lies at the source of this upward trend. This is not to say that we do not know anything. The authors refer to changing technologies that influence home production activities, and improvements in contraception that provide individuals with more control over child-rearing. These are plausibly an important part of the story, but they may also plausibly not be the whole story. As the authors also mention, it is also possible that changing social norms are contributing to this trend. It is important to note, especially for the cases of technological change and changing social norms, that dynamics are important, which is to say that these are processes in which diffusion is important. Even though washing machines and microwaves are available in all countries, these are technologies that diffuse at different rates in different countries. The same is true of social norms. I think we know relatively little of how social norms diffuse over time, but it seems reasonable to expect that changes that operate through channels such as mentoring and role models will occur slowly. Moreover, in this age of globalization I think there is no doubt that the situation or accomplishments of women in one country plausibly influence the attitudes of women in other countries, so there is an international component to the diffusion of social norms as well. In addition to these dynamic processes, there is also some change in institutions and policies over time in many countries.

To me, this suggests a very rich dynamic system of potentially interrelated economies. Holding institutions and policies fixed at their current values, I would expect to see continued evolution in the cross-country distribution of relative employment rates, basically reflecting the continued diffusion process. To borrow from the language of growth theory, I would expect to see conditional convergence. As one piece of evidence to support this view let me note that the correlation between the level of the relative employment rate in 1985 and the change in the relative employment rate between 1985 and 2000 is -0.75. This simple correlation tells us that those countries experiencing the largest increases in relative employment rates between 1985 and 2000 are those that started with the lowest relative employment rates. Such a relationship is at least suggestive of something like conditional convergence.

This picture of ongoing evolution and varied diffusion across countries is very significant in this context. Specifically, what this tells me is that if we want to use the existing data to tell us about the importance of various institutional factors on relative employment rates, then as a first step we want to ask what steady-state relative employment rate is consistent with each country's current values of its institutions? Looking at the relationship between relative employment rates and institutions from a single cross-section is likely to be quite misleading since it exaggerates the effects of those institutions which are present in countries lagging in the diffusion process. Of course, this raises another potentially interesting question—one may ask which institutions or policies are most responsible for causing the speed of diffusion to vary so much across countries?

To relate this discussion back to the Blanchard and Wolfers methodology, an important limitation of that methodology is that it is effectively a static analysis of the connection between institutions and outcomes. In principle one might think that it is easy to add dynamic elements into the analysis. However, this would seem to be tantamount to suggesting something akin to the literature on growth regressions for the current context, and I think the profession has come to feel somewhat skeptical of the ability of the growth regressions to uncover fundamental economic relationships. So I do not see that there is an easy fix to this problem.

Let me now turn to the second point that I wanted to address in my comments. Specifically, I want to discuss briefly the potential role of structural transformation as a factor that accounts for the changes in the relative labor market outcomes of women. It is well known that as economies become richer they experience a structural transformation in which economic activity moves from agriculture, to manufacturing and then to services. Kuznets considered this structural transformation one of the main stylized facts about growth and development. The authors suggest that jobs in the service sector may be more desirable to women than are jobs in the manufacturing sector. Whether this reflects fundamental difference between men and women or is just the manifestation of social norms I do not know, but certainly the evidence is supportive of the notion that women are either relatively more able to do jobs in the service sector or that they have a relative preference for them.

What I want to draw attention to is that although all economies experience this structural transformation, each economy is at a distinct phase of this transformation and the policies and institutions in place in each country affect the precise nature of the transformation. With this in mind the final piece of evidence that I would like to describe concerns the relationship between relative female employment rates and the transformation into service sector activities. The correlation of the change in the relative employment rate of women and the aggregate service to population employment rate between 1985 and 2000 is 0.82. This tells us that those countries which added the most employment (relative to population) in services were exactly those countries which experienced the greatest gains in the relative employment of women. Moreover, a similar finding emerges in the cross-section. For example, in the 2000 cross-section the correlation between employment (relative to population) in services and the female relative employment rate is 0.67. (The same value in 1985 was 0.80, but the relative convergence has caused this to diminish somewhat in 2000.) These correlations that I have reported do not tell us about causation, but I at least want to suggest the possibility that one of the causes of the cross-country differences in relative female employment rates has to do with policies that discourage provision of services in the market.

References

Akerlof, G. and Kranton, R. (2000), 'Economics and Identity', *Quarterly Journal of Economics*, 115, 715–753.

Alba, A. (1998), 'How Temporary is Temporary Employment in Spain?', *Journal of Labor Research*, 19, 695–710.

Algan, Y. and Cahuc, P. (2003), 'Job Protection and Family Policies: The Macho Hypothesis'. Unpublished paper, University of Paris I.

Altonji, J. and Blank, R. (1999), 'Race and Gender in the Labor Market', in Ashenfelter, O. and Card, D. (eds), *Handbook of Labor Economics*, Amsterdam: Elsevier, 3C, 3143–3259.

Anker, Richard (1998), Gender and Jobs: Sex Segregation of Occupations in the World. Geneva: International Labor Office.

Attanasio, O., Low, H. and V. Sánchez-Marcos (2003), 'Explaining Changes in Female Labour Supply in a Life-cycle Model', presented at the NBER Summer Institute on 'Aggregate Implications of Microeconomic Consumption Behavior', Boston, July 2003.

Bardasi, E. and Gornick, J. C. (2000), 'Women and Part-Time Employment: Workers' Choices and Wage Penalties in Five Industrialized Countries'. Working Paper no. 2000–11, ISER.

Becker, G. (1964), *Human Capital* (3rd edn), Chicago: University of Chicago Press.

Beller, Andrea H. (1982), 'Occupational Segregation by Sex: Determinants and Changes.' *Journal of Human Resources*, 17(3): 371–392.

Ben Porath, Y. (1967), 'The Production of Human Capital and the Life-Cycle of Earnings', *Journal of Political Economy*, 75, 352–365.

Berger, M. C. (1983), 'Changes in Labor Force Composition and Male Earnings: A Production Approach', *The Journal of Human Resources*, 17,

Bertola, G. (1999), 'Microeconomic Perspectives on Aggregate Labor Markets', in O. Ashenfelter and D. Card (eds), *Handbook of Labor Economics*, 3B, Amsterdam: North-Holland, 2985–3028.

—— Blau, F. D. and Kahn, L. (2002), 'Labour Market Institutions and Demographic Employment Pattern'. Discussion Paper no. 3448, Centre for Economic Policy Research, London.

—— Jimeno, J. F., Marimon R. and Pisssarides, C. A. (2001), 'EU Welfare Systems and Labor markets: Diverse in the Past, Integrated in the Future?' in G. Bertola, T. Boeri, G. Nicoletti (eds), *Welfare and Employment in a United Europe*, Cambridge, MA: MIT Press.

Blanchard, O. and Landier, A. (2000), 'The Perverse Effects of Partial Labour Market Reform: Fixed-term Contracts in France', *Economic Journal*, 122, F214–F244.

——and Wolfers J. (2000), 'The Role of Shocks and Institutions in the Rise of European Unemployment: The Aggregate Evidence', *Economic Journal*, 110, C1–C33.

Blanchflower (1996), 'Job creation and job loss: research questions arising from the use of establishment based data', in *Job Creation and Loss, Analysis, Policy and Data Development*, OECD, Paris.

Blank, R. (1989), 'The Role of Part-Time Work in Women's Labor Market Choices over Time', *American Economic Review* 79, 295–299.

——(1996), 'The Role and Influence of Trade Unions in the OECD'. Report to the Bureau of International Labor Affairs, U.S. Department of Labor: (August).

Blank, R. (1990), 'Are Part-Time Jobs Bad Jobs?,' in Gary Burtless (ed.), *A Future of Lousy Jobs*, Washington DC: Brookings Institution, 123–164.

Blau, F. and Kahn, L. (1992), 'Race and Gender Pay Differentials', in D. Lewin, O. Mitchell, and P. Sherer (eds), *Research Frontiers in Industrial Relations and Human Resource*, Industrial Relations Research Association, Madison, WI.

—— and —— (1992), 'Black–White Earnings Over the 1970s and 1980s: Gender Differences in Trends', *Review of Economics and Statistics*, 74, 276–286.

—— and —— (1997), 'Swimming Upstream: Trends in the Gender Wage Differential in the 1980', *Journal of Labor Economics*, 15, 1–42.

—— and —— (2000), 'Gender Differences in Pay', *Journal of Economic Perspectives*, 14, 75–99.

—— and —— (2003), 'International Differences in the Gender Pay Gap', *Journal of Labor Economics* 21, 106–144.

Blau, F. and Kahn, L. M. (1996), 'Wage Structure and Gender Earning Differentials: an International Comparison', *Economica*, 63, 29–62.

Blinder, A and Weiss, Y. (1976), 'Human Capital and Labor Supply: A Synthesis'. *Journal of Political Economy*, 83, 449–472.

Booth, A. L., Francesconi, M. and Frank, J. (2002), Temporary Jobs: Stepping Stones or Dead Ends?', Economic Journal, Features: Symposium on Temporary Work, F189–F213

Card, D., Kramarz, F. and Lemieux, T. (1999), 'Changes in the Relative Structure of Wages and Employment: A Comparison of the United States, Canada and France', *Canadian Journal of Economics*, 32, 843–877.

Caucutt E., Guner N. and Knowles J. (2002), 'Why Do Women Wait? Matching, Wage Inequality, and the Incentives for Fertility Delay', *Review of Economic Dynamics*, 5–4, 815–855.

Cipollone, P. and Guelfi, A. (2003), 'Tax Credit Policy and Firm Behaviour: The Case of Subsidies to Open-End Labour Contracts in Italy'. Unpublished Paper, Bank of Italy.

—— and ——. (2004), 'Tax Credit Policies and Firms' Behaviour: The Case of Subsidies to Open-End Contracts in Italy', Giornale degli Economisti, 117, 161–203.

Cohen, Piketty and Saint-Paul (eds) 'Supply Side View' in *The New Economics of Rising Inequalities*, Oxford University Press, and CEPR.

Costa D. (2000), 'From Mill Town to Board Room: The Rise of Women's Paid Labor', *Journal of Economic Perspectives*, 14, 101–122.

De la Rica, S. (2003), 'Wage Differentials between Permanent and Temporary Workers: The Impact of Firm and Occupational Segregation'. Unpublished Paper, University of Bilbao, available at http://www.ehu.es/SaradelaRica/docs/fe2.pdf

Del Boca, D., Aaberge, R., Colombino, U., *et al.* (2004), 'Labour Market Participation of Women and Fertility: The Effect of Social Policies', in T. Boeri, D. Del Boca and C. Pissarides (eds), *European Women at Work*, Oxford University Press, Oxford.

Dolado, J. J., Felgueroso, F. and Jimeno, J. F. (2002), 'Recent Trends in Occupational Segregation by Gender: A Look across the Atlantic', Discussion Paper no. 3421, Centre for Economic Policy Research, London.

Edin, P.-A. and Richardson, K. (2002), 'Swimming with the Tide: Solidary Wage Policy and the Gender Earnings Gap', *Scandinavian Journal of Economics*, 104(1), 49–67.

Farber, Henry S. (1999), 'Alternative and Part-Time Employment Arrangements as a Response to Job Loss', *Journal of Labor Economics*, 17, S142–169.

Fernandez, R., Fogli A. and Olivetti C. (2002), 'Marrying Your Mom: Preference Transmission and Women's Labor and Education Choices', Working Paper no. 9234, National Bureau of Economic Research, Cambridge.

Freeman, R. B. (1979), 'The Effect of Demographic Factors on Age-Earnings Profiles', *The Journal of Human Resources*, 14, 289–318.

Galor, O. and Weil, D. N. (1996), 'The Gender Gap, Fertility and Growth', *American Economic Review*, 86, 374–387.

Garibaldi and Mauro (2002), 'Anatomy of Employment Growth', *Economic Policy*, 34, 69–113.

Genre, V., Gomez Salvador, R. and Lamo A. (2003), 'The Determinants of Labour Force Participation in the EU'. Unpublished Paper, European Central Bank.

Goldin, C. (1990), *Understanding the Gender Gap*, Oxford: Oxford University Press, 1990.

——and Katz, L. (2002), 'The Power of the Pill: Oral Contraceptives and Women's Carrier and Marriage Decisions', *Journal of Political Economy*, 110, 730–770.

Goldin and Polachek 1987, AER (May).

Gottschalk, P. (1997), 'Inequality, Income Growth, and Mobility: The Basic Facts', *Journal of Economic Perspectives*, 11, 21–40.

Grant, J. H. and Hamermesh, D. S. (1982), 'Labor Market Competition Among Youths, White Women and Others', *Review of Economics and Statistics*, 354–360.

Greenwood J., Seshadri, A. and M. Yorukoglu (2002), 'Engines of Liberation', *Économie d'Avant-Garde* Research Reports, University of Rochester.

Grimshaw, D. and Rubery, J. (2002), *The Adjusted Gender Pay Gap: A Critical Appraisal of Standard Decomposition Techniques*. Report by Group of Experts on Gender and Employment commissioned by the Equal Opportunity Unit in the European Commission.

Güell, M. and Petrongolo, B. (2003), 'How Binding Are Legal Limits? Transitions from Temporary to Permanent Work in Spain', Discussion Paper no. 782, IZA, Bonn.

Gubta, Nabanita Datta, Oaxaca, Ronald L. and Smith, Nina (2002), 'Swimming Upstream, Floating Downstream: Trends in the U.S. and Danish Gender Wage Gaps', CLS Working Papers, 01–6, Aarhus School of Business, Centre for Labour Market and Social Research.

Hamermesh, D. S. and Grant, J. (1979), 'Econometric Studies of Labor–Labor Substitution and their Implications for Policy', *The Journal of Human Resources*, 14

——(1986), 'The Demand for Labor in the Long Run', in O. Ashenfelter and R. Layard (eds), *Handbook of Labor Economics*, I, Elsevier.

Harkness, S. (1996), 'The Gender Earnings Gap: Evidence from the U.K.', *Fiscal Studies*, 17, 1–36.

——and Waldfogel, J. (1999) 'The Family Gap in Pay: Evidence from Seven Industrialized Countries', Center for Analysis of Social Exclusion (CASE) working paper 29 (November).

Heckman, J. (1979), 'Sample Selection Bias as a Specification Error', *Econometrica*, 47, 153–161.

Jaumotte, F. (2003), 'Female Labour Force Participation: Past trends and Main determinants', *OECD Economic Studies*, 37, 51–108.

—— (2003), 'Female Labour Force Participation: Past Trends and Main determinants in OECD Countries', *OECD Economics Department Working Papers*, no. 376.

Jimeno, J. F. and Toharia, L. (1993), 'The Effects of Fixed-term Employment on Wages: Theory and Evidence from Spain', *Investigaciones económicas*, 27, 475–494.

Johnson and Stafford (1998), 'Alternative Approaches to Occupational Exclusion', in I. Persson and C. Yonung (eds), *Women's Work and Wages*, London: Routledge, 72–88.

Jones, L., Manuelli, E. R. and McGrattan, E. R. (2003), 'Why are married women working so much?' Federal Reserve Bank of Minneapolis Research Dept. Staff Report #317.

Juhn, C., Murphy, K. M. and Pierce, B. (1993), 'Wage Inequality and the Rise in Returns to Skill', *Journal of Political Economy*, 101(3), 410–442.

—— and —— (1997), 'Wage Inequality and Family Labor Supply', *Journal of Labor Economics*, 15, 73–97.

Katz, L. E. and Murphy, K. (1992), 'Changes in Relative Wages: 1963–1987. Supply and Demand Factors', *Quarterly Journal of Economics*, 107(1), 35–78.

Kidd, M. and Shannon, M. (1996), 'The Gender Wage Gap: A Comparison of Australia and Canada', *Industrial Labor Relations Review*, 49, 729–746.

Korenman, S. and Neumark, D. (1992), 'Marriage, Motherhood and Wages', *Journal of Human Resources*, 27(2), 233–55.

Layard, N., Nickell, S. and Jackman, R. (1991), *Unemployment. Macroeconomic Performance and the Labour Market*, Oxford: Oxford University Press.

Ljunqvist L. and Sargent, T. J. (1998), 'The European Unemployment Dilemna', *Journal of Political Economy*, 106, 514–550.

Lopez-Garcia, P. (2003), 'Labour Market Performance and Start-Up Costs: OECD Evidence'. Working Paper no. 849, CESifo, Munich.

Meulders, D., Plasman, O. and Plasman, R. (1994), *Atypical Employment in the EC*. Aldershot, England: Dartmouth.

Mortensen, D. T. and Pissarides C. A. (1999), 'Job Reallocation, Employment Fluctuations, and Unemployment', in M. Woodford and J. Taylor (eds), *Handbook of Macroeconomics*, Amsterdam: North-Holland.

Mulligan, C. and Yona, R. (2002), 'Specialization, Inequality, and the Labor Market for Married Women'. Unpublished Paper, University of Chicago.

Neal, Derek (2002), 'Immigrant Children and New York City Schools: Segregation and Its Consequences: Comment'. *Brookings-Wharton Papers on Urban Affairs 2002*, 206–208.

Neal, Derek, A. (2002), 'How Vouchers could Change the Market for Education', *Journal of Economic Perspectives*, 16(4), 25–44.

Neumark, David and Andrew Postlewaite (1998), 'Relative Income Concerns and the Rise in Married Women's Employment', *Journal of Public Economics*, 70, 157–183.

Nickell, S. (1997), 'Unemployment and Labor Market Rigidities: Europe versus North America', *The Journal of Economic Perspectives*, 11, 55–74.

—— and Layard, R. (1999), 'Labor Market Institutions and Economic Performance' in Orley Ashtenfelter and David Card (eds), *Handbook of Labor Economics*, 3A, Amsterdam: North-Holland.

——and van Ours, J. (2000), 'The Netherlands and the United Kingdom: a European unemployment miracle?', *Economic Policy*, 15, 135–180.

Nicoletti, G., Scarpetta, S. and Boylaud, O. (1999), 'Summary indicators of product market regulation with an extension to employment protection legislation', OECD Economics Department Working Papers, 226, OECD Economics Department.

——, Haffner, R. C. G., Nickell, S., Scarpetta S. and Zoega G. (2001), 'European Integration, Liberalization, and Labor-Market Performance', in G. Bertola, T. Boeri and G. Nicoletti (eds), *Welfare and Employment in a United Europe*, Cambridge, MA, and London: MIT Press.

O'Neill, J. and Polachek, S. (1993), 'Why the Gender Gap in Wages Narrowed in the 1980', *Journal of Labor Economics*, 11: 205–228.

O'Reilly, J. and Bothfeld, S. (2002), 'What happens after working part time? Integration, maintenance or exclusionary transitions in Britain and western Germany', *Cambridge Journal of Economics*, 26, Issue 4 (July), 409–439.

OECD (1988), 'Women's Activity, Employment and Earnings: A Review of Recent Developments' in *Employment Outlook*, Paris.

OECD (1998), 'Working Hours: Latest Trends and Policy Initiatives', *Employment Outlook*.

OECD (1999), *Employment Outlook*, Paris.

OECD (2001), 'Early Childhood Education and Care', *Starting Strong*.

OECD (2002), 'Women at Work: Who Are They and How Are They Faring?', in *Employment Outlook*, Paris.

Olivetti, C. (2001), 'Changes in Women's Hours of Market Work: The Effect of Changing Returns to Experience', Ph.D. Dissertation, University of Pennsylvania.

Pencavel, J. (1998), 'The Market Work behaviour and Wages of women, 1975–94,' *Journal of Human Resources*, 38(4), 771–804.

Pissarides, C. A. (2003), 'Company Start-Up Costs and Employment', in P. Aghion, R. Friedman, J. Stiglitz and M. Woodford (eds), *Knowledge, Information, and Expectations in Modern Macroeconomics: In Honor of Edmund S. Phelps*, Princeton, NJ: Princeton University Press.

Powell, L. M. (1998), 'Part-time versus full-time work and child care costs: evidence for married mothers', *Applied Economics*, 30, 503–511.

Rice, P. (1999), 'Gender Earnings Differentials: The European Experience', *Gender and Development WP series*, 8, World Bank.

Ruhm C. (1998), 'The Economic Consequences of Parental Leave Mandates: Lessons from Europe', *Quarterly Journal of Economics*, 108(1), (Feb. 1998) 285–317.

Saint-Paul, G. (2000), 'The political economy of labour market institutions', Oxford: Oxford University Press.

Smith J. P. and Ward M. P. (1985) 'Time-Series Growth in the Female Labor Force', *Journal of Labor Economics*, 3, 59–90.

Topel, Robert H. (1994a), 'Wage Inequality and Regional Labour Market Performance in the US', in Toshiaki Tachibanaki (ed.), *Savings and Bequests*. Ann Arbors University: Michigan Press.

——(1994b), 'Regional Labor Markets and the Determinants of Wage Inequality', *American Economic Review*, Papers and Proceedings, 84, 17–22, May.

Topel, R. H. (1997), 'Factors Proportions and Relative Wages: The Supply-Side Determinants of Wage Inequality', *Journal of Economic Perpsectives* (Spring), 11, 55–74.

Thomas, D. (1990), 'Intra-household Resource Allocation: An Inferential Approach', *Journal of Human Resources*, 25, 635–664.

Waldfogel Jane (1997), 'The Effect of Children on Women's Wages,' *American Sociological Review*, 62, no. 2., 209–217.

——(1998), 'Understanding the "Family Gap" in Pay for Women with Children', *The Journal of Economic Perspectives*, 12, no. 1., 137–156.

Wasmer, E. (1997), 'Changes in the Composition of the Labor Force. Implications for Wages and Unemployment', Ph.D. dissertation, Economics Department, London School of Economics and Political Sciences.

——(2001a), 'Measuring human capital in the labor market: the supply of experience in 8 OECD countries', *European Economic Review Papers and Proceedings*, 45, n°4–6, 861–874.

——(2001b), 'The Causes of the "Youth Employment Problem": A (Labor) Supply Side View', in Cohen, Piketty and Saint-Paul, (eds) *The New Economics of Rising Inequalities*, Oxford University Press, and CEPR.

—— (2003), 'Between-group competition in the labor market and the rising returns to skill. US and France 1964–2000', CEPR DP 2798 (2001), revised.

Watson, C. Maxwell, Bas B. Bakker, Jan Kees Martijn, and Ioannis Halikias (1999), 'The Netherlands: Transforming a Market Economy', *IMF Occasional Paper*, no. 181.

Wolf, E. (2003), 'What Hampers Part-time Work? An Empirical Analysis of Wages, Hours Restrictions and Employment from a Dutch–German Perspective', *ZEW Economic Studies*, 18.

PART II

WOMEN'S PARTICIPATION IN THE LABOR MARKET AND FERTILITY: THE EFFECTS OF SOCIAL POLICIES

Rolf Aaberge, Ugo Colombino, Daniela Del Boca, John Ermisch, Marco Francesconi, Silvia Pasqua and Steinar Strøm

Introduction

Over the last several decades the labour market participation rates of married women have increased and fertility rates have declined in most developed countries. The growth of women's participation in the labour market carries with it some positive and negative implications for the ability of countries and the European Union itself to meet a variety of social and economic targets. On one hand, the increased number of workers helps to pay pension obligations to current retirees, while on the other the declining population levels make it less likely that the current form of European pension systems can be sustained.

In Italy, as well as in other Southern European countries where we observe both low participation and low fertility rates, these issues are particularly crucial. In this report we analyse labour supply and fertility decisions in order to understand what type of social and fiscal policies can be designed to allow women to work and have children. In the first part of the report we investigate the relationship between female participation *and* fertility, both intertemporally and a cross-sectionally (at the country level), in order to determine empirically the extent to which different combinations of currently existing social and labour market policies (e.g., part-time employment opportunities, subsidised child care provision, parental leave) designed to reconcile work and child rearing simultaneously have performed (Chapter 8). This type of empirical knowledge is crucial if we are to design other policy mechanisms that will better attain these common goals of most Western European countries.

In the second part of the report we consider the impact of mothers' employment during childhood on the child's well-being, focusing on the trade-offs between her time spent in nurturing the child and household income. While we find some empirical evidence that the loss of the mother's child-care time has a negative effect on the child's well-being (e.g., socio-emotional adjustment and cognitive outcomes), it is also the case that there is evidence that the additional income from mother's employment has positive implications for expenditures on goods consumed by the child. These effects vary across countries and across family types, so the net impact of mother's employment on child's welfare can be expected to vary across national environments as well (Chapter 9).

We next consider the relationship between women's work and the interhousehold distribution of income, as well as the intergenerational income distribution, in several European countries. Women's work has an important impact on household income distribution as well as the intrahousehold income distribution, of course. Public policies directed to encourage female employment may also have the positive effect of reducing inequality in household income distribution and also may result in a more equitable distribution of resources and welfare within the household (Chapter 10).

We conclude by focusing on the decision-making process within the household in order to analyze and simulate the effect of different taxation policies on household welfare and income distribution (Chapter 11). Using all of the results we have obtained, it is possible to begin to discuss the formulation of public policies that can simultaneously promote increased labour market participation of married women, without descouraging fertility, and reduce intrahousehold and interhousehold income and welfare inequality.

Daniela Del Boca

8

Labor Supply and Fertility in Europe and the US[*]

8.1 FERTILITY AND LABOR SUPPLY: THEIR RELATIONSHIP

Over the last decades labor market participation of women increased, while fertility declined in most advanced countries. This pattern is consistent with microeconomic predictions: economic models of fertility behavior predict in fact that an increase in women's schooling levels and wage rates leads to an increase in their labor supply and to a reduction in fertility. The existence of an inverse relationship between fertility and participation was theoretically established by Becker and Lewis (1973) and Willis (1973) and empirically documented by Butz and Ward (1979) for the United States and Mincer (1985) on a cross-country basis.

A negative relationship between women's labor market participation and fertility is a cause of concern for several reasons. In most European countries the current working generation finances the pension benefits of the previous working generations and low fertility reduces the potential sustainability of the pension system. Other important implications concern lower growth, in terms of population total, and in particular, the working-age population; lower savings; and greater numbers of people with few immediate family ties, which will increase demand for formal provision of services. An understanding of this relationship is therefore relevant to policy makers in ways which go beyond theoretical speculation.

Recent analyses focusing on the temporal pattern of fertility and female participation show that as early as the mid-1980s, the sign of the cross-country correlation changed from negative to positive and became more volatile (Fig. 8.1). After 1985, the participation of women in the labor market continued to increase in all countries, but fertility rates started to decline at a lower rate or, in some countries, began to grow again.

The countries that currently have the lowest levels of fertility (Spain, Italy and Greece) are those with relatively low levels of female labor force participation,

* The content of this chapter is the responsibility of Daniela Del Boca and Silvia Pasqua (University of Turin).

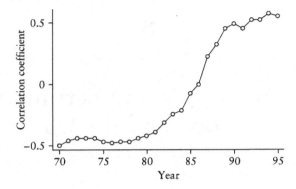

Figure 8.1. *Cross-country correlation between total fertility rate and female participation*
Source: Brewster and Rindfuss (2000).

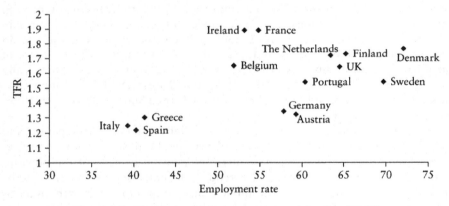

Figure 8.2. *Women's employment rates and fertility (2000)*
Source: Eurostat (2001), *Statistics in Focus*.

while the countries with higher fertility levels (Denmark, France) have relatively high female labor force participation rates (Fig. 8.2).

Various authors (Ahn and Mira 2002; Esping-Andersen 1999; Brewster and Rindfuss 2000; Billari *et al.* 2002) empirically analysed the cross-country correlation between the total fertility rate and the female labor market participation, confirming the change in sign and in the significance of the coefficient. The interpretation of the temporal change in the relationship between participation and fertility has mainly been found in the changes in social norms towards working mothers and in the effects of policies that diminish incompatibilities between childrearing and female employment: more generous parental leave, greater availability of childcare, and greater opportunities for flexible hours and part-time employment (Ermisch 1989; Hotz and Miller

1988; Del Boca 2002; Brewster and Rindfuss 2000; Benjamin 2001). The empirical evidence indicating a positive relationship between women's participation and fertility is certainly encouraging in view of pension system sustainability. Boosting female employment, if supported by such policies, will not necessarily lead to a significant decline in fertility as was experienced in the past.

Other studies of this phenomenon have shown different results, revealing a weaker and less significant correlation, but not a change from a negative to a positive sign. These analyses, pooling cross-country and time series data, allow for country effects and show that only in Mediterranean countries is there a negative correlation between fertility and female employment (Engelhardt *et al.* 2001). This result implies that it is important in these countries for female participation and fertility to be considered as a joint decision and that policies encouraging fertility may have an adverse effect on female employment and vice versa (Del Boca 2002).

Social policies have been implemented in most European countries to make childrearing less difficult in terms of being easier to reconcile with employment. In some countries the view in favor of pro-natalist action has prevailed, and government intervention has been directed towards promoting higher fertility. In others, the view that, independently of the possible consequences on fertility levels, governments are not justified in interfering with intact families' decision and in particular with how many children to have, which is essentially a private decision, has prevailed.

In this chapter, we will examine the effect of several aspects of the different institutional and social factors (related to the welfare systems and labor markets) on women's labor market participation and fertility, taking as a starting point the relevant literature, and then analysing a cross-country analysis using the European Community Household Panel Data (ECHP) dataset and taking into account country-specific factors.

8.2   TEMPORAL PATTERNS AND CROSS-COUNTRY DIFFERENCES

Several important changes over the last decades have characterized the temporal pattern of both women's labor market participation and fertility, increasing the differences across countries.

The temporal changes in fertility are determined by the combined effects of a *tempo* and a *quantum* effect: on the one hand, the total fertility has declined over the last decades (the *quantum* effect), on the other hand the age at first child has increased (the *tempo* effect). As a consequence, the number of children per family has decreased over the years, while new mothers in 1970 were older than in 1960 and again older in 1980 than in 1970 for most European countries (Gustafsson and Wetzels 2000, Billari *et al.* 2002).

A likely explanation for this fact is the increased educational levels of women. More highly educated women are more likely not to have children or to have the first child at a much later age than women with lower levels of education.

The *quantum* and *tempo* effects have had different impacts across countries, implying a rapid ageing of the population in long-lasting low fertility countries (with related problems for social security and transfer programs), especially in the south of Europe. Some studies argue that very low fertility will eventually disappear when the deferral of the first birth ends (Bongaarts and Feeney 1998), but less optimistic results have come out of later studies which use different methods (Lesthaeghe and Willems 1999).

Although the increasing long-term trend in female participation rate is similar for most countries, persistent differences in levels suggest that different countries are constrained by country-specific institutional and social factors. Analysing the behavior of OECD countries, Ahn and Mira (2002) and Engelhardt *et al.* (2001) have divided the 21 OECD countries into three groups. The high participation group, in which the participation rate (FLP) is higher than 60 per cent, includes the United States, Canada, the United Kingdom, Sweden, Norway, Denmark, Finland and Switzerland. The medium participation group includes countries where the participation rate is in the 50–60 per cent range. The low participation countries are where the female participation rate is less than 50 per cent (Italy, Spain and Greece). The two values of each of the three trends shown in Figure 8.3 represent the

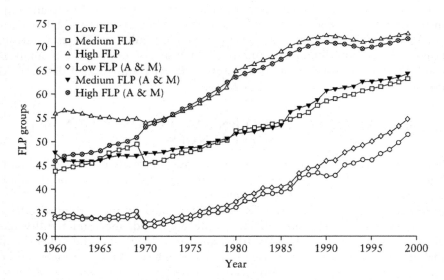

Figure 8.3. *Average level of female labor participation rates in low, medium and high participation countries*

Source: Engelhardt and Prskawetz (2002).

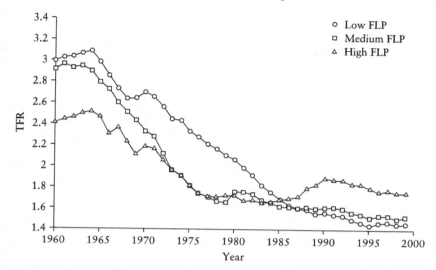

Figure 8.4. *Average total fertility rates in low, medium and high participation countries*

Source: Engelhardt and Prskawetz (2002).

differences between the studies of Ahn and Mira (2002) and Engelhardt *et al.* (2001).

Figure 8.4 shows that in those countries characterized by high participation the total fertility rate starts at 2.19 in 1970, declines to 1.65 in 1980 and then returns to 1.78 at the end of 2000. Conversely, in countries characterized by low participation, the fertility rate starts at 2.72 in 1970 and continues to decline to 1.4.

Figure 8.5 illustrates the *tempo* effect. It shows the growth of women's mean age at first birth in the three groups of countries, indicating the significance of postponement of the fertility decision. The average age in the 1960s was in the 24–26 range and grew to around 28 in the year 2000. The phenomenon of postponement has implied a reduction of completed fertility and a large number of women who remain childless. In countries with a greater decline in fertility, a higher number of women, especially educated women, has remained childless.

Because of these different temporal patterns, more and more empirical research focusing on the relationship between women's participation and fertility is being done, especially in southern European countries, where it still seems hard for women to reconcile work and motherhood, while in northern European countries more attention is being given to the effects of the high participation of mothers on wages, careers, and child outcomes (see Ermisch and Francesconi Part 2, in this volume).

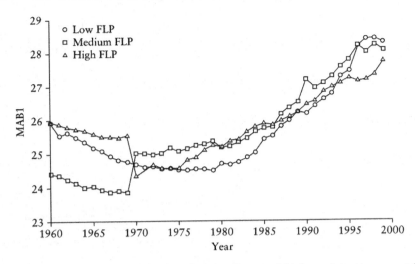

Figure 8.5. *Mean age at first birth in low, medium and high participation countries*
Source: Engelhardt and Prskawetz (2002).

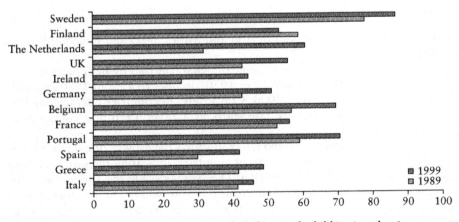

Figure 8.6. *Employment rates of mothers with child(ren) under 6*
Source: OECD, *Employment Outlook*, 2001.

In northern European countries, in fact, the employment rates of mothers with young children increased quite significantly over the last decades, while the increase was much smaller in southern Europe. The low employment rate among young women with children and the low fertility rate symbolize the difficulties encountered by women in southern European. Figure 8.6 shows the significant differences and the growth in the period 1989–1999 between the employment rates of mothers with children under 6 in Europe. Italy, Greece, and Spain are ranked at the lowest level.

Several studies have questioned whether low fertility rates represent a voluntary choice by the household to free the women from family obligations rather than being the effect of economic constraints. Bongaarts (2001) provides data on desired and realized fertility for several European countries showing that preferences fall short of achievement. This study also reports that when fertility is low, desired fertility is usually above realized fertility.

8.3   THE CHARACTERISTICS OF THE LABOR MARKET

The regulations of the labor market have an important impact on participation rates. In spite of recent institutional changes, southern European labor markets are still highly regulated: strict rules apply regarding the hiring and firing of workers and permissible types of employment arrangements. The hiring system and the high entry wage as well as very strict firing rules severely restrict employment opportunities for labor market entrants. These labor market regulations have been largely responsible for the high unemployment rates of women and youth.

If we look at unemployment among youth, in those countries where high percentages of youth are unemployed (Italy, Greece, Spain) the women's participation rate is lower (Fig. 8.7). Moreover, when the unemployment rate is high, fewer women leave the labor market during childbearing years because it is more difficult to re-enter later.

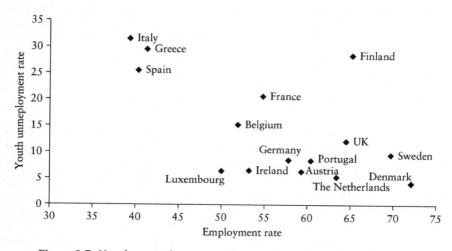

Figure 8.7. *Youth unemployment and women's employment rates (2000)*
Source: Eurostat (2001), *Statistics in Focus.*

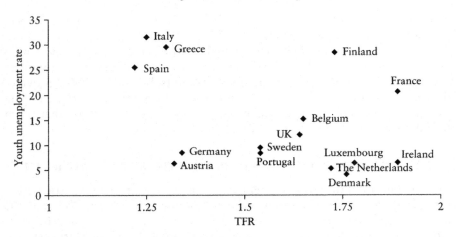

Figure 8.8. *Youth unemployment and fertility (2000)*
Source: Eurostat (2001), *Statistics in Focus*.

Empirical evidence also shows the strong difference in fertility rates between countries characterized by high unemployment rates (Spain, Italy, Greece) and countries characterized by low unemployment rates. Figure 8.8 shows that where youth unemployment is higher (Spain, Italy, Greece) the fertility rates are lower.

In countries where the unemployment rate is higher, young couples tend to postpone household formation and fertility. Young people, both men and women, wait to be well established in their jobs before getting married and having children. The lack of stable jobs among Spanish men is an important factor that forces many young people to delay marriage and childbearing: between 1987 and 1995 the proportion of employed Spanish men aged 25–39 years who held permanent work contracts fell from 55 to 37 per cent. The low level of confidence among young workers about their future employment prospects is an important determinant of the low fertility (Ahn and Mira 2001).

A negative relationship between unemployment and fertility also emerges for Italy. On the one hand women tend to participate more in the labor market to protect household income from negative shocks to the partners' wage and employment, on the other hand they do not leave work during childbearing years to protect their own labor market prospects (Bettio and Villa 1998).

The experience of unemployment not only reduces current income, but also affects the level of income that the families consider necessary for the wellbeing of their children. Tests of the hypothesis that expectations of future labor market outcomes affect current fertility decisions show that unemployment is one of the variables that most significantly affects the expectations of future wages and job opportunities and therefore may be responsible for the decline in fertility (Del Bono 2001).

The possibility to combine work and childrearing depends strongly on the occupational structure and working arrangements. Changes in the occupational structure, especially for part-time employment, have expanded employment opportunities for women (O'Reilly and Fagan 1998, also Part 1; Pissarides, Ch. 2, this volume).

However, the development of the service sector and the part-time opportunities have not increased equally in all advanced countries. While in the northern European countries, a high proportion of women work in the tertiary sector and are employed part-time, in the south of Europe the tertiary sector is less developed and part-time employment is very limited. In countries where part-time opportunities are scarce, married women are forced to choose between not working or working full-time, neither of which is necessarily their preferred option. Married women who choose to work tend to have full-time work commitments, which is not compatible with having large numbers of children.

Part-time job opportunities are very limited in southern European countries when compared to northern and Central European countries (Appendix A, Figure 8.A.1). The positive link between part-time jobs and women's participation in the labor market has been shown in studies based on cross-country analyses. Empirical analyses of several countries show that being a mother (compared with being childless) decreases the probability of choosing full-time work and increases the probability of both not working or of working part-time (see Petrongolo, Ch. 4, this volume).

The availability of part-time jobs increases the probability that women are employed in all European countries (Bardasi and Gornick 2000, Tanda 2001). Greater opportunities for part-time employment also reduces the costs of having children, and has a positive impact on fertility rates. Figure 8.9 shows that in countries where part-time opportunities are higher, fertility rates are also higher (The Netherlands, Denmark, UK, Sweden).

In Italy, the availability of part-time opportunities has a positive impact on both the probability of women participating in the labor market and the probability of having children (Del Boca 2002). However part-time work may have also negative effects on wages and career prospects (especially in countries where it is widespread). Part-time jobs tend to be more frequent in low-qualified occupations with a negative impact on women's career opportunities. UK and US mothers are more likely to work in part-time jobs and earn lower wages compared with women without children. Mothers working part-time also have significantly lower hourly wages in Sweden but not in Germany (see Ch. 2 pp. 12 this volume).

When we look at the employment conditions of women before and after childbirth we see that after the first birth, mothers either become unemployed or inactive or experience downward occupational mobility. That is, even if a woman remains employed she may end up in an occupation that is inferior to

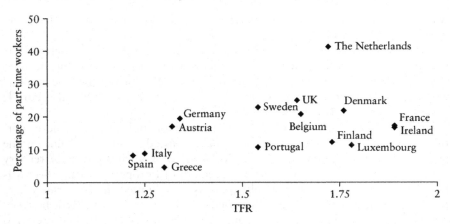

Figure 8.9. *Part-time and fertility (2000)*
Source: Eurostat (2001), *Statistics in Focus*.

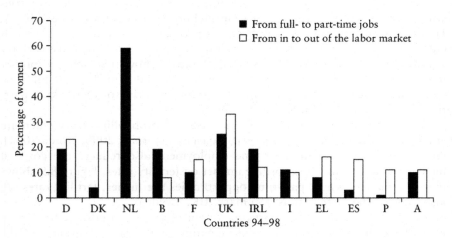

Figure 8.10. *Transitions in Europe around first childbirth*
Source: Del Boca, Pasqua, Pronzato 2003.

the one held before the birth in terms of quality, payment and responsibility (Gutiérrez-Domènech 2002). This may stem from the fact that mothers might sometimes be willing to supply labor that involves fewer responsibilities during the childrearing years and/or because employers may be reluctant to hire mothers for high profile positions since they believe that their family role may absorb most of their energy and interfere with their productivity.

A comparison across European countries (Figure 8.10) shows that that only in the Netherlands, Belgium and Ireland the probability of changing from a full-time activity to a part-time activity after the birth of the first child is higher than the probability of leaving the labor market. In southern European countries, a smaller number of women change their status after childbirth. As we have discussed above, the proportion of women working in these countries is much lower than in the rest of Europe, and they are predominantly employed in full-time, permanent jobs.

8.4   FROM MATERNITY TO PARENTAL LEAVE

It is usually claimed that maternity leave increases female participation because women are not forced to exit from the labor market after childbirth to take care of their newborn children. Therefore, maternity leave constitutes an important policy for helping women to reconcile household responsibilities with work activities.

In 1992, the European Union issued a directive which mandated a paid maternity leave of 14 weeks, and in 1998 another directive mandating a 3-month parental leave was also approved. However, maternity leave policies (of compulsory and optional leave) still differ markedly across Europe in terms of both duration and benefits. Denmark, Finland and Italy are the most generous countries in terms of duration of base maternity leave, while France, Spain and Portugal have longer optional parental leave periods (see Appendix A, Table 8.A.1).

The benefits received during the base period are particularly low for Greece, where benefits are not paid either during the optional period. Spain, Portugal, the Netherlands and the United Kingdom also offer no benefits during the optional period. In the United States, maternity leave has only recently been introduced with the Family and Medical Leave Act (1993) (FMLA), and its coverage is still quite limited: only 12 weeks of unpaid leave for women working full time in firms with at least 50 employees. Before 1994, however, many employers created maternity leave programs as a response to the growing presence of women in the workforce (Sundström 1994; Kelly and Dobbin 1999).

Maternity leave is likely to have a positive impact on women's employment rate since more women would enter employment if they knew they had access to leave. A relatively strong correspondence between the generosity of child-related policies of maternal employment (including maternity leave) and women's employment profiles emerges from cross-country comparisons. In northern European countries, where policies are more generous, female participation in the labor market is higher (Gornick *et al.* 1997).

Quite different results, however, have been reported for the United States. During the period 1980–1990, the labor supply of new mothers did not increase more in states where maternity laws were enacted. After 1993, when the FMLA (1993) was introduced, the effect of maternity leave appears limited, probably because 12 weeks is such a short period, the coverage is not universal, and in many cases leave is unpaid (Klerman and Leibowitz 1999).

The expected effect of the duration of leave is in fact ambiguous: in theory, the longer women stay out of the labor force, the greater the loss they incur in terms of skill deterioration and lost opportunities for promotion and training. A negative relation between maternity leave and female employment is therefore expected. However a longer leave may also be seen in a positive light since it gives mothers more time to recover while retaining job security. Therefore, the positive effect of maternity leave on fertility and female employment seems to depend strongly on the length of leave and on the generosity of the benefits that women receive during the leave. A comparison of the effect of compulsory and optional maternity leave regulations in European countries shows that a long compulsory maternity leave period seems to have a negative impact on the probability of women working, possibly increasing the costs of hiring women. In contrast, the length of the optional maternity leave has a positive effect on women's employment rate.

France is an example of the negative effect on female employment of long maternity leave. In France, in fact, parental leave has been associated with a benefit called the Allocation Parentale d'Education (APE). The full-rate APE can be considered as a kind of mother's wage, but it is only temporary in that it applies only until the youngest child reaches the age of 3. This is a strong incentive for mothers to leave the labor market, especially when they have relatively low wages or precarious jobs. Périvier and O'Dorchai (2003) argue that:

[t]he APE has had positive consequences for most women who have taken it up at a partial rate or who have chosen the full-rate but could fall back on a secure job. Usually, these women are skilled. However, it has had the strong perverse effect of removing from the labor market those women who, generally speaking, were unskilled. Once the three years of entitlement to the APE had expired, these women were generally no longer able to find a job because of the training opportunities foregone and their inactivity during too long a period. In conclusion, it has encouraged unskilled women to return home and has strengthened the disparity and inequality, that were already strong to start with, between skilled and unskilled women.

(p. 117)

If we look at the labor demand side, it is evident that by imposing additional costs to the employers, maternity leave policies may have a negative impact on women's job opportunities, careers and wages or, more precisely, on what is defined as the 'family gap', which is the wage difference between women with and without children (Waldfogel 1998). Employers, in fact, may find it risky to hire young women who may be absent from work for long periods. Moreover, they also prefer to employ women in jobs with fewer responsibilities, where they can easily be replaced during maternity leave. Again, the effects on wages and career depend on the length of the leave.

In fact, in the 1980s and 1990s the gender gap in pay decreased in the United States because of equal pay and equal opportunity policies, while the 'family gap' increased because of the lack of family-friendly policies, including maternity leave and childcare. The results show that a short period of maternity leave does not affect human capital accumulation and therefore does not negatively affect new mothers' wages. On the contrary, the possibility of returning to the same job after the leave period has a positive effect on women's pay, because of gains in firm-specific work experience and job tenure. Similar results were found for Europe (Ruhm 1998).

If we look more closely at the Nordic countries, it can be seen that formal parental leave has no effect on Swedish women's wages, probably because most women in Sweden work in the public sector. Instead, interruptions due to unemployment prove to cause greater losses than interruptions due to maternity leave and childcare. Longer leave periods have a negative impact on wages, most likely because of the signaling effect, that is to say, employers tend to penalize those who take longer leave because this is a sign of lower job commitment (Albrecht *et al.* 1999). A negative impact of interruptions is also found for young women in Germany, but in this case the effect for interruptions due to maternity leave is greater than the effect of interruptions due to unemployment (Kunze 2001).

Further, in a comparative analysis of Finland and Norway, some evidence was found for the hypothesis that the extension of parental leave may have positively influenced fertility. The effect is most significant for Finland where more extensions were available during the period of analysis (about 1960–1990), and is mainly limited to the probability of a second or third birth (Rønsen 1998). If the studies mentioned above mainly concentrate their attention on the effects of maternity leave regulation for women workers, it is also interesting to consider the impact on decisions made when parental leave is also available.

In Appendix A, Table 8.A.2 (p. 152) reports paternity and parental leave legislation in European countries. Paternity leave is explicitly directed to the fathers of newborn children, while parental leave can be used either by the mother or the father. As can be seen, only northern European countries offer fathers the opportunity to stay at home for some days following the birth of the child, while in most southern European countries extremely limited paternity leave is provided, if at all.

On the contrary, all European countries give fathers the possibility of parental leave, but in 1995 only 5 per cent of the fathers in the European Union took advantage of this opportunity. This is generally interpreted as being an indication of the secondary role of fathers in childrearing, while a possible income constraint could be an important cause. Since on average men have a higher labor income than women, and parental leave benefit is a portion of the wage, it is less costly, in terms of household income loss, for women than for men to take the optional parental leave. In fact, a higher percentage of fathers taking parental leave is found in North Europe where benefits during the optional period represent a higher percentage of the average wage.

While parental leave has relatively limited negative effects on women's wages, it has a significant negative effect on men's earnings. Moreover, mothers who contribute more to the household income are less likely to leave their jobs both before and after the birth and they tend to return earlier to their jobs (Wenk and Garret 1992). Swedish families are more likely to have a second baby in cases where the father takes parental leave for the first child, suggesting that policies encouraging an active participation of the father in childcare may stimulate fertility (Oláh 1996).

Another relevant aspect to be considered is that maternity/parental leave regulation usually guarantees only entitlement to permanent workers, while the extension of the benefit to part-timers and temporary workers is still quite limited. In Europe, and in particular in southern European countries, employment has traditionally been based on permanent jobs. Only recently some elements of flexibility have been introduced into southern European labor markets, with the introduction of temporary jobs, especially for young people. The growth of the proportion of youth with temporary and unstable jobs has increased uncertainty, causing delays in marriages (or cohabitation) and postponement of fertility due to lower coverage in terms of parental leave and benefits (De la Rica and Iza 2003).

As a consequence, young women may wait for a stable and protected job before deciding to have a child, especially in areas where the unemployment rate is high. Postponement may result in a lower fertility rate.

8.5 CHILDCARE SYSTEMS

The presence of children affects mothers' preferences with respect to non-market time versus market time. Social policies directed at reducing the costs that children incur by increasing the availability, quality and affordability of childcare may affect fertility and participation rates. Studies on temporal patterns have shown that the increased availability of childcare is one possible explanation for the change in fertility over time and for the observed changes in the relation between women's participation and fertility (Ahn and Mira 2001; Engelhardt and Prskawetz 2002).

However childcare systems have not evolved in the same way in all developed countries. In some countries (as in Anglo-Saxon countries) the view that the choice of having children is a private one prevails, and government support is targeted only to poor families with children. In other countries (as in northern countries) children are considered to be public goods and public policies cover their costs independently of family income. The organization and financing of childcare for children in different age groups in different countries are different across Europe (see Appendix A,

Table 8A.2 p. 152). In the United Kingdom, a model of private provision and financing of childcare prevails, while in Sweden, public organization and financing prevails, and in southern Europe (Italy and Spain), there is a mixture of private and public childcare. Coverage for younger children is higher in Sweden while coverage for older children is higher in Italy. The different characteristics of childcare services have different implications on the labor supply of mothers.

Figure 8.11 shows the availability of childcare in several countries (proportion of children under 3, and from 3 up to the mandatory school-enrolment, who benefit from formal childcare arrangements). For children under 3, the supply of childcare varies across countries considerably. Nordic countries have the highest proportion (40%) while in southern Europe it is much lower (5–6%). For older children the coverage tends to be much higher and tends to be more uniformly distributed across countries.

Childcare availability also has important effects on fertility, while childcare costs do not seem to be an important factor. Figure 8.12 shows that in most of the high fertility rate countries childcare availability is relatively high, while in southern European countries where childcare availability is very low (Italy, Spain, Greece) fertility is also low.

In southern European countries, childcare does not seem to be designed to accommodate market work of both parents, especially given that part-time opportunities are scarce. Public childcare is only available in some areas of these countries, and with limited hours. These constraints have resulted in lower growth in the participation of southern European mothers with younger children than in other countries.

The decision to work and to have a child are, in fact, both positively influenced by the availability of childcare. Given the low availability of childcare and the limitation in daily hours, a large proportion of Italian mothers, for example, have to rely on family support systems, mainly on the help of

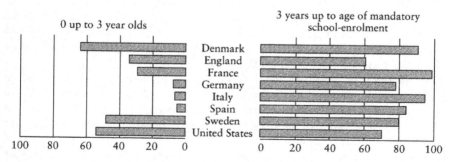

Figure 8.11. *Proportion of children using childcare*
Source: OECD (2001).

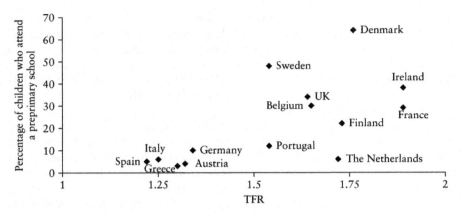

Figure 8.12. *Childcare availability and fertility*
Source: Eurostat (2001), *Statistics in Focus*.

grandparents. The role of the extended family on women's decisions to work and to have children is relevant, and the substitutability between formal childcare and informal help by the family is fundamental (Del Boca 2002). These results indicate, in fact, that the participation of women with children in the labor force is affected by childcare availability as well as the availability of informal childcare. Family support, both in the form of transfers and in the form of help with the children, increases the probability of women's participation as well as their probability of having children. Similar results also emerge for Spain, where a high opportunity cost is associated with childbearing because of the lack of 'social care services' and is compensated for by a strong family support network (Del Boca 2002; Del Boca, Locatelli, Vuri 2003; Baizan *et al.* 2002).

Another important issue concerns the quality of childcare. If high quality childcare is available, the preferences of mothers for time spent at home relative to time spent at work become weaker. This is particularly true for older children (3–5 years of age) and in families where only one child is present and childcare use responds also to the child's needs for socialization in addition to education and care (Del Boca 2002).

On average, in countries where childcare is publicly provided, childcare quality is higher and more homogeneous. The problem of quality is more relevant in systems where childcare is mostly privately provided (and where a wider variety of types of services are supplied) because private services are usually less subject to monitoring.

Quality is related to cost. The ratio of specialized personnel to the number of children and higher levels of training are positively related to quality care, but high-quality care costs more. Childcare costs are part of the family decision making in two ways. First, childcare costs can be thought of as a part of the cost of rearing a child and thus influence those decisions for which the cost of children is a relevant factor. In addition, in families where the mother is the principal caregiver, the cost of childcare can be considered as a tax on the mother's net wage and will result in a decrease in mothers' employment and working hours. The higher the cost of childcare, the higher the cost of each additional child. This leads to the prediction that higher childcare costs will also tend to lower fertility (Cigno 1991; Del Boca 2002; Ermisch 1989).

The results of several studies for the United States, the United Kingdom and Canada show that childcare cost is a very important variable with significant effects on participation of mothers (Blau and Robins 1988; Ribar 1992; Connelly 1992; Kimmel 1998; Powell 2002). In northern European countries, instead, where public childcare is readily available, the cost of childcare is less influential on the mother's decision to work (Gustafsson and Stafford 1992). Similar results emerge for Italy: childcare costs are significant only in those areas where there are several childcare places available (Del Boca 2003).

8.6 CHILD BENEFITS

As we have discussed above, any governmental measure aimed at reducing the costs of children can be expected to have a positive effect on the demand for children. A theoretical distinction is drawn, however, between measures aimed at reducing the direct costs of children (direct expenditures) and measures reducing the opportunity cost of children (foregone earnings) (Cigno 1991).

The magnitude of these effects may depend on the work status of the beneficiary. Higher cash benefits have a greater effect on unemployed women than highly paid executives. On the other hand higher cash benefits may lead to an increased demand for children but also to a demand for higher quality. Child benefits may also be expected to have distinct effects on women with different numbers of children. If the same benefits are paid for each child regardless of birth order, benefits can have an increasing influence on the decision to have a greater number of children since their cost would be lower with each additional child (economies of scale).

Studies based on time series found a positive relation between fertility and cash policies. Family benefits were found to result in increased fertility of 0.2–0.3 children per woman (Blanchet and Eckert-Jaffe 1994, using French data). Other studies suggest the existence of a timing effect: higher family benefits would encourage early entry into motherhood but not necessarily a large family size (Barmby and Cigno 1990, and Ermisch 1989). A cross-country comparison, which considers benefits for one-child, two-children and three-children families separately, indicated a positive but very limited effect of child benefits on fertility (Gauthier and Hatzius 1997). These results vary widely across countries and by birth order. The cross-country comparison shows that while cash benefits do not affect fertility in Anglo-Saxon countries, they have a positive effect in Scandinavian countries, since they are likely to be correlated with other family support policies. In southern European countries the effect is significant only for the first child, while in other countries (France and Sweden for example) it is significant for the third child. These differences reflect important differences in family support policies across countries. Studies based on macro data reveal a number of methodological pitfalls, since it is difficult to measure the incentive effects of transfers to a population which, in any case, would have had several children.

The influence of child transfers on fertility has not been widely studied on individual data. Studies on the role of financial incentives on fertility at the individual level (Lefebvre *et al.* 1994 and Laroque and Salanie 2003 for Canada and France respectively) report very weak effects.

The analysis of cash benefits must take into account two important factors. First, child benefit effects may be greater for lower income households, that is, fertility would increase in households where the average number of children is higher. The second aspect concerns the potential discouraging effects on mothers' labor supply. Given the low participation rates of mothers in several countries and the greater response of low income women to changes in tax-transfer systems (see Aaberge, Colombino and Strom, chapter 11 this volume) these effects are likely to be significant and raise crucial policy questions. These conclusions underline the importance of estimating fertility and part-icipations decisions simultaneously (Francesconi 2002; Del Boca 2002; Laroque and Salanie 2003; Colombino and Di Tommaso 1996; Colombino 2000).

8.7 FAMILY PATTERNS AND FAMILY STRUCTURE

Strong interdependence exists between the patterns and structure of family relationships and women's participation rates and fertility rates. On average the proportion of women working is lower among married couples while the share of women with children tends to be higher among married women than among women cohabiting with a partner in the context of a consensual union, and among those living alone. Micro-level data show that the correlation between participation and divorce is positive, while the relationship between fertility and divorce is negative but in most cases ambiguous (Vuri 2001). When comparing different countries, however, important differences emerge. Southern European countries are characterized by a family structure which have peculiar characteristics compared with the rest of Europe. On the one hand, the strong ties with the family of origin support women's choices to work and have children. Grandparents support their adult children by providing both time for childcare which compensates for the rigidity of the service system (especially in Italy), and financial transfers. This responsibility is likely to have a significant effect on women's participation and fertility. Del Boca (2002) shows that the presence of grandparents in the vicinity increases the probability of women working and having children.

The role of the family in supporting children goes far beyond the completion of children's schooling. Del Boca and Lusardi (2003) show that 45 per cent of young households were gifted the house in which they live by their parents, and for most of the rest the support of the family was essential for the down-payment accumulation. Because of the limited access to credit and housing markets, the southern European family traditionally provides income support and co-residence to its children during their usually lengthy search for a stable, 'secure' job. (Martinez-Granado and Ruiz-Castillo 2002).

Strong family ties encourage late departure from the parental home. The proportion of children living with their parents has actually increased in the southern European countries in the last decade, while it has decreased in north Europe. The responsibilities of mothers towards their adult children is often combined with the need to informal elderly care which partly explains the low participation of women above the age of 40 (Marenzi and Pagani 2003).

While the extended family may be important to soften the constraints that young people face in finding a suitable job and housing, it may negatively affect the reproductive behavior of young people. Paradoxically, the stronger the traditional family ties are, the lower the fertility rates. Correlations between total fertility rates and proportion of co-residence of adult children show that fertility is lower in countries where a higher proportion of youths continue living with their parents into their late 20s (Fig. 8.13).

A late departure from the parental home often results in the postponement of marriage and parenthood with a shorter time interval for childbearing. Staying at home until into their thirties, young Italians find it harder to accept respons-ibilities: with family support, they have the opportunity to wait for a job that is exactly what they are looking for, and to postpone marriage until their mid–late thirties. Livi Bacci (2001) describes this phenomenon as 'the posponement sindrome' (*la sindrome del ritardo*).

The effects on fertility of late departure from the parental home are twofold. On the one hand, men have less domestic experience because they go straight from co-dependency with their family to co-dependency with their wives, without ever having lived alone or with friends.[1] Thus Italian husbands do not help with domestic chores, even if their wives are in full-time employment, and their contribution is much lower than that of their European counterparts. Ichino *et al.* (2002), in a comparative work, show that Italy is the European country where husbands help their wives less and where full-time mothers

---

[1] In Italy as well as in Spain most children go to college in their home town and reside with their family.

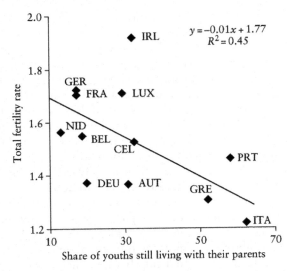

Figure 8.13. *Fertility and share of youth living with parents*
Source: Social, Employment and Migration WP-15, 2002 OECD (p. 22)

spend less time with their children. The excessive burden of child-rearing on women has been considered as an important cause of Italy's low fertility. Del Boca *et al.* (2003) show that husbands' help in the home is an important factor in support of women's work, and as a form of formal childcare.

Another interesting interpretation of this relationship is given within the 'familistic view.' Dulla Zuanna (2004) reports survey results suggesting that in Italy children are 'valued' more than in other northern European countries where family size is much larger. According to his approach, the high value could paradoxically explain the low Italian birth rate, since Italians invest a large amount of time, money and attention in their children, and, rather than having several children, they prefer to have just one child. These results appear to be coherent with the notion of substitution between quantity and quality of children (Willis 1973).

Another important aspect is related to the flexibility of forms of relationships: in countries where the proportion of births out of wedlock are more frequent and cohabiting couples are more frequent, fertility is actually higher. A higher marriage rate is not associated with higher fertility; while more neutral marriage laws, depending on the form of relationship, can support fertility. Differences across countries are partly explained by legal provisions, and in particular by the extent to which rights are extended to mothers and children living outside marriage.

Cross-country correlations between total fertility rates and several proxies of the dominance of traditional forms of family relationships suggest a different pattern. One indicator of family patterns is divorce rates (an indicator of the frequency of disruptions in marriages). Figure 8.14 shows a positive correlation between divorce and fertility rates at the end of the 1990s (Sleebos 2002).

Another relevant indicator is the proportion of births out of wedlock (i.e. birth occurring outside marriages, as a proportion of all births). Figure 8.15

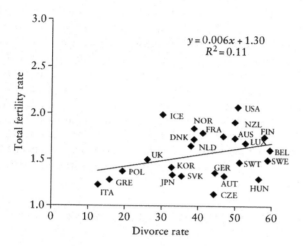

Figure 8.14. *Fertility and divorce rate*
Source: Social, Employment and Migration WP 15, 2002 OECD (p. 21).

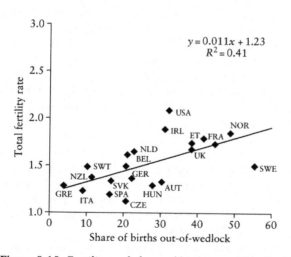

Figure 8.15. *Fertility and share of births out of wedlock*
Source: Social, Employment and Migration WP 15, 2002 OECD (p. 21).

also shows a positive correlation between share of births outside wedlock and fertility.

Billari and Kohler (2002) and Sleebos (2002) analysing different set of countries reach similar conclusions, suggesting that countries where divorce and out-of-wedlock births are more frequent, have lower fertility rates than other countries. Further support for this cross-country pattern is provided by the large increase in the proportion of out-of-wedlock births in Sweden, France, the United Kingdom, and United States (countries with relatively high total fertility rates) compared to Italy and Spain. In France and the United Kingdom, the share of out-of-wedlock births increased from around 7 per cent in 1960 to more than 40 per cent in 2000. The increase was sharper in Sweden (from 11 to 55%) and less significant in Italy and Spain (from 2 to 9%). Long-term commitments in southern European countries have been an obstacle rather than a fortune for fertility: while such associations obviously do not imply causal relations, they provide empirical evidence against the assumption that higher marriage rates are a necessary condition for increasing fertility, and suggest that marriage laws that are more neutral with respect to the form of relationship may be an important condition for sustaining fertility (Billari and Kohler 2002).

8.8   COMPARING THE EFFECTS OF SOCIAL POLICIES

As we have discussed above, the compatibility between labor market participation and fertility can be the outcome of several factors: changes in education levels and wages, changes in labor market regulations, and changes in the service sector. In northern countries, governments have developed policies with the objective of simultaneously encouraging the labor force participation of women and fertility. These programs support dual-earner families and the burden of childrearing is shifted to the state. Public childcare availability, generous optional maternity leave as well as part-time opportunities have allowed women to choose either to remain in the labor market during their childbearing years and maintain a continuous and stable relationship with the labor market, or to take care of their children themselves by taking advantage of long optional maternity leave provision.

In Anglo-Saxon countries, governments have implemented programs only for the poor, and they have allowed the market to produce services which respond to families' needs for childcare during working hours. In this context, where long optional parental leave is not available, mothers have less choice: they may choose between part-time work combined with the use of private childcare, or leaving the labor market.

The southern European countries, on the contrary, have targeted programs mainly to working mothers (employment protection, public childcare mainly for dual-earner families), leaving the burden of childrearing to the family. The development of private services has been constrained in several ways by competition with the public sector and by strict regulation. The outcome has been employment protection for those already employed at the cost of low employment and low fertility. In areas where childcare availability is higher, women can combine work and childrearing without leaving the labor market, while in areas where childcare is not available mothers can continue working through their childbearing years only with the support of the family.

Examination of policies to assist women with children from 0 to 3 years, such as childcare and optional paternal leave, reveals that different combinations characterize different countries (Figure 8.16). For example, in countries with longer optional maternity leave, but low levels of childcare availability, as well as very few part-time opportunities, women may take time out of work to take care of their children. These interruptions imply negative effects on wages and career prospects and also low participation.

Northern Europe (Denmark and Sweden), on the other hand, is characterized by shorter optional maternity leave (although paid at a higher percentage of wages), but wide availability of childcare, as well as part-time opportunities. More women in these countries have the option to use childcare, managing not to take time out of their jobs during childrearing. The negative impact on wages and career prospects is less relevant.

Finally, in most southern European countries (particularly Italy and Greece) characterized by low optional maternity leave, low childcare and very limited part-time options, women do not have the option to use childcare, and need to rely on family support in order to continue working when their children are young. The outcome is very low participation, but high continuity in the labor market attachment.

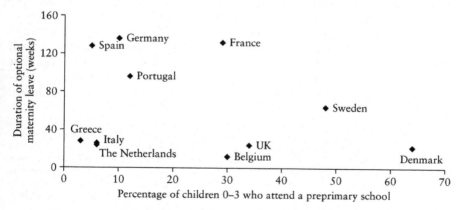

Figure 8.16. *Childcare availability and optional maternity leave (2000)*
Source: Eurostat (2001), *Statistics in focus.*

8.9 PARTICIPATION AND FERTILITY DECISIONS: EMPIRICAL RESULTS FROM ECHP

The analysis in the previous sections has suggested the importance of labor market and social policies in a woman's decision to work and/or to have children. However, empirical analysis of participation and fertility is quite complex since these decisions are affected both by individual characteristics (for which we need data at the individual level) and by policies (which are the same across individuals living in the same country).

We use here the European Community Household Panel (ECHP)[2] and select all women aged 21–45, married (or cohabiting) from Denmark, the Netherlands, France, Italy and Spain, available for the years 1994–1999 (see Del Boca, Pasqua and Pronzato 2003). The dependent variables are whether the wife is working at the time of the interview and whether or not she had a child in the last two years. The variables considered include personal characteristics (wife's age, education and non-labor income), family characteristics (husband's income, presence of children in the household), environmental variables (regional unemployment rate, percentage of part-timers, availability of childcare).[3]

One of the limitations of the economic analysis of fertility is the omission of factors such as fecundity, tastes, and other marriage-specific traits which are unobservable to the researcher. To take into account and isolate these effects, we use a fixed effect model with panel data. Unfortunately there are no data available to estimate the effects of all social policies across different European countries over time (optional parental leave for example).

We also estimate a random effect model and we compare the coefficients associated with time-varying variables (Tables 8.1 and 8.2). The fixed effect and random effect estimates of the wife's age are both positive and significant in the employment equation. This is not true in the fertility equation where the fixed effect estimate is positive and the random effect is negative and significant. Schooling is a time-invariant variable and therefore it can be used only in the random effects estimates. As expected, it has a positive sign in the employment equation, but also a positive effect on the probability of having a child. This effect can be interpreted in part as a permanent income effect given that fathers' education is not included in the analysis (assortative mating). Moreover, higher education might also positively affect the preference for children,

---

[2] The ECHP is a standardized multi-purpose longitudinal survey co-ordinated and supported by Eurostat, which allows study and comparison of the member states in the European Union. The survey involves annual interviews of a representative panel of households and individuals in each country, covering a wide range of topics on living conditions such as income, employment, poverty and social exclusion, housing, health, migration and other social indicators. The unit of analysis is the household and, within the household, all individuals older than 16, although it is possible to gather demographic information on family members under sixteen as well.

[3] A detailed description of the variables and the characteristics of the ECHP data set is in Del Boca, Pasqua, Pronzato (2003).

Table 8.1. *Employment equation*

	Fixed effects	Random effects
Age	0.040**	0.035**
Schooling	–	1.251**
Wife non-labor income	−0.081**	−0.140**
Husband total income	−0.003	−0.009**
Children in the HH	−0.454**	−0.868**
Unemployment (regional)	−0.086**	−0.096**
Part-time (regional)	0.095**	0.001
Childcare (regional)	0.020*	0.011
The Netherlands	–	−1.750**
France	–	−0.498**
Italy	–	−1.154**
Spain	–	−1.119**
1995	–	−0.023
1996	–	−0.043*
1997	–	−0.041
1998	–	−0.042
1999	–	−0.055
Constant	–	−1.612**
Hausman specification test	168.55	
Obs.	12,466	49,299

Key: * = significant at 90%; ** = significant at 95%.

for example, to provide a better socialization to an otherwise single child. The fixed and random effect estimate of the wife's labor income are both negative and significant in the employment equation, while they are positive and significant in the fertility equation. Similar results are found for the husband's income. The presence of children in the household has a negative effect both on participation and on fertility, and there is no variation across estimation methods. The fixed effect and random effect estimates of the coefficient of the regional unemployment rate are both negative in the employment equation. In the fertility equation, the fixed effect estimate is negative while the random estimate is positive. The different sign of the coefficient in the fixed effect and in the random effect estimates can be rationalized by looking at the regional level data: where the unemployment rate is high, the fertility rate is also higher (such as in the southern regions of Italy and Spain).

The fixed effect coefficient of the regional part time are positive both in the employment equation and in the fertility equation, while the random estimate is positive in the employment equation and negative, but not significant, in the fertility one. The fixed and random effect estimates of childcare are all positive (however only the fixed effect estimate is significant). These results are coherent with the predictions of our modeling framework developed in Del Boca (2002).

Table 8.2. *Fertility equation*

	Fixed effects	Random effects
Age	0.002	−0.135**
Schooling	−	0.470**
Wife non-labor income	0.124**	0.116**
Husband total income	−0.000	−0.007**
Children in the HH	−1.920**	−0.025
Unemployment (regional)	−0.011	−0.018**
Part time (regional)	0.005	−0.010
Childcare (regional)	0.037**	0.009
The Netherlands	−	0.275
France	−	0.121
Italy	−	0.246
Spain	−	−0.071
1995	−	−0.042
1996	−	−0.054
1997	−	−0.004
1998	−	−0.117**
1999	−	0.158**
Constant	−	2.471**
Hausman specification test	950.57	−
Obs.	16,764	49,585

Key: ** = significant at 95%; * = significant at 90%.

The year dummies capture the effect of changes in macroeconomic conditions. The year omitted is 1994. The year dummies are negative and nonsignificant in the employment equation, and first negative and then positive but only marginally significant in the fertility equation. The country variables indicate the effect of living in the Netherlands, France, Italy or Spain relative to Denmark (the omitted category), conditional on personal family and environmental characteristics. The effects are all positive but non-significant in the fertility equation while negative and significant in the employment equation. This means that in spite of the different characteristics of households and environments, there are country specific effects (cultural attitudes, for example) that have important impacts on the probability of working.

Which set of estimates is to be preferred? The tests statistics reported indicate overwhelming rejection of the null hypothesis of independence between the unobserved individual effect and the covariates.

8.10 CONCLUSIONS

The analysis of the temporal and cross-country patterns of women's labor market participation shows how several factors affect the compatibility between childrearing and work (labor market characteristics, social services, and family wealth). The most significant factors which facilitate reconciliation of childrearing and work are the opportunities for part-time arrangements, the availability of childcare and parental leave options.

The combination of these options seems to allow different solutions for combining work with having children. Empirical evidence and comparative results show that it is more difficult to combine work and having children in southern Europe than in the rest of Europe. The primary reason for low participation and fertility in these areas seems to be the mismatch between the types of jobs sought by married women with children (part-time) and the types of job available (full-time) in a situation where affordable childcare is lacking. Married women who choose to work tend to have full-time commitments and this is not conducive to having a large number of children. Thus the labor market structure imposes large fertility costs.

This imbalance could be addressed by increasing the provision for childcare which would simultaneously increase job opportunities for women and reduce the costs of taking full-time jobs. By creating more flexible employment opportunities, more women would be able to continue working during their childbearing years. The fixed effect estimates of the impact of some of these variables (part-time childcare, unemployment) on household behavior are consistent with our predictions and reasonably precisely estimated.

APPENDIX 8.A

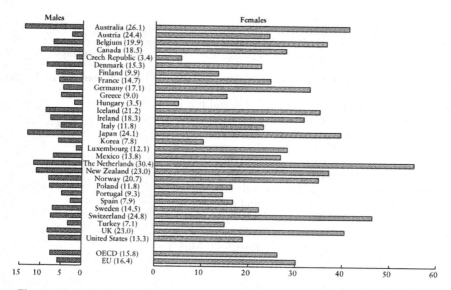

Figure 8A.1. *Incidence of part-time employment as a proportion of employment*

Table 8A.1. *Parental/childcare leave for 1999–2001*

	Duration of base maternity leave (weeks) (1)	Maternity benefits during base leave (% of average wages)	Duration of optional parental leave (weeks) (2)	Parental benefits during optional leave (% of average wages)	Total duration of leave (1) + (2)	Paternity leave
Sweden	14	66	64	66	78	10 days
Denmark	28	100	22	83	50	10 days
UK	18	90	24	15.3	42	None
The Netherlands	16	100	24	14.2	40	None
Belgium	15	77	12	50.3	27	3 days
Germany	14	100	136	25.1	150	None
France	16	100	132	42.4	148	3 days
Portugal	16	100	96	12.7	112	None
Italy	22	80	26	30	48	None
Spain	16	100	128	7.28	144	2 days
Greece	16	50	28	0	44	1 day

Source: Missoc 2001.

Table 8A.2. *Formal day care programs for young children*

	Organization/Financing		Coverage	
	0 to 3 years	3 to 7 years	0 to 3 years	3 to 7 years
Italy	Mainly public organization and financing.	Public and private organization and financing.	6%	95%
Spain	Both organization and financing is mainly public.	Both organization and financing are mainly public.	5%	84%
Denmark	Financing mainly public; provision is mainly public.	Both organization and financing are wholly public.	64%	80%
UK	Mixed public and private provision of centers. Mostly private.	Public and private provision. Mostly private.	34%	60%

Source: OECD (1999; 2000).

APPENDIX 8.B

Table 8B.1. *Descriptive statistics*

	Denmark	The Netherlands	France	Italy	Spain
% of women working	78.5	56.0	64.7	48.5	39.4
% of women that had a child in the past 2 years	23.2	18.1	21.9	18.9	18.1
Wife's age	33.9	35.0	34.4	35.5	35.2
% of women with tertiary education	39.6	18.4	24.0	8.6	21.6
% of women with secondary education	42.7	56.7	46.5	43.0	20.5
% of women with less than secondary education	17.8	24.9	29.5	48.4	57.9
Wife's non-labor income (Euro PPP)	3.7	0.7	1.9	0.5	0.5
Husband's total income (Euro PPP)	16.7	20.0	18.8	15.0	14.3
% of household where there is already at least one child	64.1	64.0	72.5	74.7	75.1
% of part-time workers (regional)	21.6	36.4	15.7	6.7	7.9
Unemployment rate	6.8	5.5	11.9	13.5	21.6
Childcare provided by employer (regional)	1.4	20.9	6.1	3.3	4.7
Number of observations	5,286	10,314	6,811	14,385	12,503

9

Parental Employment and Children's Welfare*

9.1 PARENTAL EMPLOYMENT AND CHILDREN'S WELLBEING: RELATIONSHIP CONCERNS

The last thirty years have witnessed a formidable growth in the body of social science research that investigates the effects of children on parents' behavior, and especially on mothers' labor market behavior. The previous chapter has explicitly dealt with some of the processes that explain such relationships. Comparatively much less attention has been devoted to the opposite types of effects, those of parental behavior on children's outcomes. This chapter aims at reviewing some of the most recent empirical research in this field. In particular, we will be concerned with the effect that parental employment has on different aspects of children's wellbeing. The desirability of public policies that facilitate women's and especially mothers' labor force participation should be evaluated also (and perhaps quite considerably) in relation to these intergenerational effects.

The level of most nations' investments in children is massive. Government expenditures on elementary, secondary and post-secondary schooling are enormous. Among industrialized countries at the end of the 1990s, the proportion of GDP per capita devoted to primary and secondary schooling was on average about 3.6 per cent (Hanushek 2002). In the United States, the expenditures per primary-school student were approximately $6,000 a year, while the expenditures per secondary-school student were nearly $7,800 a year. These figures were respectively $5,700 and $6,500 in Italy, $5,800 and $7,300 in Norway, and $3,300 and $5,200 in the United Kingdom. In addition, huge resources are spent by governments and parents for housing, feeding, clothing, and transporting children, for providing nonparental care services, and for assuring provision of healthcare services. Another cost (and perhaps one of the most important and difficult to assess) refers to the implicit value of the time that parents spend monitoring, teaching, and caring for their children.

---

* The authors of this chapter are John Ermisch and Marco Francesconi who bear full responsibility for any error or imperfection.

Related to these parental time investments are the employment patterns that parents go through during their offspring's childhood. Mothers' paid work in particular could be seen as a key factor in the process that shapes children's welfare. This is because, on the one hand, it represents a direct reduction of the time that mothers spend with their children and on the other hand, by increasing family income, it potentially expands the resources that can be devoted to children. To document the importance of this trade-off at an aggregate level, Figure 9.1 shows the correlation between average child poverty rates (one

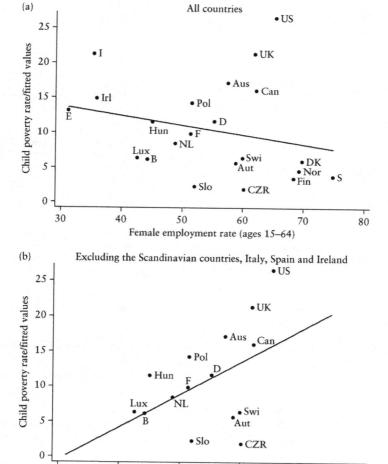

Figure 9.1. *Child poverty rates versus female employment rates—A cross-sectional/ cross-national relationship*

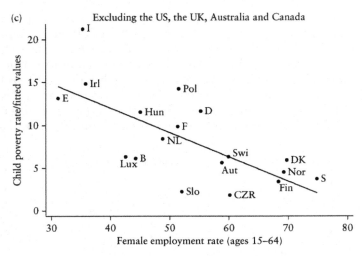

Figure 9.1. *(Continued)*

Note: Child poverty rates (π_n) for each country n are taken from Bradbury and Jäntti (2001, Table 3.2). Children are poor if their household has an equivalent disposable income less than 50 per cent of the overall median household income. Employment rates for women aged 15–64 (ρ_n) for the United States, Australia, Canada, Switzerland, and Norway are from Organisation for Economic Cooperation and Development (2002, various tables). For all the other countries they are taken from European Commission (2002, various tables). The straight line in each panel represents the linear prediction based on the linear regression: $\pi_n = a_1 + a_2\rho_n + \varepsilon_n$, where ε_n is a random shock, and a_1 and a_2 are parameters.

Legend: For each country in parentheses below we report the year(s) in which child poverty rates and female employment rates are measured. US = United States (1994); UK = United Kingdom (1995); I = Italy (1995); Aus = Australia (1994); Can = Canada (1994); Irl = Ireland (1987, 1991); Pol = Poland (1992, 1991); E = Spain (1990, 1991); D = Germany (1994); Hun = Hungary (1994, 1996); F = France (1989); NL = Netherlands (1991); Swi = Switzerland (1982, 1990); Lux = Luxembourg (1994, 1995); B = Belgium (1992); DK = Denmark (1992); Aut = Austria (1987, 1991); Nor = Norway (1995); S = Sweden (1992); Fin = Finland (1991); Slo = Slovakia (1992, 1997); CZR = Czech Republic (1992, 1997).

measure of ill-being) and average female employment rates for a total of 22 countries.[1] Panel (a) suggests that this correlation is negative, but small and not significantly different from zero. But if the four Scandinavian countries (Norway, Sweden, Finland and Denmark) and Italy, Spain and Ireland are excluded from the analysis (Panel (b)), the correlation becomes strongly positive: an increase in the female employment rate by 1 per cent leads to a 0.46 per cent increase in child poverty. Conversely, if the United States,

---

[1] The child poverty rates in this figure are taken from Bradbury and Jäntti (2001). Children are poor if their household has an equivalent disposable income less than 50 per cent of the overall median household income. The female employment rates are taken from different sources (see the note to Fig. 1) and refer to the group of women aged 15–64. Using published information on mothers' (rather than women's) employment rates would have been preferable for our purposes, but would have also restricted the analysis to a smaller number of countries.

the United Kingdom, Australia and Canada are excluded from the original pool of countries (Panel (c)), a 1 per cent increase in the female employment rate is associated to a 0.3 per cent reduction in the child poverty rate.

The relationship between child poverty and women's labor market involvement is thus not clear cut. The negative relationship in Figure 9.1(c) is the result of high-child-poverty/low-female-employment in 'familistic' welfare regimes (such as Spain, Italy and Ireland), and low-child-poverty/high-female-employment in the 'social-democratic' welfare regimes that are prevalent in the Scandinavian countries. Conversely, the positive relationship in Figure 9.1(b) is driven by the strong positive correlation between child poverty and women's employment in countries with a 'liberal' welfare regime (the United States, the United Kingdom, Australia and Canada). We should emphasize that the correlations shown in Figure 9.1 confound the effects of female employment on child poverty with the effects of income on child outcomes and the influence of common factors, such as institutions, that both improve child outcomes and augment incomes. In addition, most of the microeconometric evidence on the relationship between children's wellbeing and mothers' employment available to date comes from such countries, especially the United States and the United Kingdom. Therefore, part of the results discussed in this chapter cannot be easily generalized to all countries, exactly because they are characterized by different institutions (labor markets, schools, government interventions, and so on) and different behaviors of parents (and, possibly, children's responses). For our purposes parental employment will be taken to refer to mothers' and fathers' decisions on their labor supply, while children's wellbeing will cover a wide range of outcomes, including cognitive development in early childhood, educational attainment, and other outcomes that are measured when children are young adults (e.g. early childbearing and unemployment experiences).

Within the social sciences, the idea that the family plays an important role in shaping children's socio-economic outcomes is hardly a new one. As noted by Parsons (1975), Knight (1935) identified the family as the principal social institution that fosters income inequality through behavior that forges intergenerational links between parents' and children's wealth. Likewise, empirical analyses of the determinants of socio-economic success date as far back as the 1920s (e.g. Ginsberg 1929). The main objective of these early contributions was to study the relationship between fathers' and sons' occupations, using cross-tabulations known as occupational mobility tables that were meant to summarize the relationship of interest. Indeed, a huge body of sociological research on intergenerational social mobility has stemmed from this approach, continually refining its econometric estimation and deepening its theoretical underpinnings.[2] These, however, are topics that we shall not be covering here,

---

[2] See, among others, Glass (1963) for Britain, and Blau and Duncan (1967) for the United States. For more recent contributions, reference should be made to the studies of Hauser and Featherman (1977), Featherman and Hauser (1978), Halsey, Heath and Ridge (1980), Goldthorpe (1980), Erikson and Goldthorpe (1992), and Breen and Goldthorpe (2001).

principally because there are already a number of studies that have reviewed the pertinent strands of literature, their main findings and the questions they have left open (e.g. Solon 1999; Bjorklund and Jäntti 2000).

Haveman and Wolfe (1995) provide us with a comprehensive survey of the empirical research on the links between investments in children and children's attainments.[3] Their review included studies which analysed the relationship of a wide range of family and neighborhood characteristics with several measures of children's outcomes (e.g. high school graduation, years of schooling, out-of-wedlock fertility and earnings). Although our study is more limited than theirs in that it focuses only on parents' employment decisions as a form of parental investment in children, it is intended to expand the coverage offered by Haveman and Wolfe (1995) in two important directions. First, we discuss a number of more recent contributions, some of which are based on data from countries other than the United States and others use statistical techniques that were not employed by most of the studies surveyed in Haveman and Wolfe. This will allow us to check whether the results are, or are not, broadly consistent across countries as well as across statistical methods. Secondly, we pay special attention to the specific mechanisms that lie behind the estimated relationship between parental employment patterns during childhood and children's wellbeing. This focus will, in turn, allow us to gain a more solid interpretation of the estimates that are currently available in the literature and, consequently, we will have a better understanding of the links of interest.

Section 9.2 outlines the theoretical perspective and the statistical framework within which we discuss the impact of parental work on children's welfare. These are important because they tell us how to measure such impact and how to interpret the results that try to identify it. Section 9.3 contains a review of some of the most recent empirical studies that have analysed this impact. The children's outcomes that we emphasize include cognitive development, educational attainment, health and other outcomes (such as unemployment and early childbearing). Any attempt to measure the relationship between parental employment patterns and children's wellbeing must take account of the ways other parental factors and decisions during childhood might influence children's long-term development. For that reason, we also ought to consider how far outcomes are affected by processes such as children's experience of life in a single-parent family (or step-family), childhood family income, and parental education. Section 9.4 contains a review of findings relating to such processes. Section 9.5 summarizes the main results of this research, puts them into the context of the female labor supply literature, and offers some alternative ideas for future analyses in this area.

---

[3] The seminal work by Becker, and in particular that summarized in Becker (1981/extended in 1991), has provided (and continues to provide) researchers with the framework within which such links have been analysed across the social sciences.

9.2 THE IMPACT OF PARENTAL EMPLOYMENT ON CHILDREN'S WELLBEING: MEASURING AND EVALUATING THE EFFECTS

In explaining the determinants of children's wellbeing, economists and other social researchers have emphasized the role of parental (or family) circumstances and decisions, while often downplaying the role of other factors and institutions (see Haveman and Wolfe 1995). These include the society at large (or the state) that influences the opportunities faced by parents and children, and the choices that children themselves make.[4] In what follows we will be liable for the same omissions. In addition, we will only focus on some of the salient aspects of the framework that analysts may want to use in investigating the relationship between parental employment and children's welfare, leaving aside other (potentially even more important) decisions and investments, such as childcare, school quality and peer interactions. Strategic interactions between the two parents or between parents and children, which could affect the decisions of all family members, are not considered either.

A convenient way of organizing a coherent interpretation of the determinants of children's wellbeing and guiding analysts in their choice of variables has been provided by a production function framework (Todd and Wolpin 2003). Within this framework, researchers draw an analogy between the knowledge acquisition process of individuals and the production process of firms. Indeed, most of the existing studies of the determinants of children's outcomes are based on the assumption that the inputs into the child outcome production process are subject to choices made by parents (and possibly other institutions, such as schools).

It has long been emphasized that a problem in estimating a (household, health, or education) production function is given by the fact that non-experimental data on all relevant inputs and on child endowments are never readily available (Rosenzweig and Schultz 1983). Only a limited number of contributions, however, have implemented a production function approach that accounts for such a problem. For instance, many have included family income as a proxy for missing data on family inputs, with the presumption that richer families purchase more of such (unobserved or unobservable) inputs (e.g. Baum 2003; Brooks-Gunn, Han, and Waldfogel 2002; McCulloch and Joshi 2002; Ruhm 2000).[5] However, when income is held constant, an increase in

---

[4] For example, at present the majority of studies that analyse the determinants of children's development and school attainments include either characteristics of the family of origin or characteristics of the schools that children attend that presumably shape children's opportunities, but not both. Exceptions are Goldhaber and Brewer (1997), Ludwig (1999), and Dustmann, Rajah and van Soest (2003). See also the discussion in Todd and Wolpin (2003).

[5] Rosenzweig and Schultz (1983) define this type of models as 'hybrid equations' to emphasize that the estimates obtained by such equations are generally biased estimates of the true technical relationship embodied in the production function. In general, the sign and magnitude of the bias depend on the properties of the utility functions which families and children are posited to optimize. We also will adopt this terminology in describing the estimation procedures of the studies reported in our review (see S. 2.3).

the expenditures on a particular input (say, tutors' time) must imply a reduction in expenditures on other goods (e.g. educational trips, museum visits and theatres). To the extent that these other goods also influence children's attainments, the effect of an increase in tutors' time expenditures on attainment would be confounded with the decreased purchases on these other inputs. The inclusion of this and other proxies, which are meant to compensate for missing data on parents' (or schools') inputs, makes the interpretation of the 'effect' of observed inputs quite difficult, and can lead to biased estimates for the inputs of interest here, namely parental employment patterns (Todd and Wolpin 2003).

Another problem is the interpretation of the parental employment parameter. If educational toys or books available to the child can be unarguably seen as inputs in an education production function, parents' employment patterns (regardless of how or when in the child's life-cycle these patterns are measured) are more problematic. This is because parents' employment patterns per se may have little to do with the actual inputs that parents use to invest in their children's cognitive development and human capital. We illustrate this point with a simple example. Consider the case of two families, a and b, with exactly the same number of members (i.e. one mother, one father and one child).[6] Assume that the child's human capital H is produced through a bundle of educational goods and services that parents can only buy on the market, such as toys, books, schools and tutors (which we denote by X), and through time devoted to the child (which we denote by t). That is:

$$H = \varphi(X, t, \mu), \tag{1}$$

where μ represents family- and child-specific endowments ('ability') that are known to the child and parents but not controlled by them, for example, genetic traits or environmental factors.[7] Suppose that families a and b are identical in all observable aspects (age structure, education, type of school attended, resources, and so on), except that the mother in a is in a full-time job, while the mother in b does not work. The time in employment is denoted by h, and thus, $h_a > 0$ while $h_b = 0$. Total maternal time (T) can then be allocated to childcare–t; market time–h; and leisure–l, so that $T_i = t_i + h_i + l_i$, for $i = a$, b. If both families allocate the same level of expenditures on educational goods

---

[6] To make things easier in this example, we also consider only a static environment, assuming away any dynamic labor supply consideration.

[7] The hybrid equations that we mentioned before and that are widely used take instead a different form, which could be summarized by:

$$H = \Psi(X_s, h, Y, w, \mu), \tag{2}$$

where X_s is a subset of the X inputs that are used to produce H, Y is money income of the household, and w denotes mother's earnings. That is, a subset of inputs, X_s, mother's employment, h, and the *determinants* of other inputs (through the reduced-form demand function for H) are regressed against H. Given X_s, the 'effect' of h in (2) is interpreted as if it were the relevant production–function relation.

and services to the child (i.e. $X_a = X_b$)—allocation that is driven by parental preferences, which have been assumed to be identical—we would expect the mother in family a to spend less time with her child compared to the mother in the other family $(t_a + l_a < t_b + l_b)$. This is because the mother in a works. However, the time devoted to the market is only one component of the total time available to mothers, and it is not even the input required in the human capital production of children. Indeed, the mother in family a could devote as much (and, possibly, more) time to stimulating her child's human capital than the mother in family b, that is, $t_a \geq t_b$ and $l_a \leq l_b - (t_a - t_b)$.

If we relax the assumption of equal resources across these two families, and allow family a to be better off than family b (as a result of the mother's working in a), the picture becomes even more complicated. The non-working mother in family b will have more time available to spend with her child but will have fewer financial resources to buy the educational goods and services needed for the child's human capital production. Conversely, the working mother in family a could compensate the possibly lower time spent with her child with a greater amount of educational goods and services. So, we may have to compare situations in which we observe both $t_b + l_b > t_a + l_a$ and $X_b < X_a$. But once again, the mother in family a may still devote more time to her child than the mother in b (through a reduction in her leisure time) and magnify the positive income effect she enjoys through her paid work.

A further complication arises when we allow for preference heterogeneity or for unobserved family-specific endowments in the child's human capital production function (Rosenzweig and Schultz 1983; Currie and Cole 1993; Rosenzweig and Wolpin 1995; Ermisch and Francesconi 2002).[8] In such cases, the interpretation of maternal (and paternal) employment in terms of a human–capital–production–function parameter is complicated by the limited availability of 'events' that vary randomly between children with working mother, and children with non-working mothers.[9] Unfortunately, time (and space) differences in mother's wages or other income components, which could be seen as potential instruments for mother's employment, will also be determinants of

---

[8] So far the term μ in (1) has not played a role. But variations in μ will generally affect (parental) decisions and, consequently, have important econometric implications. In particular, the notion that the human–capital–production inputs, X, are behavioral variables means that even if only information on the technology of human capital–production were desired, having measures of all important behavioral inputs, X, and H in (1) would not be adequate to describe the human capital technology.

[9] There are only a few studies that address endowment (or preference) heterogeneity in the estimation of the technology that produces children's human capital. In the child health literature (where parental employment is however not of primary importance), early examples are Rosenzweig and Schultz (1983) and Grossman and Joyce (1990) studies, which employ instrumental variables techniques. Other more recent examples are Rozenzweig and Wolpin (1995), Strauss (1990), and Currie and Cole (1993) studies, which employ data on siblings, half-siblings and cousins to examine how maternal choices and characteristics affect child health outcomes. The study by Ermisch and Francesconi (2002) employs sibling differences to analyse the effect of parental employment on educational outcomes.

children's wellbeing. The application of a production–function approach is, therefore, at one end, problematic, and at the other end, invalid when the specification of the estimating models includes variables that are hard to justify in a human–capital–production function.

A second approach to modeling the relationship between childhood parental employment and subsequent child outcomes is given by conditional demand functions (Pollak 1971). Ermisch and Francesconi (2002) show that, with separable parental utility,[10] H can be expressed simply as a function of the endowments of all children in the household, denoted by the vector μ, and the total resources devoted to human capital investment in children, R. That is,

$$H = \theta(R, \mu). \tag{3}$$

Clearly, mother's (and father's) employment will be subsumed in R. A problem with this approach is that, for econometric purposes, R is generally not independent of μ. While Y (family income) and w (mother's wage rate) would appear to be natural instruments for R, these are problematic. In fact as Browning and Meghir (1991) point out, these variables are presumably endogenous. In particular, both Y and w are likely to reflect parents' endowments, which are correlated with their children's endowments μ (e.g., through genetic and cultural transmissions).

Finally, another approach to analysing the response of children's welfare to parental employment is based on the formulation and estimation of a dynamic structural model in which parents (and possibly children) make decisions on labor market and location behaviors, and childcare and education choices. In this environment, child outcomes are the result of a production process in which inputs are optimally chosen by parents who maximize household utilities under a number of constraints. Mother's and father's employment patterns enter the problem through time and budget constraints, and their effect on child's welfare reflects the role played by the optimizing choices of parents (and eventually other decision makers). This approach is still in its infancy, but its potentials are far reaching. Input endogeneity is directly modeled, and the estimation techniques allow for heterogeneity in tastes and constraints. Two recent examples are Liu, Mroz and Van der Klaauw (2002) and Bernal (2002). The first investigates the interactions between parental inputs and school inputs as determinants of child cognitive development, with mothers making decisions not only on their labor market participation but also on household location (which, in turn, affects the child quality production function both directly and through the school environment). The second focuses on the effects of labor supply and childcare decisions of women immediately following birth on children's cognitive development. They will be reviewed in the next section.

[10] This implies that parents have preferences characterized by a utility function which has future child outcomes of children separable from parents' 'standard of living' (or consumption).

9.3 A SELECTIVE REVIEW OF RESULTS

Efforts to identify the effect of parental employment on children's outcomes span the social sciences. Although the four conceptual frameworks outlined in the previous section (production function, conditional demand function, structural approach, and hybrid equations) have been primarily used by economists, many of the contributions by non-economists can be interpreted within one of such approaches. While we discuss studies from other disciplines (psychology, sociology and demography in particular), we will mainly focus on studies by economists. Most of the literature refers to the effect of maternal employment, and only very few studies have looked at the effect of father's employment patterns. We emphasize, where possible, the findings on this latter effect. Similarly, we try to distinguish the effect of mothers' full time work from that of mothers' part-time work.

We begin our review of recent contributions by discussing the relationship between parental employment patterns and early childhood outcomes (e.g. cognitive development). This is by and large the broadest literature. This may be because a greater number of researchers from different disciplines have engaged in analysing such outcomes. It may also be because many of the relevant outcomes can be observed fairly soon after birth, thus imposing fewer data requirements than those imposed by outcomes that can be observed only after a long period of time—such as earnings. Our review continues by presenting recent studies on education attainment, and a set of other miscellaneous outcomes (e.g. unemployment and early childbearing).

In Tables 9.1–9.3, we provide information for each study on the data source, sample selection and timing issues, that is, when (or at what age of the child) the outcomes and the other conditioning variables have been measured. We then list the outcomes and define the estimation method.[11] Finally, the last two columns contain one the set of conditioning variables used in estimation, and the other the main results concerning the parental employment variables.

9.3.1 *Cognitive development and early childhood outcomes*

Studies largely informed by child developmental psychology have paid particular attention to socio-emotional adjustment (primarily behavior problems) and cognitive outcomes (primarily receptive verbal ability and early achievement scores). Research on such outcomes has focused on large samples of children, with the bulk of the studies analysing data from the National Longitudinal Survey of Youth (NLSY) for the United States. A smaller number

---

[11] For studies that adopt a production–function approach without accounting for child- and family-specific endowments (the term μ in equation (1)), we label their estimation method as 'reduced-form' to emphasize that they do not account for any particular source of unobserved heterogeneity.

Table 9.1. *Parental employment and children's cognitive development and early childhood outcomes*

Study	Data source and sample(s)[a]	Timing issues	Outcomes[b]	Estimation method[c]	Comments[b]	Effect of parental employment on children's outcomes[d]
Baum (2003)	NLSY: sample sizes vary depending on the outcome (between 1600 and 2000 observations). Children born between 1988 and 1993 to mothers who were between the ages of 23 and 30 in 1988	Outcomes are measured at ages 3–4 (PPVT) and at ages 4–5 (PIAT). Mother's employment is measured over the first three years of the child's life	PPVT; PIAT-M; PIAT-R	OLS (reduced-form production functions; no control for endowment heterog.)	Outcome variables are averaged, so that there is only one test observation per child. Other controls: large set of socio-demographic variables of the child (e.g. sex, birth order and age), of the mother (e.g. education and age), and of the test. Plus an extensive set of supplemental background variables (including mother's AFQT, and grandmother' education), family income, and childcare variables	For all outcomes: Mother's employment in the child's first year (weeks worked): PIAT-M: (−) 5% Mother's employment in years 2 and 3 (weeks worked): PIAT-M: (+) 10% Negative effects of maternal employment are offset by positive effects of increased family income
Bernal (2002)	NLSY: 374 mother–child observations	Outcomes are measured at ages 3–5 (PPVT) and at ages 5–7 (PIAT). Maternal employment is measured over different child's ages, from birth to age 5	PPVT; PIAT-M; PIAT-R	SML (structural estimation method)	Other variables included are: mother's age, education, and race, presence of father, number of siblings, birth order, father's income, child's birth weight, and childcare choice	For all outcomes: Mothers' employment in the first five years of the child's life: Full-time: (−)
Brooks-Gunn, Han and Waldfogel (2002)	NICHD-SECC: 900 European American non-Hispanic children (all born in 1991)	Outcomes are measured at: 15, 24 and 36 months of the child. Mothers' employment status is measured at 1, 3, 6,9,12,15, 24 and 36 months	MDI (= 110.58 at 15 months; = 95.49 at 24 months); Bracken School Readiness (= 46.59 at 36 months)	OLS (reduced-form production functions; no control for endowment heterog.)	Other controls: mother's age and education at child's birth, mother's PPVT-R, mother's marital status, child's sex. Plus controls for family income, presence of older siblings, mother's depression at 1-month postbirth, home environment score, childcare quality, and mother's sensitivity	School readiness: Mother's employment by 9th month of the child: Full-time (−) 5% Part-time (−) ns Stronger effects for children whose mothers are not sensitive, for boys and for children of married women. MDI: (+) ns

Study	Sample	Outcome	Method	Details / Covariates	Results
Horwood and Fergusson (1999)	CHDS: 1265 children born in Christchurch (New Zealand) in a four-month period in mid-1977, followed from birth to age 18	Word recognition (age 8, 10 and 12); reading comprehension (age 10 and 12); mathematical reasoning (age 11); scholastic ability (age 13). Mother's employment is measured either at the time the outcomes are assessed or from birth up to the time of assessment	OLS (reduced-form production functions; no control for endowment heterog.)	Mother's work is measured in terms of hours worked per week and distinguished four groups (0 hours, 1–19 hours, 20–39 hours, 40+hours). Other covariates: child's intelligence; mother's age at birth, mother's education, family socioeconomic status, mother's ethnicity, family structure, child's birth order, family size, mother's emotional responsiveness	For all outcomes and all groups of mother's hours of work: (+/−) ns. The only exception is for the word recognition test at age 12 for which compared to nonworking: Mother's working 20+ hours per week: (−) 1%; Mother's working 1–19 hours per week: (+) 1%
Joshi and Verropoulou (2000)	NCDS children: 1730 individuals who were 5–17 in 1991; BCS, 9003 individuals (born in 1970)	NCDS: PIAT-M; PIAT-R; aggression; anxiety BCS: Maths and reading tests scores	Multi-level models and OLS (reduced-form production functions; no control for endowment heterog.)	NCDS: Outcomes are measured in 1991 (when children were aged 5–17). Mother's employment is measured in the first 4 years of the child's life and in 1991. BCS: Outcomes are measured in 1980. Mother's employment is measured in the first 4 years of the child's life (in 1970–1974). Other controls are: sex, age, number of older siblings, mother's education, mother's test scores (measured at age 7 of the child), mother's general ability (measured at age 11 of the child), housing tenure, family structure (in 1991)	NCDS: Mother is employed in the first year of the child's life: PIAT-R: (−) 5% Mother's part-time employment when child aged 1–4: Non-anxiety: (+) 5% BCS: No significant effect
Liu, Mroz and Van der Klaauw (2002)	NLSY: 7164 children aged 5–15 in 1986 with up to six	PIAT-M	ML (production function; structural estimation method)	Outcome is observed between age 5 and age 15. Mother's. Mother's employment variables: part-time and full-time employment variables	Full-time work: (−) 1% Part-time work: (+) 1%

Table 9.1. (*Continued*)

Study	Data source and sample(s)[a]	Timing issues	Outcomes[b]	Estimation method[c]	Comments[b]	Effect of parental employment on children's outcomes[d]
	possible time-period specific observations per child	employment refers to the two-year period before assessment			(defined in terms of annual hours over the two-year period before assessment). Other variables: child's sex, race and age, mother's age, mother's marital status, mother's education, mother's AFQT score, plus school-district level average characteristics (including high-school dropout rate, average teacher salary, and per child school-district expenditures), residential moves across 24 geographic areas over the two-year period before assessment (endogenous)	
Ruhm (2000)	NLSY: approximately 3000 child-mother cases, some with more than one observation per test	Outcomes are measured at ages 3–4 (PPVT) and at ages 5–6 (PIAT-M and PIAT-R). Maternal employment is measured over the first three years of the child's life	PPVT; PIAT-M; PIAT-R	OLS (reduced-form production functions limited controls for endowment heterog.)	Three maternal employment variables: hours worked; proportion of weeks worked; weeks after birth of child until mother resumes employment. One paternal employment variable: father's average weekly work hours in years 1 through 3 of the child. Other controls: basic child, maternal and household characteristics (e.g. age, sex, and education) a host of other maternal, family and other characteristics (e.g. marital status, AFQT scores, poverty indicator, drug use, attitudes, birth weight, BMI) and maternal employment characteristics (including wages, occupation and hours)	Mother's labor supply during the first three years: PPVT: (−) ns PIAT-M: (−) 5 % PIAT-R: (−) 5 % Father's employment during the first three years: (+/−) ns (for all outcomes)

| Waldfogel, Han and Brooks-Gunn (2002) | NLSY: 1872 children (903 non-Hispanic Whites, 582 non-Hispanic African American, and 387 Hispanics), who were born between 1982 and 1989, and who could be followed from birth to age 7 or 8 in 1990, 1992, 1994 or 1996 | PPVT-R is measured at ages 3–4; PIAT-M and PIAT-R are measured at ages 5–6 and ages 7–8. Mother's employment mainly refers to employment during the first three years of the child's life. It also refers to employment status after age 3 up to the year before assessment | PPVT-R; PIAT-M; and PIAT-R | OLS (reduced-form production functions; no control for endowment heterog.) | Four measures of maternal employment status: employed during the first year of life; employed during the second or third year; employed after age 3 up to the year before the assessment; currently working. Other covariates are: sex, presence of older and younger siblings, family income, ever in poverty, mother's age at birth, mother's education, mother's AFQT score, mother's marital status at year of child's birth, home environment score, child care type, child ever breastfed | Mother's employment in the child's first year of life: Whites: PPVT-R: (−) 1% PIAT-M (ages 5–6): (−) 5% PIAT-M (ages 7–8): (−) 1% PIAT-R (ages 5–6): (−) 5% PIAT-R (ages 7–8): (−) 5% No effect Mother's employment in the second and third year of the child's life: Whites: PIAT-R (ages 7–8): (+) 5% African Americans: PIAT-R (ages 7–8): (+) 5% Hispanics: PIAT-R (ages 5–6): (−) 5% PIAT-M (ages 7–8): (−) 5% Any employment after age 3–4: Whites: PIAT-M (ages 7–8): (+) 5% Blacks and Hispanics: No effect Currently working: Whites: PIAT-M (ages 5–6): (−) 5% PIAT-R (ages 5–6): (−) 5% Blacks: No effect Hispanics: PIAT-M (ages 5–6): (+) 5% |

Key: [a]NLSY = National Longitudinal Survey of Youth; NICHD-SECC = National Institute of Child Health and Human Development Study of Early Child Care; CHDS = Christchurch Health and Development Study (1977 New Zealand birth cohort); NCDS = National Child Development Study (1958 British birth cohort); BCS = British Cohort Study (1970 British birth cohort).

[b]PPVT = Peabody Picture Vocabulary Test; PPVT-R = Peabody Picture Vocabulary Test-Revised; MDI = Bayley Mental Development Index; PIAT = Peabody Individual Achievement Test; PIAT-M = Peabody Individual Achievement Test Mathematics subtest; PIAT-R = Peabody Individual Achievement Test Reading subtest; BPI = Behavior Problems Index; SPPC = Self-Perception Profile for Children; AFQT = Armed Forces Qualification Test; BMI = Body Mass Index.

[c]OLS = ordinary least squares; SML = simulated maximum likelihood; ML = maximum likelihood.

[d](−), (+) = negative, positive effect; statistical significance level indicated (ns = not significant).

Table 9.2. *Parental employment and children's educational attainment*

Study	Data source and sample(s)[a]	Timing issues	Outcomes[b]	Estimation method[c]	Comments[b]	Effect of parental employment on children's outcomes[d]
Ermisch and Francesconi (2002)	BHPS: about 1000 young adults (born between 1970 and 1981) matched to their mothers and, if present, fathers or stepfathers	Children's outcome is measured over the 1990s when children were aged 16 or more. Parental employment is measured from birth to age 15 of the child (and distinguished by child's developmental stage)	Highest educational qualification (A level or more)	Logit and LP models; sibling-difference models (conditional demand functions)	Other variables: child's age and gender, mother's and father's education, birth order, whether respondent is the only child, age of the mother at birth, age of the father at birth, childhood family structure (ever in a lone-parent family and ever in a stepfamily), measures of occupational prestige for the mother and the father (averaged over the entire childhood of the child)	Mother's part-time employment: Level estimates: (−) ns Sibling-difference estimates: (−) 10% Mother's full-time employment: Level estimates: (−) ns Sibling-difference estimates: (−) 5% (Stronger negative effects for children of less educated mothers) Father's employment: Level estimates: (+) 5% Sibling-difference estimates: (−) ns
Joshi and Verropoulou (2000)	BCS: 9003 individuals (born in 1970)	Outcome measured at age 26. Maternal employment is measured when the child was aged under 5	Highest educational qualification	OLS (reduced-form production functions; no control for endowment heterog.)	Gender-specific regressions. Other controls are: father's social class (at the child's birth), mother's and father's education, child's reading and maths scores at age 10, housing tenure, and free school meals	Mother's employment: For boys: (−) 5% For girls: (−) 1%

Study	Sample	Outcome	Method	Controls	Results
Kiernan (1996)	NCDS: 3300 men and 3300 women (born in 1958)	No educational qualification	Outcome measured at age 33. Maternal employment is measured when the child was aged 16	Bivariate analyses and logistic regressions (reduced-form production functions; no control for endowment heterog.)	Gender-specific regressions. Sample is also stratified by whether the child at age 16 lived with both biological parents or with a lone mother. Other controls are: mother's age and education; child's school performance at age 7, whether the child left school at age 16, and a measure of family's financial circumstances (child aged 16)	Mother's non-employment: For men: no effect For women (living with either both parents or lone mother): (+) 1%
O'Brien and Jones (1999)	620 children aged 13–15, interviewed in 6 schools located in Barking and Dagenham (East London) in early 1994	Highest/lowest GCSE grades	Outcome measured at age 16. Maternal and paternal employment variables were measured once when children were aged between 13 and 15	Logit regressions (reduced-form production functions; no control for endowment heterog.)	Other variables included are: sex, race, religion, housing tenure, family structure, number of siblings, child's expectations about further education, child working, having a boyfriend/girlfriend, mother's and father's occupation, praising by mother, praising by father, joint activities with parents, presence of rules about going out at night and watching TV	Low educational outcome: Mother's full-time work: (−) ns Mother's part-time work: (−) 5% Father's work: (−) ns High educational outcome: Mother's full-time work: (+) ns Mother's part-time work: (+) 10% Father's work: (+) ns

Key: [a]CPS = Current Population Survey; PSID = Panel Study of Income Dynamics; NLSY = National Longitudinal Survey of Youth; NICHD-SECC = National Institute of Child Health and Human Development Study of Early Child Care; CHDS = Christchurch Health and Development Study (1977 New Zealand birth cohort); BHPS = British Household Panel Survey; NCDS = National Child Development Study (1958 British birth cohort); BCS = British Cohort Study (1970 British birth cohort).
[b]AFDC = Aid to Families with Dependent Children; TOSCA = Test of Scholastic Abilities; School Certificate is the first of a series of national examinations in New Zealand that provide evidence of academic achievement and are a prerequisite to University entry (students typically sit School Certificate at around the age of 16 and may elect the number of type of subjects on which they wish to be assessed); GCSE = General Certificate of Secondary Education (UK certificate obtained after a national examination generally taken when the child is age 16).
[c]OLS = ordinary least squares; SML = simulated maximum likelihood; LP = linear probability.
[d](−), (+) = negative, positive effect; statistical significance level indicated (ns = not significant).

Table 9.3. *Parental employment and children's other outcomes*

Study	Data source and sample(s)[a]	Timing issues	Outcomes[b]	Estimation method[c]	Comments[b]	Effect of parental employment on children's outcomes[d]
Antecol and Bedard (2002)	NLSY: 15+ year olds. Sample sizes vary depending on the outcome (between 800 and 1300 children)	Children's behavior is measured up until the end of age 14. Maternal employment is measured at age 15 of the child in terms of average weekly hours of work	Smoke regularly, drink regularly, being sexually active, use marijuana regularly, being convicted of a crime before age 15	Probit models (reduced-form production functions; no control for endowment heterog.)	Other variables: gender, race, family structure (months with biological father), birth order, mother's education, and average net family income	Mother's average weekly hours of works: Smoking: (−) ns Sex: (−) ns Marijuana: (+) ns Conviction: (+) ns Drinking: (+) 10%
Ermisch and Francesconi (2001c)	BHPS: about 1000 young adults (born between 1970 and 1981) matched to their mothers and, if present, fathers or stepfathers	Children's outcomes are measured over the 1990s when children were aged 16 or more. Parental employment is measured from birth to age 15 of the child (and distinguished by child's developmental stage)	Economic inactivity; psychological distress; childbearing (women only) by age 21	Logit models; sibling-difference models (conditional demand functions)	Other variables: child's age and gender, mother's and father's education, birth order, whether respondent is the only child, age of the mother at birth, age of the father at birth, childhood family structure (ever in a lone-parent family and ever in a stepfamily), measures of occupational prestige for the mother and the father (averaged over the entire childhood of the child)	Mother's part-time employment: Economic inactivity: Ages 6–10: (−) 5% Psychological distress: Ages 0–5: (−) 5% Early childbearing (women only): Ages 11–15: (−) 5% Mother's full-time employment: Economic inactivity: Ages 11–15: (−) 5% Psychological distress: Ages 6–10: (−) 1% Ages 11–15: (+) 5% Early childbearing (women only): Ages 6–10: (+) 1% Ages 11–15: (−) 1% Father's employment: Economic inactivity: Ages 0–5: (−) 10% Psychological distress: Ages 0–5: (−) 5% Early childbearing: Ages 0–5: (+/−) ns

Study	Sample	Measurement	Outcomes	Analysis	Controls	Results
Kiernan (1996)	NCDS: 3300 men and 3300 women (born in 1958)	Outcomes measured at age 33. Maternal employment is measured when the child was aged 16	In employment; ever-unemployed; owner-occupier; on income support; labor market earnings; net household income; partnership formation and dissolution; teenage motherhood	Bivariate analyses and logistic regressions (reduced-form production functions; no control for endowment heterog.)	Gender-specific regressions. Sample is also stratified by whether the child at age 16 lived with both biological parents or with a lone mother. Other controls are: mother's age and education; child's school performance at age 7, whether the child left school at age 16, and a measure of family's financial circumstances (when child aged 16)	Mother's non-employment: For men: In employment: (−) 1% Ever-unemployed: (+) 10% Owner occupier: (−) 1% On income support: (+) 5% In lowest quartile of earnings: (+) 1% For women: Ever-unemployed: (+) 10% Owner occupier: (−) 1% On income support: (+) 5% In lowest quartile of net household income: (+) 1% Teenage motherhood (+) 1% (only for daughters of lone mothers)
Joshi and Verropoulou (2000)	BCS: approximately 9000 individuals (born in 1970), around 4700 women and 4000 men	Teenage motherhood (only for women) is measured before age 20. Unemployment is measured between school leaving and age 26 and the longest spell must be at least 4 months. Maternal employment is measured when the child was aged under 5	Teenage motherhood; unemployment	OLS (reduced-form production functions no control for endowment heterog.)	Gender-specific regressions. Other controls are: father's social class (at the child's birth), mother's and father's education, child's reading and maths scores at age 10, housing tenure, and free school meals	Mother's employment: Teenage motherhood (women only): (+) ns Unemployment: For women: (−) ns For men: (−) ns

Table 9.3. *(Continued)*

Study	Data source and sample(s)[a]	Timing issues	Outcomes[b]	Estimation method[c]	Comments[b]	Effect of parental employment on children's outcomes[d]
Wolfe, Wilson, and Haveman (2001)	PSID, 873 women aged 0–6 in 1968 and aged 21–27 in 1989; and 720 women aged 8–12 in 1968 and aged 30–34 in 1989	Individuals are followed for 22 years (from 1968 to 1989). Outcomes are measured when individuals were teenagers, and mother's employment is measured when their daughters were aged 6–15	Teenage nonmarital (or out-of-wedlock) birth	Probit models (reduced-form production functions; no control for endowment heterog.)	Other variables: race, mother's education, birth order, average number of siblings (ages 6–15), proportion of years lived with one parent (ages 6–15), average family income-to-needs ratio (ages 6–15), proportion of years in poverty (ages 6–15), proportion of time received AFDC	Mother's employment: (+) ns

Key: [a] PSID = Panel Study of Income Dynamics; NLSY = National Longitudinal Survey of Youth; BHPS = British Household Panel Survey; NCDS = National Child Development Study (1958 British birth cohort); BCS = British Cohort Study (1970 British birth cohort).

[b] AFDC = Aid to Families with Dependent Children.

[c] OLS = ordinary least squares; SML = simulated maximum likelihood; LP = linear probability.

[d] (−), (+) = negative, positive effect; statistical significance level indicated (ns = not significant).

of studies for Britain have used data from the 1958 National Child Development Study (NCDS) and the 1970 British Cohort Study (BCS). Greater data availability (due, for example, to the fact that many outcomes here can be measured just a few years after birth, and therefore even short household panels can be used) and a long-standing psychological literature have led to a vast production of research in this area. Space limitations have urged us to include in our discussion only a small group of studies.[12] Table 9.1 lists such studies.

The lack of consensus that characterized the early cognitive development literature seems to have been replaced by a somewhat more consistent set of results. First, maternal employment in the first year of life has a different effect on later emotional and cognitive outcomes than does maternal employment begun thereafter. In particular, there is some systematic evidence that employment begun in the first year of life may have negative effects for some groups of children (especially 'white' children in the United States), whereas employment after the first year of the child's life appears to have more positive effects (Baum 2003; Han, Waldfogel and Brooks-Gunn 2001; Waldfogel, Han and Brooks-Gunn 2002).[13] Secondly, a non-negligible number of studies finds that the negative effects on cognitive outcomes can be associated with maternal work over the first five years of the child's life and not just with work during the first year only (e.g. Joshi and Verropoulou 2000; Bernal 2002; Liu, Mroz and Van der Klaauw 2002). This suggests that policy concern over the impact of early mother's work on later child outcomes (such as family leave legislation or job flexibility) should perhaps extend to all families with children of pre-school age.

Thirdly, some of the negative effects of either first-year or first-five-years maternal employment seem to persist over time for some groups of children. Thus, early maternal employment is likely to have long-term consequences on children's wellbeing. This holds in studies that include an extensive set of controls, even though they are not easily interpretable because they fail to control for endowment heterogeneity (Han, Waldfogel and Brooks-Gunn 2001; Joshi and Verropoulou 2000). It holds also in studies that estimate structural models (Liu, Mroz and Van der Klaauw 2002). Children's scores in

[12] Some of the early psychological literature has been reviewed elsewhere (e.g. Harvey 1999; Ruhm 2000). Interestingly, there is a remarkable lack of consensus over which maternal employment affects children's achievement (see, among others, Parcel and Menaghan 1994 and Harvey 1999). Even when studies are based on the same data source, estimates range from maternal employment being detrimental (Baydar and Brooks-Gunn 1991; Desai, Chase-Lansdale, and Michael 1989; Belsky and Eggebeen 1991) to its having virtually no effect (Blau and Grossberg 1992) to its being beneficial (Vandell and Ramanan 1992). As noted by Todd and Wolpin (2003), given that these studies use standard regression models, differences in results are likely to be due to sample selection criteria and to the choice of conditioning variables.

[13] This is in line with the earlier evidence presented in Belsky and Eggebeen (1991) and Baydar and Brooks-Gunn (1991). Han, Waldfogel and Brooks-Gunn (2001) argue that these results are not found in Harvey's work (1999) because Harvey did not follow the same children over time and because she pooled Whites, African American and Hispanics together. Notice, however, that also Horwood and Fergusson (1999) find no significant effects of mother's labor supply on academic achievement for a large cohort of children born in New Zealand in 1977.

cognitive and developmental tests (measured in childhood or early adolescence) are considered to be strong predictors of later outcomes by many psychologists (e.g. Harris 1983). In interpreting the evidence on the relationship between family resources (e.g. income) and educational outcomes—such as college enrolment, delay of college entry, final graduation and length of time to complete school (which can be taken as 'later' outcomes)—economists increasingly emphasize the importance of long-run factors associated with greater family resources or higher family income (e.g. Carneiro and Heckman 2002). Parental employment in general (and maternal employment in particular) could be one such factor, to the extent that it is systematically associated with greater family resources. In other words, childhood parental employment can provide one of the links between long-term factors that promote cognitive and non-cognitive ability and child outcomes measured later in life. We will come back to this in the next subsection.

Fourth, among the studies listed in Table 9.1, only two of them report estimates of the relationship between children's early outcomes and father's employment (i.e. Harvey 1999; Ruhm 2000). In both studies, father's work choices do not appear to have any significant effect.

9.3.2 *Educational attainment*

Table 9.2 summarizes the primary micro-data analyses of the effect of parental employment on children's educational achievements. Most of these studies are implicitly based on a production–function framework, in which parental employment is seen as one of the inputs into the production of children's human capital. As explained in Section 9.2, this interpretation is problematic and is made even more difficult for models that include family income in the set of explanatory variables without controlling for endowment heterogeneity (Hill and Duncan 1987; Haveman, Wolfe and Spaulding 1991; Kiernan 1996).

For a sample of youths from the Panel Study of Income Dynamics (PSID), the early study by Hill and Duncan (1987) shows that, while years of schooling and maternal hours of work are not correlated for girls, boys' schooling decreases with mother's employment. Later research, which again uses American data from the same source (Haveman, Wolfe and Spaulding, 1991) or from the Current Population Survey (CPS) (Graham, Beller and Hernandez 1994) actually found opposite results: that is, mother's employment is positively (and significantly) related to her children's educational achievements. From this evidence it is difficult to draw any general conclusion.[14] But by focusing our attention on the results of studies that use data from other countries, we may

---

[14] In a more recent study Duncan, Teachman and Yeung (1997) use sibling models and find that the number of years in which mothers worked more than 1000 annual hours when their children were aged 0–5 reduce a child's schooling at age 20, while the number of years in which mothers worked more than 1000 annual hours when their children were aged 6–10 or 11–15 increase a child's schooling. None of these effects is, however, statistically significant at conventional levels.

find evidence that more consistently points either to positive or negative or no effects. This is true in part for Britain.[15] Using data from the 1958 NCDS, Kiernan (1996) finds that daughters of working lone mothers are less likely to have attained no qualifications (at age 33) than their contemporaries in the reference group of intact families with a working mother. In this study, therefore, it is both the structure of the family of origin (living with a lone mother) and the employment patterns of mothers that are consequential to daughters' schooling (see also subsection 9.4.4). However, for children of working mothers in general (and, particularly, those in intact families) and for boys, Kiernan does not report any significantly greater or smaller educational achievement with respect to children of non-working mothers. Using data from the more recent 1970 BCS, the study by Joshi and Verropoulou (2000) shows instead that there is a negative and significant association between mothers' early employment and their offspring's later achievements, although this is not very large (see also subsection 9.4.3).[16]

These results are confirmed by the more recent study by Ermisch and Francesconi (2002), which, unlike the earlier studies, uses a conditional demand function approach and applies sibling difference (or mother fixed effects) models (see S. 9.2). Ermisch and Francesconi show that it is possible to give a causal interpretation to the associations between parental employment when the child was very young (say he/she was a pre-schooler), and educational attainments of children as young adults: such associations are in fact parameters of a conditional demand function.[17] They find a negative and significant effect on the child's educational attainment as a young adult of the number of months his/her mother was in full-time employment when the child was aged 0–5. The effect of mother's months in part-time employment during these ages is also negative, but smaller, and less well determined. In the context

[15] The study by Horwood and Fergusson (1999) for New Zealand, however, points towards evidence of no effects. In particular, it reports no significant impact of mother's work on tests measuring scholastic ability at age 13 as well as on school certificate attainments that are a prerequisite to university entry (and are measured at age 16).

[16] In the East London study by O'Brien and Jones (1999), teenagers, interviewed a day or two before sitting their GCSE exams, show the best chances of getting high results in these exams if they come from families where the mother has a part-time job (and not a full-time job). According to the children also, the time they spend with their mother was greatest where she works part-time, and about the same in the sole or dual full-time earner couples.

[17] As discussed in Section 2, estimation is complicated by heterogeneity in preferences, productivity in human capital investment and children's endowments relevant to educational attainment, and by the fact that parents may compensate or reinforce children's endowments. While a sibling difference estimation strategy may eliminate heterogeneity that is common across siblings, it is generally not sufficient to identify the 'effect' of parents' employment. That rests on the assumption that the idiosyncratic endowments of children are not revealed to parents until after the youngest child is sufficiently old (e.g. he/she has completed his/her pre-school years). Estimation based on comparisons between families must also make this assumption, but additional stronger assumptions are required (e.g. no correlation in endowments across generations or no effect of parents' endowments on their employment).

of a conditional demand–function framework, these results suggest that a higher full family income increases the educational attainment of children, and given full family income, a mother's higher wage reduces her children's educational attainment.

Only two studies report estimates for father's employment (O'Brien and Jones 1999; and Ermisch and Francesconi 2002). In both, the effect on children's educational attainment is small and not statistically significant. But while the first study finds some positive impact, the second shows a reduction in the probability of achieving higher educational qualifications as father's years of paid work increase.

From the body of evidence shown in Table 9.2 and discussed here, it is hard to come up with a clear cut view of the effect of parental work on children's educational outcomes. Some of the studies, particularly early studies that use American data, find a negative and significant effect of mother's work, others find either no significant effect or a positive impact. But more recent research, which has focused on the experience of other countries (particularly in Britain), seems to point to a more consistent finding, namely that longer mothers' employment is typically associated with reduced educational achievements of children. This finding emerges quite clearly within the conditional demand–function framework developed in Ermisch and Francesconi (2002), but it also holds, at least partially, in other reduced form analyses of large scale British data.

9.3.3 Other outcomes

A huge number of other outcomes could be affected by childhood parental patterns. The range (and extent within each) of such outcomes would vary depending on the interest of the survey. Here we are primarily concerned with providing an overview of only a few recent studies but focusing on several outcomes. These are reported in Table 9.3. For a review of results from earlier (exclusively American) studies see Haveman and Wolfe (1995).

All the studies listed in Table 9.3 are (implicitly) based on a production–function approach with the exception of the study by Ermisch and Francesconi (2001c), which, again, draws its interpretation and specifications from a conditional demand–function framework. In addition, except for Ermisch and Francesconi (2001c), the other studies fail to control for endowment heterogeneity, which, as argued in Section 2.2, have less desirable properties since the effect of parental work on children's outcomes is likely to be a biased estimate of the true technical relationship embodied in the (health or wellbeing) production functions.

In the case of teenage (or early) childbearing, Kiernan (1996) finds that mother's employment (or non-employment) does not affect their daughters' chances of having a teen birth. But daughters from 'lone-mother' families, where the mother is not in employment, have odds of becoming teenage mothers that are significantly higher than the reference group of women from intact families with a working mother. Conversely, both Joshi and Verropoulou (2000) and Wolfe, Wilson and Haveman (2001) find that mothers' employment increases the risk of an early birth for their daughters, but in both studies the effect is not significant. Interestingly, the mother's employment is measured over the first five years of the child's life in the former study, and over the ages 6–15 in the latter. By considering instead the employment patterns of parents over the entire child's childhood, Ermisch and Francesconi (2001c) obtain different results. They find that mothers' full-time employment, when their daughters were aged 6–10, significantly increased their daughters' risk of an early birth. But this is virtually offset by the lower risk of childbearing if mothers are in full-time paid work when their daughters are adolescents (aged 11–15). On the other hand, a mother's part-time employment in the first 10 years of the child's life does not affect the chances of an early birth, and actually it decreases them if mothers are part-timers when their daughters are aged 11–15.

The results on economic inactivity (or unemployment) are overall more coherent. Kiernan (1996) finds that British women and men are more likely to have experienced unemployment since they left school (and up to age 33) if their mothers were not working in their childhood (at age 16). This is in line with the results reported in Ermisch and Francesconi (2001c), whereby mother's full-time employment when the child was aged 11–15 is correlated to a lower risk of economic inactivity measured when the child is 16 or older. Similarly, mother's part-time work when the child was aged 6–10 has a negative impact of the risk of inactivity later in life. The estimates in Joshi and Verropoulou (2000) are in the same direction (for both men and women) but are not statistically significant.

Table 9.3 shows several other outcomes that cannot be fully assessed as they are measured in one study at most and, thus, comparisons cannot be drawn. They are however interesting to illustrate. For Britain, Kiernan (1996) correlates mother's non-employment (when the child was aged 16) with a number of socio-economic outcomes observed when the child was aged 33, namely: whether the young adult is on income support (the most important government programe for non-working low-income individuals), whether the child is an owner-occupier, and whether he/she is in the lowest quartile of the earnings or the net household income distributions. She finds that the non-working mother situation is typically associated with worse outcomes for both men and women: that is, higher chances of being on income support and being at the bottom of the income or earnings distributions, and lower chances of owning the house they occupy. Also for Britain, but on a different outcome, Ermisch and Francesconi (2001c) observe that young adults' chances of psychological distress are lowered by mother's part-time employment when the child was aged 0–5, or by mother's full-time employment when the child was aged 6–10 (but they seem to be heightened if the mother worked full-time when her child was aged 11–15). Finally, for a large sample of 15-year-old Americans, Antecol and Bedard (2002) find that mothers' work is positively related to the probability that young people are more likely to drink regularly, but is uncorrelated to smoking, using marijuana and being convicted of a crime before age 15.

There is comparatively less evidence on the effects that fathers' employment has on all these outcomes, as it has also been the case for the outcomes discussed in the previous two subsections. Ermisch and Francesconi (2001c) find that a greater employment activity of fathers when their children were aged 0–5 leads generally to better outcomes, in terms of lower probabilities of unemployment and psychological distress. None of the other studies in Table 9.3 contains results on fathers' work.

9.3.4 *Summary of results and discussion*

Our review so far has yielded a number of interesting findings. Clearly, because of sample selection criteria (or data constrains), choice of conditioning variables and model specifications, they vary quite considerably and they are not always consistent. Here we summarize the most salient and robust results, although in this operation we will not do justice to their subtleties and to the specific nuances of the studies that produced them. We will however emphasize some of the plausible interpretations of these results, and their interplay with potential public policy initiatives. We will also discuss the credibility of such interpretations in terms of the adequacy of the econometric modeling and in terms of their clear links to theory. To help this discussion, we report some of the key estimates in Table 9.4. The table lists only a few studies across (cognitive and educational) outcomes and econometric methods, and reports statistically significant quantitative effects of mothers' work on each of the outcomes.[18]

A.   *Does mothers' employment affect children's well-being? And are the effects between part-time work and full-time work different?*
Table 9.4 shows that there are some adverse effects of a mother's employment on cognitive outcomes. It appears that the most detrimental impact is produced by maternal employment in the first year of the child's life. Waldfogel, Han and Brooks-Gunn (2002) find that maternal employment in the first year decreases the receptive vocabulary of 3–4-year-olds by more than 3 points, the reading/verbal achievements of 5–8-year-olds by about 2 points, and the mathematics achievements of 5–8-year-olds by another 2–3 points. These findings are for non-Hispanic white children, who instead seem to gain some positive effects from second- and third-year maternal employment. Other ethnic groups (and

---

[18] Other outcomes are not reported due to their large response heterogeneity and due to space limitations.

Table 9.4. *Significant effects of parental employment on children's cognitive and educational outcomes—selected studies*

Study, type of outcome, and timing of the employment measure	Mean outcome	Effect of		
		Mother's employment	Mother's part-time employment	Mother's full-time employment
Waldfogel, Han and Brooks-Gunn (2002)				
First year of child's life				
Whites				
PPVT-R (ages 3–4)[a]	86.7	−3.23 (1.18)		−4.13 (1.22)
PIAT-M (ages 5–6)[a]	99.4	−1.96 (0.98)		−2.97 (1.02)
PIAT-R (ages 5–6)[a]	106.3	−2.28 (0.99)		−2.82 (1.01)
PIAT-M (ages 7–8)[a]	100.6	−2.88 (0.88)	−2.92 (1.22)	−2.85 (0.88)
PIAT-R (ages 7–8)[a]	104.1	−2.31 (0.99)		−2.53 (1.02)
Second and third year of child's life				
Whites				
PIAT-R (ages 7–8)[a]	104.1	2.41 (1.16)		
Blacks				
PIAT-R (ages 7–8)[a]	104.1	3.80 (1.54)		
Hispanics				
PIAT-R (ages 5–6)[a]	106.3	−3.44 (1.56)		
PIAT-M (ages 7–8)[a]	100.6	−3.68 (1.56)		
Third and fourth year of child's life				
Whites				
PIAT-M (ages 7–8)[a]	100.6	3.32 (1.30)		
Currently working Whites				
PIAT-M (ages 5–6)[a]	99.4	−2.32 (1.08)		
PIAT-R (ages 5–6)[a]	106.3	−2.12 (1.05)		
Hispanics				
PIAT-M (ages 5–6)[a]	99.4	3.59 (1.65)		

Table 9.4. (*Continued*)

Study, type of outcome, and timing of the employment measure	Mean outcome	Effect of		
		Mother's employment	Mother's part-time employment	Mother's full-time employment
Ruhm (2000)				
First year of child's life				
PPVT (ages 3–4)[b]	0.00	−0.065 (0.027)		
PIAT-M (ages 5–6)[b]	0.00		−0.072[c] (0.037)	
Second and third year of child's life				
PPVT (ages 3–4)[b]	0.00		0.081[c] (0.036)	
PIAT-R (ages 5–6)[b]	0.00	−0.081 (0.029)		−0.091[c] (0.042)
PIAT-M (ages 5–6)[b]	0.00	−0.059 (0.030)		−0.109[c] (0.043)
Joshi and Verropoulou (2000)				
Any employment (ages 0–5)				
Highest academic qualifications (men)[e]	2.5	−0.12 (0.047)		
Highest academic qualification (women)[e]	2.5	−0.10 (0.039)		
Ermisch and Francesconi (2002)				
Years of employment (ages 0–5)				
Achieved A level or more (ages 18 or more)[f]	0.641		−0.039 (0.022)	−0.071 (0.028)

Notes: Standard errors are in parentheses.

[a]These outcomes are measured in raw scores. The corresponding effects of mother's employment (again measured in scores) and deviations (− = negative; + = positive) from the means.

[b]These outcomes are measured in standardized scores normalized to have a mean of zero and a standard deviation of one, that is, they are transformations, on an age-specific basis, of the raw scores (that were originally designed to have a normal distribution with a mean of 100 and a standard deviation of 15). The corresponding effects of mother's employment are changes measured in terms of a standard deviation rise (+) or decline (−).

[c]These estimates compare the effect of part-time work versus no work.

[d]These estimates compare the effect of full-time work versus part-time work.

[e]These outcomes are measured on a 6-point scale where 0 = no qualification and 5 = degree. The corresponding effects of mother's employment are deviations (− = negative; + = positive) from the means.

[f]These outcomes are measured in probability terms (computed at sample values). The corresponding effects of an extra year of mother's employment are marginal effects indicating the deviations (− = negative; + = positive) from the mean outcome.

especially African-American children) seem to experience no negative effect of first-year employment, but Hispanic children tend to show 3.5-point lower scores (in reading and math) if their mothers work when they are aged 2 or 3.

Some of these findings also emerge in the study by Ruhm (2000). For example, in this study a 20-hour per week increase in mother's employment throughout the first year of the child's life is correlated with a 0.7 standard deviation decline in verbal ability at ages 3 and 4. For this outcome, there is also a partially offsetting benefit for working during the next two years. But unlike the previous study, Ruhm's estimates show some negative effects of second- and third-year mother's employment: the math and reading performances of 5–6-year-olds are reduced by 0.06 and 0.08 standard deviations, respectively. Both studies, however, point to full-time work as having larger costs (or lower benefits). Waldfogel and colleagues find that children of mothers who work for more than 20 hours a week in their first year experience an additional reduction in test scores from about 10 per cent (in the case of PIAT-R, ages 7–8) to 50 per cent (in the case of PIAT-M, ages 5–6). Ruhm finds that the contrast between part-time and full-time work is sharper in the second and third years, where part-time work is correlated (albeit insignificantly) with improvements in all cognitive outcomes but switching from part-time to full-time employment reduced the reading and math scores by 0.09 and 0.11 standard deviations, respectively.

One important difference between these two studies is in terms of the magnitude of the effects. Waldfogel, Han and Brooks-Gunn argue that their effects are fairly small, although they express concern for the fact that such effects persist to ages 7 and 8. Ruhm, on the other hand, claims that the effects he finds are substantial and equivalent to those predicted by a 2- or 3-year decrease in maternal education. However, what matters is perhaps not just the effects on these early outcomes per se, but also the consequences on later outcomes. Using data from the British NCDS on test scores measured at age 7 and outcomes at age 33, Currie and Thomas (2001) provide evidence that early reading and math test performance is strongly related to future educational outcomes, which, in turn, strongly affect later labor market outcomes (e.g. employment and wages). These results therefore indicate that such effects may indeed translate into persistent economic costs.

Another way of assessing the longer-term consequences of a mothers' employment is given by the other two studies reported in Table 4. They both refer to the British experience. Joshi and Verropoulou (2000) find that young women attain 10 per cent less of a grade if their mothers had been employed before they were 5, and young men 12 per cent of a grade less. In other words, young people are on average about one-tenth less likely to advance one rung of the qualification ladder, such as the step between GCSE and A-level, or A-level and a non-degree higher education. These estimates are unarguably small. But one problem with these results is that the difference between, say, no quali- fication and some qualification is the same as that between higher vocational degrees and university degrees, while instead there may be heterogeneous responses at different points of the educational distribution. Another problem is that they do not control for any type of unobserved factor, either at the individual or at the family level. In any case, these results are confirmed in the second British study. For children with mothers working full-time an additional year when they were aged 0–5, Ermisch and Francesconi (2002) find that the probability of achieving A-level or more is reduced by 7 percentage points (from 64 to 57 per cent).[19] An additional year of part-time employment (again when the child was aged 0–5) also leads to a reduction in the probability of educational achievement by about 4 percentage points, but this effect is significant only at the 10 per cent level. To the extent that education and later socio-economic success are correlated, these effects have important long-lasting consequences.

B. Do we know why?

Having established the set of results just outlined is only part of the job. Perhaps, the most important part is to uncover the mechanisms that explain them. What are the forces behind such results? To address this question, we will draw our arguments from the discussion in Section 9.2.2. There we have emphasized the problems of estimating and interpreting cognitive and human–capital–production–functions. The estimation is complicated by the endogeneity of several potential inputs as well as the unobservability of others. The interpretation of the parental employment parameters is instead problematic because parents' employment may not be seen as a specific input that parents use to invest in their children's human capital. Most of the studies reviewed so far are, however, based (implicitly or explicitly) on a production–function framework, and many of such studies do not incorporate endowment heterogeneity in their estimation. So these results and their interpretations warrant some caution.

Most of the developmental studies in Table 9.1 (p. 164) (including those reported in Table 9.4) are based on the observation that early years, and especially the first year, of a child's life are crucial to development, because it is in this period that an infant develops a sophisticated cognitive conception of objects and people (Harris 1983).[20] Given this observation, there are two main explanations why maternal (but not paternal) employment is potentially detrimental to children (see also Baum 2003). First, such employment decreases the quantity of time that mothers spend with their children. Spending less time in maternal care is detrimental if non-maternal childcare arrangements are of inferior quality. The few studies that have been able to control for childcare quality when examining mother's work effects find that it does play an

[19] For non-British readers, 'A (Advanced)-level' corresponds to education beyond high school, but short of a university degree.

[20] Attachment theory, which posits that children whose mothers are absent during critical periods of early child development are less likely to form secure attachments with their mothers (Bowlby 1969) has been very influential for many psychology and sociology contributions in this area.

important role (NICHD Early Child Care Research Network 1997) as does the type of care (Han, Waldfogel and Brooks-Gunn 2001). In addition, high-quality care, if available to low-income children, seems to make a greater difference in their development than it does to children in high-income families (Desai, Chase-Lansdale and Michael 1989; Vandell and Ramanan 1992). Secondly, marketplace work may decrease the quality of maternal time spent with children if working mothers are subject to emotional distress, overload or exhaustion, and consequently may be more contentious in the home. In sum, one set of explanations of why we observe the negative effect of mothers' employment on children's outcomes operates through the lower-quality of non-maternal childcare, which to some extent is correlated to lower family income, and the higher level of distress experienced by working mothers. But both such aspects are difficult to measure in any large-scale representative survey. More importantly, there is a substantial degree of disagreement on their genuine impact. For example, Parcel and Menaghan (1994) argue that non-working mothers are more likely to be depressed and to withdraw from their children. Similarly, Moore and Driscoll (1997) observe that maternal employment may have positive side effects on mothers by actually reducing their depression.

An alternative explanation is offered in the study by Ermisch and Francesconi (2002). This study offers a direct interpretation of the effect of mothers' (or fathers') employment as a parameter of a conditional demand function. Very simply, they show that higher mothers' employment produces a positive income effect and a negative substitution effect on time allocated to each child. The sign of the effects is, therefore, ambiguous a priori, and must be established empirically. In societies where (or times when) the income effect dominates—because, let us say, higher incomes can afford greater leisure and maternal childcare time—then we expect to observe a positive association between mother's work and child outcomes. In societies where the substitution effect is greater instead, we expect a negative association. So, in the case of a negative effect (which is the result obtained by Ermisch and Francesconi, and shown in Table 9.4), the conditional demand framework provides a straightforward interpretation. A higher full family income when maternal employment was measured (in the case of the Ermisch–Francesconi study, this is when the child was aged 0–5) increases children's human capital, because this increases parents' time allocated to human capital investment in children. Thus, the effect of poverty on a child's education partly works through lower parents' time inputs. For a given full family income, higher mother's earnings in the first five years of life of her child reduce the child's educational achievements, because more time is allocated to the labor market.

Ermisch and Francesconi (2001c and 2002) point out that the relationship between any child outcome and mother's time depends, in general, on all preference and production parameters. For econometric purposes, between-family variation in mother's employment time is not likely to be exogenous because of variation in preferences, production functions and parental endowments across families. So, any estimation based on comparisons (between families (which has been used in most of the studies listed in Tables 1–3) will lead to biased estimates of the effect of mothers' (or fathers') employment on their children's outcomes. This suggests that comparisons within households (i.e. sibling-difference or mother fixed effects estimators) may instead be used. But even these are generally not sufficient to identify the 'effect' of parents' employment. It can be shown, in fact, that these differences between siblings in mother's employment are not likely to be independent of the differences in child endowments when parents know their children's endowments and respond to them. The identification of the effect must rest on assumptions, most of which are related to the process that reveals information about child endowments to the parents.

These difficulties are likely to open up new directions of research. Especially promising seems to be that offered by structural models. Early examples in this area are the studies by Bernal (2002) and Liu, Mroz and Van der Klaauw (2002). Although computationally demanding, such models have the advantage of a clear interpretation (as they are based on theory), and allow for powerful predictions of parents' and children's behavior given any change in the state of the world through a change in their constraints, even changes along dimensions that are invariant in the data. Other research directions are possible and should be encouraged. In particular, new and relevant evidence is likely to emerge from studies that stress the availability of more detailed parental data over the child's childhood as well as from studies that emphasize the use of experimental data (e.g. Grogger, Karoly and Klerman 2002).

C.   *Is there any effect of father's employment?*
There are comparatively fewer studies that measure the impact of fathers' work on children's outcomes (Harvey 1999; O'Brien and Jones 1999; Ruhm 2000; Ermisch and Francesconi 2002). Generalizations are therefore hard to infer. In any case, regardless of estimating method and model specification, all these studies show very small point estimates, with generally large standard errors around them. One way of reading this result is that paternal employment is inconsequential to children's wellbeing. But this may be an oversimplification. An alternative view starts with noticing that most fathers (at least in the studies reviewed here) were employed full-time for most of the time during their children's childhood.[21] The lack of any substantial variation in working patterns across families and over time makes it very unlikely that any difference in children's outcomes would be associated with father's employment in a way that is statistically significant. Moreover, there is the usual problem with a production–function interpretation, if what is included in the analysis is father's time spent in employment without any control for time and resources

---

[21] This is not surprising given that the majority of studies refers to the experiences in the United States and Britain from the 1960s onward.

directly devoted to his children. Fathers who spent an identical amount of time in paid work might have devoted substantially different amounts of time (and resources) to their children and to activities that could be relevant to their development and future achievements.

The fact that child outcomes are possibly invariant to paternal employment patterns does not mean that fathers have no role in shaping their children's welfare. Perspectives in economics (Becker 1991, see in Becker 1981), sociology (Coleman 1988) and psychology (McLoyd 1989) all acknowledge that fathers' economic contributions represent a key resource for children's development. Fathers' financial contributions provide wholesome food, adequate shelter in safe neighbourhoods, commodities (such as books, computers and private lessons) that facilitate children's academic success, and support for college attendance. Besides this role, a substantial body of research shows that positive father involvement and strong emotional ties between fathers and children contribute to children's development, wellbeing and attainment (for a review, see Lamb 1997). In the case of non-resident fathers in single-mother families, Amato and Gilbreth (1999) find that payment of child support, feelings of closeness and authoritative parenting are positively associated with a number of measures of children's welfare. Although fathers can provide services to their children (e.g. care and support), it is not clear how such a provision operates as a substitute for, or complement to, mothers' provisions. Clearly more research on these and related issues is needed. Quite critical to this research will be the availability of better data on fathers' and stepfathers' time, especially on the time spent with their children.

9.4 THE IMPORTANCE OF OTHER FAMILY PROCESSES AND DECISIONS DURING CHILDHOOD

Parental employment during childhood is just one of the many factors that have a potential bearing on children's cognitive development and success in later years. It may even be a relatively minor one, when viewed as part of a constellation of other factors, which cannot be 'controlled' by parents (such as their genetic endowments), and other parental 'characteristics and decisions', including parents' personality and emotional stability, parenting practices and the quality of homecare that children receive from their parents. In this context, social scientists have concentrated on a subset of parental characteristics and decisions during the childhood of their children or beyond. In many instances, they have done so without considering childhood patterns of parental work. Here we only focus on a few of these characteristics (regardless of whether the studies have conditioned on parental employment), and only over the child's childhood.[22]

---

[22] In particular, we will not consider *inter-vivos* financial and non-financial transfers and bequests.

9.4.1   Family income[23]

In Section 9.2.2, we pointed out the problem of using family income, together with parental employment, in estimating child outcomes. To reiterate on the same point, it is hard to interpret the 'effect' of the mothers' (or fathers') labor supply on any child outcome keeping everything else (including family income) constant. This is the interpretation we would give to the results obtained from a regression of child outcomes on child and parental characteristics. It is however difficult to imagine a situation in which the mother changes her labor market behavior but family income remains unchanged. In any case, there is a substantial literature (particularly in economics) that evaluates the effects of income on several child outcomes (e.g. Hill and Duncan 1987, and references therein). This research has generally predated the literature concerned with the effects of parental employment and, in many instances, has not controlled for observed differences in parental employment. Quite convincingly, this research establishes that parental income is positively associated with a wide range of children's outcomes, such as cognitive test scores, socio-emotional wellbeing, mental health, behavioral problems, teenage childbearing, educational outcomes and economic status in early adulthood (see Mayer 2002, for a review of this literature). There are however two important issues of contention. The first is on the magnitude of the impact. The second is on its interpretation.

The first issue is itself related to: (a) the income variable used in the analysis (e.g. current income versus permanent income), and (b) when, in the child's life, income is measured (i.e. during early childhood, middle childhood, or adolescence). In their comprehensive survey, Duncan and Brooks-Gunn (1997a) find that having higher income during early and middle childhood has large positive effects on a number of measures of ability and achievement observed when children are aged between 2 and 8 years and also on earnings and hours worked observed when children are aged between 25 and 35.[24] On the other hand, Hill and O'Neill (1994), Blau (1999) and Mayer (2002), among others, for the United States and Lefebvre and Merrigan (1998) for Canada stress that most of these income effects are small in absolute terms and small relative to the effects of other factors associated with differences in child outcomes, such as ethnicity and parental education. There is however more agreement in suggesting that permanent income is more important to children's outcomes than short-term income. In particular, studies that measure parental income averaged over ten or more years, produce estimates that are two to five times larger than estimates generated from studies that measure income in only one year (Mayer 2002). Furthermore, while Duncan and Brooks-Gunn (1997a)

---

[23] Throughout this subsection (and later) we use the terms family income, parental income, and household income interchangeably to mean the total income of the household where the child (for who the outcomes are measured) lives.

[24] The effects of family income on children's behavior and physical and mental health seem to be smaller and not statistically significant.

document that family economic conditions in early and middle childhood are far more important for shaping children's outcomes than they do during adolescence, other researchers such as Mayer (2002) state that the robustness of these findings has yet to be established.

The issue of interpretation is instead related to the question of whether we estimate the causal effect of parental income on children's outcomes. Sometimes when analysts talk about the effect of family income, they mean the effect of family income and all its correlates. Others mean the effect of income per se.[25] Reviewing the techniques that have been used to address this issue is not the scope of our study.[26] Mayer (2002) notes that most of these techniques rely in one way or another on changes in parental income. Examples of such changes are given by comparisons of outcomes for siblings when their parents' income differed ('sibling fixed effects' models), or by exploiting the fact that the same individual is observed more than once ('child fixed effects' models), or by comparing outcomes for children of sisters ('grandparent fixed-effects' models). One criticism of these various forms of fixed effects models is that they can lead to income effect estimates that are biased downward. Indeed Blau (1999) reports very small (and even negative) child fixed effects estimates of family income on cognitive test scores for children of mothers drawn from the National Longitudinal Survey of Youth.[27] Blau's grandparent fixed effects estimates are smaller than the estimates obtained from a model with a standard set of controls (e.g. mother's education, child's age, gender and survey year) but do not differ from those obtained when a measure of mother's ability is included in the regressions.

Some of this discussion reiterates the point made earlier on the importance of long-run family effects in shaping children's outcomes. In line with this argument, Cameron and Heckman (2001) and Carneiro and Heckman (2002) find that college enrolment in the United States is strongly and positively affected by a permanent income measure of family income over the first eighteen years of the life of a child. Whereas family income observed in late adolescence turns out to have no additional effect on college enrolment. Consistent with the argument based on long-run family factors are the results presented in Case, Lubotsky and Paxson (2002), according to which, American parents' long-run average income is positively related to their children's health. They show that this parental income–child health relationship partly reflects higher-income parents' ability to manage chronic conditions (e.g. asthma, bronchitis, hearing problems, heart conditions, epilepsy and mental retardation), and that poorer

---

[25] This distinction is important especially for its implications in terms of public policy. Increasing the income of low-income families is relatively simple. Finding policies that change the correlates of income is likely to be more difficult.

[26] The interested reader could find some relevant material on this topic in Duncan and Brooks-Gunn (1997a) and in Mayer (2002).

[27] Blau's (1999) estimates from the child fixed-effects models are based on annual not permanent income, which partly accounts for the fact that they are quantitatively very small.

children are not more likely to have a particular chronic condition but are simply more likely to be in poor health if they have it. While more research is needed to unravel the mechanisms behind the income–health gradient, Case, Lubotsky and Paxson (2002) rule out several possible ones. They find that health insurance does not play a crucial role in protecting health upon the arrival of a chronic condition, not is health during childhood a systematic reflection of health at birth, nor can a simple genetic model explain the gradient.

9.4.2   *Parental joblessness and financial difficulty*

Closely related to income are other measures of family socio-economic status, such as parental joblessness and financial difficulty of the family of origin. Although Mayer (2002) argues that the effect of financial difficulties or economic strain (and presumably parental joblessness) cannot be easily interpreted in the context of the effect of family income on children's wellbeing, in any case such measures are quite informative of the household environment in which children grow up. It is probably not true that all low-income children experience financial difficulties (measured for example by whether children receive free school meals), because for example they and their families adjust to the low incomes and report no economic strain. Similarly, some families experiencing (and reporting) financial difficulties may still continue to have middle-class incomes (because, perhaps, one of the parents becomes ill or unemployed, while the other continues to earn). Yet these alternative measures of economic status may be relevant to understand the impact of family characteristics and decisions on their offspring's welfare as they capture facets of the life children experience that are not captured by family income. In addition they are also intimately linked to the parents' working patterns.

Gregg and Machin (1999) analyse longitudinal data from the 1958 NCDS cohort to examine models of relative success or failure in the early years of adulthood. They find that growing up in a family in financial distress matters, and it matters more than lone parenthood, for a large set of outcomes. In particular, it increases the likelihood of juvenile delinquency by age 16, and decreases the chances of staying on at school after the minimum school leaving age, achieving higher levels of education, being employed and receiving higher wages later in life. Similar conclusions are reached in McCulloch and Joshi (2002), who study a sample of young children whose mothers were part of the original NCDS. In analysing a different outcome, namely the Peabody Picture Vocabulary Test (PPVT), which is an indicator of a child's cognitive functioning, they conclude that current income is not a complete yardstick for children at risk of impaired development. In particular, their indicators of more long-term deprivation (such as lack of car access and social housing) suggest that a more sustained experience of poverty is more damaging. Also Ermisch, Francesconi and Pevalin (2003) find that childhood parental joblessness plays a key part in shaping people's outcomes in their early adulthood (e.g. unemployment, smoking and early childbearing). Their results, however, indicate that lone parenthood in general has a greater impact on people's lives.

9.4.3 *Parental education*

A vast empirical literature in economics, sociology and developmental psychology has focused on the effect of parents' (particularly mothers') education on children's outcomes (e.g. Duncan, Brooks-Gunn and Klebanov 1994; McLanahan and Sandefur 1994; Haveman and Wolfe 1995; Duncan and Brooks-Gunn 1997b). In US and UK studies, parental education has been consistently found to be a strong predictor of children's wellbeing, from test scores and psychological adjustments at early ages through highest schooling attainment and early labor market outcomes in young adulthood (e.g. Duncan and Brooks-Gunn 1997a; Dearden, Machin and Reed 1997; Ermisch and Francesconi 2001a).[28] This seems to be true also for a variety of countries across the world (Behrman 1997). In addition, Ermisch and Francesconi (2002) find that the adverse effect of mothers' full-time employment on children's educational attainment is substantially smaller for more-educated mothers. So a widely held wisdom is that a key return to investments in women's education is manifested in increased schooling (and, generally, greater wellbeing) of the next generation.

One recent study has questioned the validity of this wisdom. Behrman and Rosenzweig (2002) point out that the positive relationship between the schooling of mothers and the schooling of their children may be biased because it reflects both the correlation between education and inherited 'ability' and the correlation between education and 'assortative mating' among mothers. To account for such correlations, they exploit the differences in mother's schooling using a sample of mothers who are identical twins as well as the differences in father's schooling in a sample of fathers who are identical twins. They find that increasing men's education would increase the educational level of the next generation by a small amount, net and gross of assortative mating. But, surprisingly, raising the schooling attainment of women seems to have no (or even negative) impact on children's schooling. They argue that this pattern of results is consistent with the hypothesis that women's time in the home is a critical factor in childrearing and children's human capital formation. In a previous study, the same authors and other colleagues found, however, strong evidence that increased women's schooling leads to greater educational achievements of their children in rural India (Behrman *et al.* 1999). These conflicting results emphasize the importance of the labor-market contexts and cultures within

---

[28] Haveman and Wolfe (1995) outline how economists have traditionally viewed the impact of parents' education on children's attainment within theories of family behavior. (See Becker (1981/ extended in 1991)).

which such relationships are estimated, and stress the need for further research even on a topic that, until recently, seemed to be quite uncontroversial.

9.4.4 *Lone parenthood*

Another important determinant of child outcomes is the type of family in which children grow up, in particular, whether both parents live in the household with the child. In many countries the proportion of children growing up with both biological parents has declined dramatically over time. Bumpass, Raley and Sweet (1995) estimate that over half of all American children born in the early 1980s will have lived apart from at least one of their parents before reaching age 18. Ermisch and Francesconi (2000) find that that proportion is not less than 40 per cent for British children born in the 1990s. The dissolution of parents' marriages and cohabiting unions, and the ensuing period of lone parenthood that this entails affect children's life chances to the extent that expenditures on children are smaller after the dissolution.

The increase in family instability and lone parenthood has stimulated considerable concern among policy makers and the public more generally. It has stimulated also a huge research interest among social analysts who have tried to measure its impact on child outcomes. Early surveys of the relevant literatures, which mainly used data from the United States, have found that growing up in a non-intact family had negative consequences for children's wellbeing across a broad range of outcomes, including educational attainment and teenage childbearing (McLanahan and Sandefur 1994; Haveman and Wolfe 1995; McLanahan 1997). Not all types of non-intact families have however similar consequences, in the sense that living in some types of non-intact families is more difficult for children than living in others. Although this conclusion must be tentative, there is some evidence that growing up with a divorced or never-married mother is associated with lower educational attainment and more behavioral and psychological problems, while growing up with a widowed parent is also never associated with poorer outcomes for children (McLanahan 1997).[29] Similarly, a number of studies demonstrate that remarriage is not a panacea for divorce or non-marital childbearing (see many of the studies reported in Duncan and Brooks-Gunn 1997b). Nor is life in multi-generational households with grandparents (McLanahan and Sandefur 1994; Chase-Lansdale, Brooks-Gunn and Zamsky 1994), although grandmothers may be in a position to reinforce the mother's authority and are likely to feel committed to their grandchildren (Cherlin and Furstenberg 1986), and can

---

[29] Analysing administrative Canadian data, Corak (2001) finds that the main consequences of parental divorce are reflected on children's marital behavior. But the consequences on labor market outcomes (earnings and incomes) are relatively modest and statistically insignificant. In line with these results, Lang and Zagorsky (2001) and Biblarz and Gottainer (2000) also find that parent absence due to death has less of an impact on children's outcomes than parent absence due to divorce.

thus provide a set of resources to mitigate—but not substitute for—the absence of the natural father (Deleire and Kalil 2002).

Current research is also inconclusive on whether family structure is more important than family income (or parental work and education) in determining children's eventual success. Although family structure is related to poverty (and financial difficulties), the two are not proxies for one another. Based on evidence presented in Haveman and Wolfe (1995) and in McLanahan (1997), family structure seems to be more important than poverty in affecting behavioral and psychological problems, whereas poverty appears to be more important than family structure in determining educational attainment.

Some of these findings are confirmed by more recent research. For example, Ermisch and Francesconi (2001b) and Ermisch, Francesconi and Pevalin (2003) use a 'sibling-difference' model to analyse British household panel data. They find that young adults who experienced single parenthood as children have significantly lower educational attainments. As opposed to the earlier American studies, family structure seems to be as important as (and possibly even more important than) poverty in affecting this outcome. Family structure is also found to be associated with a number of other disadvantageous outcomes for young adults, including a higher risk of unemployment, a higher risk of having a child before a woman's twenty-first birthday, a higher chance of being a heavy smoker and a higher likelihood of experiencing psychological distress in early adulthood. Most of these unfavorable outcomes are more strongly associated with an early family disruption (in pre-school ages), which is in line with some of the results for the impact of family income and parents' employment on educational attainments (Hill, Yeung and Duncan 2001; Ermisch and Francesconiz 2002).[30]

Other recent studies, however, provide us with somewhat different evidence. The research by Ginther and Pollak (2000), which also uses a sibling-difference approach, finds no significant impact of experiencing single parenthood on young Americans' educational attainments. Björklund and Sundström (2002) detect no significant impact of parental separation on the final educational attainments (measured when aged 33–48) of Swedish children using a sibling-difference method with a sample of full biological siblings, who have all lived with both parents for at least part of their childhood. These results suggest that the negative association between educational attainments and parental separation apparent in between-family comparisons would mainly reflect non-random selection of families into single parenthood. Comparison with the

---

[30] A number of British studies, which examine birth cohort data, confirm these basic findings. (See, among others, Kiernan (1992, 1996, 1997), Ní Bhrolcháin, Chappel and Diamond (1994). and Cherlin, Kiernan and Chase-Lansdale (1995)). Other studies, which use the same cohort data, find instead that growing up in a family in financial distress matters more than lone parenthood (e.g. Gregg and Machin 1999; McCulloch and Joshi 2002). The differences in conclusions between these two groups of studies are possibly due to differences in estimation techniques and in sample inclusion criteria and to the choice of conditioning variables.

British results and the earlier American evidence suggests that 'selection' may differ among countries, and also that the institutional and policy context is likely to matter for the longer-term impact of parental break-up on children. For instance, it is probably the case that Sweden provides more support (in a broad sense) to lone-parent families than Britain and the United States do.

9.5 CONCLUSIONS

Parental employment during childhood appears to have both short-term and long-term consequences on children's wellbeing. The short-term effects of increased early maternal employment operate through 'worse' socio-emotional adjustment and cognitive outcomes, which are measured when children are aged between 4 and 12. The long-term effects have their strongest manifestation on lower educational attainments for children who are in their late teens and early twenties. The effects of paternal employment seem to be far more modest. Thus, growing up in a family in which the mother chooses to work appears to have some adverse consequences on children's welfare, suggesting the negative effect of the loss of maternal childcare time.

Other parental decisions, however, are at work, which can shape children's outcomes. For example, closely related to employment, we have family income. There is evidence that children in poor or low-income households tend to have lower educational and labor market attainments than children from more affluent families. Therefore, if stronger labor market involvement means higher family income, children's life chances may be unaffected by the decision of both parents to work. They may even be enhanced if the income effect dominates. Another important process is given by the structure of the family in which children are brought up. Growing up in a single-parent or step-parent family (or experiencing a parental separation or divorce) has a negative effect on several child outcomes, measured either in early childhood or later in life. With lone parenthood and divorce becoming more widespread and with the attempt in many countries of moving low-income families from welfare to work, it is hard to see how children of single parents (who are generally poor) will get on. The higher family income that their parents' employment is meant to provide must in fact compensate them for both the lack of parental time and the absence of one of the two biological parents. Unless single parents are in relatively high-pay jobs, this double goal may be difficult to be achieved.

It must be said that there are several other factors that could affect children's wellbeing in even more fundamental ways than childhood parental employment patterns (or family income or family structure) do. Among them, we have for example parents' personality and emotional stability, parenting practices, the quality of homecare that children receive from their parents, and the type of friends and networks with which children are involved while growing up. These tie in with the point frequently made by Heckman and colleagues (e.g. Cameron and Heckman 2001; Carneiro and Heckman 2002) that it is the long-term influence of family background and family income that best explains the observed relationship between child outcomes and parental behavior. Likewise, most of our results have been found for high-income countries (especially the United States and Great Britain), so they should be interpreted with care and cannot be straightforwardly generalized to other countries and cultures. It is possible that in other contexts or in low-income countries, increased labor force participation and employment of mothers lead to better child outcomes. All these factors are difficult to measure and integrate in one analytical framework coherently. Our understanding of the processes that link them to children's wellbeing is just at its initial stages.

10

Changes in Labor Market Participation and Family Income Distribution*

10.1 HOW DO WOMEN'S AND MEN'S WORK AFFECT INCOME DISTRIBUTION?

The trend of increasing female employment and decreasing male employment has raised questions about its effects on income distribution both across and within households. The decline in the participation of husbands in the labor market can have two different effects on wives' labor supply: an 'added worker effect' that increases wives' labor supply in order to maintain the same level of income and the same household living standard; and a 'discouraged worker effect' which reduces wives' labor supply since women believe that it is more difficult to find work when their husband cannot find a job.

At the macroeconomic level, the increased participation of women in the labor market seems to be a response to the decline in male employment and wages. At the micro level, however, this process seems to be more complicated since the decline in male employment and wages appears to be greater in low-income families, whereas the increase in female participation is greater in high-income families (Davies *et al.* 1992). Empirical results for the United States and for Europe, in fact, show weak evidence in favor of the 'added worker effect' (Lundberg 1985, Ercolani and Jenkins 1999, Pasqua 2001), but if family background is taken into account, wives' labor supply is more responsive to husbands' unemployment where the role of women in the labor market is better-accepted (Del Boca *et al.* 2000).

In order to explain the increase in women's participation in the labor market in households where the husband is employed, it is important to take into account the fact that people do not marry randomly, but as the result of a process known as 'positive assortative mating:' men with higher education and incomes tend to marry women with higher education and incomes. If a positive 'assortative mating' effect exists, better educated women, with better

* This chapter is responsibility of Silvia Pasqua (University of Turin).

opportunities in the labor market, tend to get married to better educated men, who are generally employed and earn relatively high incomes. On the contrary, lower educated women tend to marry lower educated men, who are characterized by lower incomes and a higher probability of being unemployed (Jacobsen and Rayack 1996). Recent empirical analyses have shown that in about 50–60 per cent of dual-earner couples, both spouses have the same level of education, whereas there is a wider discrepancy in their earnings (Winkler 1998, Davies *et al.* 1992, Aaberge *et al.* 2000). As a consequence of 'assortative mating' we observe a simultaneous increase in the number of families in which both spouses work and an increase in the number of households where nobody works (Gregg and Wadsworth 1996). The conclusion is that the growth in female employment is due more to greater job opportunities (for more highly educated women) and increased availability of part-time jobs and childcare services (see Del Boca and Pasqua Ch. 8, in this volume), making it easier to reconcile family work and extra home activities, than it is to economic constraints (for less well-educated women) to make up for the loss of a job or the low wage of their spouses (Juhn and Murphy 1997).

If better educated women only—usually married to better educated men ('assortative mating') with 'good' jobs and high incomes—enter the labor market, the outcome may be increasing income inequality. However, in countries where we observe high female participation, women with middle and low levels of education also work, and this may contribute to reducing inequality.

In the United States, at the beginning of the 1970s, the value of the probability of being a working woman decreased in proportion to the husband's wage; while at the end of the 1980s, the opposite was true. In particular, in the two decades considered, more women from the middle classes started to work and this had an equalizing effect on household income distribution (Juhn and Murphy 1997; see also Chs. 3 and 5, Pt. I in this volume).

In the United Kingdom, female employment used to be higher in the top half of household income distribution, but between 1980 and 1990 it also increased in middle- and low-income families, and had an equalizing impact. The rates of poverty doubled during that decade, but without the increase in female employment, the number of families in poverty would have been significantly higher.

In general, the effect of an increase in labor force participation by women on household income distribution depends on the initial level of female employment: it becomes unequal when few women work, and equalizes when more women enter the labor market.

Figures 10.1 and 10.2 report female employment rates and inequality for European countries in 1997, and for Italian regions in 1998. These are useful examples to use in order to understand the potential relation between women's work and inequality since vast differences exist in the rates of female employment. In both cases, only households where both spouses are present and of an appropriate working age have been considered, since if we were to consider other types of households also (e.g. single parents with or without children,

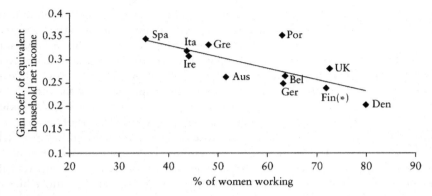

Figure 10.1. *Inequality and women's employment in European countries (1997)*

Source: author's elaboration using ECHP dataset.

Key: (*) = referred to 1996.

households in which one of the spouses is retired), the inequality measures could be affected by different sources of inequality (e.g. social benefit, pensions).

Inequality is measured using the Gini coefficient of equivalent household net income[1] for European countries and the Gini coefficient of total household net income for Italian regions.[2] As we can see in both cases household income is distributed more equally where women work more. In Figure 10.1 only Portugal appears as an outlier, with both a high percentage of working women and high inequality, while the other countries lie quite close to the trend line.

In the Italian case (Fig. 10.2), the result is similar: most southern regions, characterized by low female employment, are also characterized by high household income inequality, while in northern regions where women work more, inequality is lower.

The analysis of the impact of women's work on household income distribution in different European countries can be carried out using different techniques. One of the most common methodologies is the decomposition of total inequality by type of household (dual-earners, male-breadwinner and other types of household) and/or by sources of income (wife's earnings, husband's earnings and other sources) (Betson and van der Gaag 1984, Cancian and Reed 1998, Aaberge *et al.* 2000, Pasqua 2002, Del Boca and

[1] The equivalent household net income has been calculated using the OECD equivalence scale that assigns value 1 to the first adult in the household, 0.7 to other adults and 0.5 to children younger than 14.

[2] Obviously, total household net income is affected by taxes, government transfers and capital share in total income. However, the relation between inequality and women's employment do not change when we consider only household net labor income (neither for Europe nor for Italy). Unfortunately the datasets used do not report gross incomes.

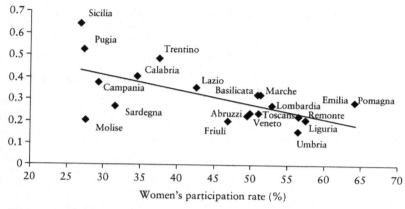

Figure 10.2. *Inequality and women's employment in Italian regions (1998)*
Source: author's elaboration using SHIW dataset.

Pasqua 2003). This is, however, merely a descriptive technique that does not permit consideration of the reasons why more women entered the labor market and the possible effects of those entries on men's labor supply and earnings distribution.

The impact of women's earning on household income distribution can also be analysed at different stages of a typical life cycle: young households with no children (stage 1), households where children are present and the youngest is under 6 years of age (stage 2), and households where children are between 6 and 18 (stage 3). Women's full-time employment decreases from stage 1 to stage 2 and increases again in stage 3. On the other hand, part-time employment increases constantly during a woman's life cycle. The effect of women's work seems to be equalizing in all stages, but the effect is weakest in the second stage, when women work least (Lehrer 2000).

In the following two sections we present differences in inequality in income distribution between dual- and single-earner families (S. 10.2) and between men's and women's earnings (S. 10.3), using data from the European Community Household Panel (ECHP) dataset for the year 1997 and from the Bank of Italy Survey on Household Income and Wealth (SHIW) for the years 1977 and 1998.

10.2 DUAL-EARNER AND SINGLE-EARNER HOUSEHOLDS

The growth in women's participation in the labor market has increased the percentage of dual-earner households, since female-breadwinner families

Table 10.1. *Inequality in equivalent household net income*
for dual- and single-earner households in European
countries (ECHP, 1997)

	All households	Dual-earner households		Single-earner households	
	Gini coeff.	Gini coeff.	Population share	Gini coeff.	Population share
Denmark	0.203	0.190	83.5	0.227	14.3
Finland (*)	0.239	0.232	70.3	0.211	26.4
Germany	0.249	0.221	64.7	0.261	31.7
Austria	0.263	0.242	53.6	0.254	44.9
Belgium	0.265	0.235	65.4	0.270	29.2
United Kingdom	0.281	0.258	69.3	0.299	26.0
Ireland	0.308	0.239	42.7	0.308	48.2
Italy	0.319	0.246	44.9	0.297	51.7
Greece	0.332	0.320	51.0	0.301	48.0
Spain	0.345	0.285	32.2	0.308	58.1
Portugal	0.352	0.326	63.3	0.331	34.7

Key: (*) = referred to 1996.

represent a minor phenomenon in most European countries.[3] As a consequence it is important to understand whether income is distributed more equally within the group of dual-earner or single-earner households. In fact, if income distribution is more equal within the group of dual-earner households, the effect of women's work on income inequality can be positive; otherwise the opposite is true.

Table 10.1 shows the inequality in the distribution of the equivalent household net income in the population subgroups of dual- and single-earner households (population shares are also presented) in several European countries. Data are elaborated from the ECHP (European Community Household Panel) dataset and refer to the year 1997. As before, only married couples in which both spouses are present and of an appropriate working age are considered.[4] Countries are ordered by increasing inequality in income distribution among all households (first column).

[3] In the ECHP dataset female breadwinner households represent on average 3% of the sample.
[4] Some countries present in the dataset have been excluded for different reasons: Luxembourg, because it is not present in the version of the dataset used, the Netherlands and Sweden because the data on participation in the labor market and on incomes refer to different years, and France because the data report gross incomes rather than net incomes as reported for the other countries. Finland was not included in wave 5 and therefore relative data are taken from wave 4 (1997, income refers to 1996).

Table 10.2. *Inequality in total household net income for dual- and single-earner households in Italy (SHIW, 1977 and 1998)*

	All households	Dual-earner households		Single-earner households	
	Gini coeff.	Gini coeff.	Population share	Gini coeff.	Population share
			1977		
Italy	0.317	0.237	24.1	0.309	61.4
Northern regions	0.297	0.211	31.1	0.304	55.4
Southern regions	0.343	0.271	13.5	0.303	72.5
			1998		
Italy	0.305	0.236	39.0	0.312	44.8
Northern regions	0.266	0.231	49.1	0.291	34.6
Southern regions	0.335	0.242	26.3	0.301	56.1

In every country but Finland and Greece, income is distributed more equally among dual-earner than single-earner households. Ireland and Italy, in particular, show the greatest difference in inequality between the two population subgroups. Only in Italy, Ireland and Spain, which are all high inequality countries, is the percentage of dual-earner households lower than that of single-earner ones. All these facts seem to indicate that women's work has a positive impact on household income distribution: as more women are employed, the percentage of dual-earner households rises, and, since income is usually distributed more equally within dual-earner than within single-earner households, inequality is lower.

Analogous results have been found for Italy (Table 10.2). Here we consider two years, 1977 and 1998 from the Historical Archive of the Bank of Italy Survey on Household Income and Wealth (SHIW). Over this period the percentage of dual-earner families increased on average from 24.1 per cent to 39 per cent , but the increase was greater in the northern regions than in the southern ones. On the contrary, inequality within the subgroups of dual- and single-earner households did not change substantially, but the greater incidence of dual-earner families on the population resulted in a more equal income distribution.

Therefore, Italian regional differences also seem to indicate a positive impact of women's work on inequality in household income distribution: where women work less (southern regions) and the percentage of dual-earner households is lower, income inequality is higher. Similar results hold true for the United States in an analysis of the period 1968–1980: household income was distributed more equally in the subgroup of dual-earner households than in the subgroup of single-earner ones (Betson and van der Gaag 1984).

10.3 INEQUALITY IN WOMEN'S AND MEN'S EARNINGS DISTRIBUTION

The impact of husbands' and wives' work on the distribution of family income also depends on the inequality that characterizes women's and men's earnings distribution. As is well known, a gender gap exists between men's and women's wages in all European countries (see Olivetti in Ch. 5, Pt. I, this volume). Comparing the distribution of labor income between male and female workers, we usually find that the distribution of women's labor income is much more unequal (see Table 10.3).[5] Denmark is the only country in which earnings are more equally distributed among women than among men, probably due to the fact that women across the educational board have a job. However, no clear relation ever seems to emerge between the percentage of women working and inequality in women's earnings distribution. This may be due to the fact that we are considering total annual labor income, which is affected by the number of hours worked. Where many women work part-time (as in the UK, Belgium and Germany, see Del Boca and Pasqua in this volume), a high percentage of women has low annual earnings.

Data for Italy (Table 10.4) show how both in 1977 and in 1998 the Gini coefficient for earnings does not differ substantially between women and men at the national level.[6] However, in the South, where women work less, inequality in wives' earnings distribution is higher than inequality in men's earnings distribution, while the opposite is true for the northern regions. In particular the Gini coefficient was relatively high for women in the southern regions in 1977 but then more women entered the labor market, leading to a more equal household income distribution.

In order to understand better the effect of men's and women's earnings on inequality, the decomposition of the inequality measures by sources of income can be performed. This allows us to compute what percentage of total inequality is due to each source of income. Usually three main sources of income are considered: men's earnings, women's earnings (including also zero values) and a residual category, 'other sources,' that includes both household non-labor income and labor income from other family members. The percentage of total inequality 'explained' by each source depends not only on the inequality that characterizes the distribution of that particular source, but also on the correlation between that source and the total income and on the factor share in total income.

The results of inequality decomposition by sources of income in European countries show that in high-inequality/low-female-employment countries (mainly southern countries), inequality in wives' earnings distribution is higher

---

[5] Finland has been excluded since data on total household income are net while data for wives' and husbands' labor income are reported as gross amounts.

[6] The incidence of part-time is relatively low in Italy.

Table 10.3. *Inequality in women's and men's labor income in European countries (ECHP, 1997)*

	% of women working	Gini coeff. of women's labor income	Gini coeff. of men's labor income
Denmark	79.9	0.230	0.239
United Kingdom	72.6	0.390	0.299
Belgium	63.6	0.301	0.271
Germany	63.2	0.383	0.267
Portugal	63.0	0.392	0.351
Austria	51.6	0.350	0.259
Italy	43.7	0.294	0.279
Greece	48.1	0.358	0.314
Ireland	44.1	0.401	0.330
Spain	35.4	0.406	0.338

Table 10.4. *Inequality in women's and men's labor income in Italy (SHIW, 1977 and 1998)*

	% of women working	Gini coeff. of women's labor income	Gini coeff. of men's labor income
	1977		
Italy	25.7	0.279	0.278
Northern regions	32.2	0.237	0.250
Southern regions	15.2	0.370	0.312
	1998		
Italy	44.6	0.279	0.281
Northern regions	54.5	0.261	0.274
Southern regions	31.6	0.306	0.288

than in low-inequality/high-female-participation ones because of the presence of many zero values in women's labor income distribution. Therefore the main equalizing impact of female work seems to be due more to the 'employment effect' (the increase in the percentage of women working, and therefore with positive labor income), rather than to the decrease in the inequality in female earnings distribution. Despite this, the contribution of women's earnings to total inequality remains low in almost all high-inequality/low-female-employment countries as a consequence of the relatively small proportion of household income earned by wives (Pasqua 2002). In Norway, inequality in women's earnings distribution decreased between 1973 and 1997 and therefore female labor income contributed less and less to inequality in household labor income distribution (Aaberge *et al.* 2000).

Another standard method for assessing the impact of women's work on inequality is the use of counterfactual distributions. This method consists in comparing actual inequality in income distribution with the inequality calculated on household income minus the wife's earnings (as if women had no earnings at all). This is obviously a gross approximation of the impact of women's work on income distribution because it does not take into account the fact that the husband's labor supply would respond to the loss of the wife's earnings (Aaberge and Aslaksen 2003).

When the counterfactual distribution analysis is applied, it appears that women's earnings have an equalizing impact on household income distribution (Cancian and Reed 1998 for the US, Pasqua 2002 for European countries, and Del Boca and Pasqua 2003 for Italy).

10.4   INTRA-HOUSEHOLD INCOME DISTRIBUTION

The changes in the labor market participation of men and women have implications not only for income distribution across households, but also for the distribution of resources within the household.

The growth in women's employment rates and the decline in men's employment rates have important welfare effects, both through the changes in resources available to household consumption and through the changes in the balance of power within the households. Empirical evidence from a variety of countries has shown that wives' contributions to household income have increased and that the income received by wives or by husbands has different effects on the demand patterns, when total income is held constant.

The implications of these results are at odds with the neoclassical model which assumes that families behave as though they have a single utility function which represents their preferences. This would imply that an increase in family resources has the same effect on family welfare regardless of which family member receives it. If family members 'pool' their incomes and allocate total resources to maximize a single objective function, it would be only the total income that affects demand.

However, a large number of studies from several countries has rejected the 'income pooling' hypothesis, finding that earned and unearned income received by a husband or by a wife have different effects on demand pattern, and that children appear to do better when their mothers control a larger fraction of family resources.

In fact, increases in the wife's income, relative to the husband's income, are associated with greater expenditures in restaurant meals and childcare (Phipps and Burton 1992, using Canadian data) and with reduced expenditure on alcohol and tobacco. The shares of each spouse's income also affects the amount spent on women's personal necessities (Bourgignon *et al.* 1994, using

French data). The results seem to indicate that in families where women have the higher income, they may have greater control over family resource allocation namely, when the woman's income is the higher one, family choices reflect the woman's preference ordering to a higher degree.

Similar results have been found by analysing the demand for leisure in families at different stages of their life cycle, both in Italy and in the United States. While income pooling is rejected for families without children or with older children, when children are very young the spouses' decisions concerning leisure show greater interdependence (Del Boca 1997; Lundberg 1988).

In studies analysing developing countries, particular focus has been placed on family and child health. Here, income controlled by the mother has a greater positive effect on family health, on human capital (especially on child education) and on leisure (recreational activities) than does income under the control of the father (Thomas 1990; Schultz 1990; Pasqua 2001). The strongest result emerges for child survival probabilities: the effect of the mother's income is almost 20 times stronger than that of the father's.

Resources under each spouse's control are assumed to strengthen the individual's bargaining power by increasing her or his opportunity cost of being married. The more attractive are the individual's opportunities outside the family, the stronger is the individual's influence on intra-family resource distribution, and consequently the final allocation more closely reflects her or his preference ordering. In this context, therefore, the external alternatives available to the wives and to the husbands are particularly relevant (McElroy and Horney 1982).

The effect of extra-household variables on women's spending patterns can be analysed in countries where there is a large regional variation of legal, demographic and labor market structures. In the United States, for example, it has been found that in states characterized by a legal structure that allow more generous divorce settlements, women invest more on their human capital (Carlin 1991). In Italy, in regions characterized by a more favorable marriage market, women are less likely to work, while in regions where more job opportunities are available they are more likely to work (Del Boca 1997).

The results presented show how the growth of women's participation and economic independence can have several important implications not only for income distribution and equality, but also for intra-household resource allocation and for household consumption decisions. More resources for women may in fact imply more spending for children, which to some extent is likely to compensate for the negative effect on children's wellbeing caused by the reduction in time dedicated to them when both parents work (Ermisch and Francesconi, in this volume). Finally, the growth in women's employment also has an important impact on the future labor supply decisions of their daughters: in countries where labor market participation of women is low, empirical evidence shows that women's employment decisions are positively affected by the employment decisions of their mothers (Del Boca *et al.* 2000).

10.5 CONCLUSIONS

All empirical evidence presented in this chapter seems to indicate that women's work has an important impact on household income distribution as well as on income distribution within families. These findings suggest that public policies intended to encourage female employment may also have the positive effect of reducing inequality in household income distribution and of producing a more equal distribution of resources within the family. Moreover, increases in the share of household income earned by women may also imply a shift towards larger expenditures on children's health and education.

Affordable childcare, child benefits and part-time opportunities may have an important impact on household income distribution since they affect the labor supply decisions of women living in low-income households who are more responsive to economic incentives than high-income women and men. The earnings of low-income-level partners, in fact, appear to be complements rather than substitutes, and this has important implications for income distribution (see Aaberge, Colombino and Strom, in this volume). In order to consider these aspects, we need to take into account the fact that husbands' and wives' labor supply decisions are determined simultaneously, as we have seen in the previous chapter.

11

Taxes, Transfers, Labor Supply and Household Welfare*

11.1 MOTIVATIONS FOR STUDYING LABOR SUPPLY AND TAXATION

There are important links between female labor supply and taxes. First, income taxation affects labor supply. Also, labor supply generates the basis for tax revenue. Secondly, married women are the most responsive component of the labor force with respect to changes in incentives. As we illustrate in this chapter, their behavior turns out to be crucial in designing and evaluating tax-transfer policies.

Taxes are collected in order to finance government spending. Many trends contribute to increasing demand for government spending. The fact that individuals are living longer, and that cohorts born in the late 1940s and 1950s were rather large, imply that in the coming decades there will be an increasing number of ageing individuals. In addition to the expected increase in government spending on pensions, one should also expect a sharp increase in the government spending on a variety of health issues, ranging from hospital services, elderly homes and pharmaceuticals. Disability pensions and unemployment benefits are two other government programs that have increased recent government spending in EU-countries due to high and persistent unemployment over many years. In recent years there has thus been a growing concern in western societies regarding the increase in government spending and hence about the costs of taxation, that is to say, the loss in efficiency due to disincentives and distortions on worker behavior caused by taxation. The perceived disincentives on labor supply appeared to be the major justification for reducing marginal tax rates in many European nations during the 1980s and the early 1990s where the marginal tax rates faced by top earners dropped from 70–80 per cent to around 40–50 per cent (see e.g. Blundell 1996).

Taxes and transfers are also implemented with the direct aim of changing incentives and distribution of resources. There is a growing interest in

* The content of this chapter is the responsibility of Rolf Aaberge (Statistics Norway, Oslo), Ugo Colombino (Department of Economics, Turin) and Steiner Strøm (Department of Economics, Turin). We thank Andrea Cornia and Valerie Leehene for their useful comments.

reforming the welfare system, or the various institutions devoted to supporting incomes or the consumption of disadvantaged households. While this last issue is in principle distinct, there is an obvious connection with the former: both call for a redesign of the 'tax-and-benefit' system with the aim of implementing a new configuration of incentives that could eventually lead to more efficiency and not more inequality, given total tax revenue.

In order to be able to undertake tax reforms that enhance the efficiency of the economy, one needs to know how taxes and transfers affect behavior. Here we will concentrate on labor supply. Labor supply consists of participation and hours worked in the labor market, given participation. Economists assume that individuals make their labor supply choice based on preferences that depend on the outcome of working, that is, earnings, and foregone leisure. Preferences can be represented by a function that increases with income and leisure (the utility function). It is assumed that individuals choose their labor supply so that utility is maximised, given a budget constraint and given their perceived opportunities in the labor market. The budget constraint transforms time allocated to labor into gross income, and then—through the tax rule—into net income.

Most of the individuals are married or cohabiting. Therefore, to address the labor supply decisions in a population properly, we have to account for the interaction between spouses. Thus in most cases below, the 'utility function' relates to households with household consumption and leisure of the spouses as the main arguments in the utility function.

Most tax reforms involve a change in marginal tax rates. As a first approximation, reform effects can be discussed in terms of labor supply responses to changes in marginal tax rates. A reduction in marginal tax rates, for example, has two opposing effects on labor supply. First, lower tax rates on the margin make it more profitable to supply more labor. This is called the substitution effect of tax rate changes. Secondly, lower tax rates make it possible to reduce labor supply and still enjoy the same level of consumption. This is called the income effect of tax rate changes. It is the net of these two effects that determine whether a cut in tax rates may increase labor supply. Substitution and income effects vary across households, depending on their taste for leisure and how interesting and challenging their jobs are, on their economic situation before taxes are changed, and whether the jobs they have, or can move to, are flexible enough to meet their preferences for working longer hours. An important part of empirical labor supply is to identify those individuals who are the most responsive to tax rate changes. If the top earners are the most responsive ones, then tax reforms should be targeted at cutting tax rates at the top. However, many of those having high wage incomes often occupy jobs from which they derive a lot more than income. They work long hours because they may enjoy their jobs. Thus, their responses to economic incentives are weakened. Tax reforms must take this into account. If the enhancement of efficiency is the main concern of the authorities, they must target the tax cuts towards those who respond most strongly to economic incentives, not necessarily cutting tax rates for the individuals paying the highest marginal tax rates.

Economists tend to picture the trade-off between equality and efficiency as inescapable. In a widely used textbook in public economics, Stiglitz (1986, p. 481), the reader is warned that the price of redistributing income is a loss in economic efficiency. If this is true, then tax reforms that enhance the efficiency of the economy will imply more inequality. However, if high-income earners are less responsive than low-income earners to economic incentives, then a tax reform that enhances efficiency and reduces inequality may be available. To get an adequate answer to this question, a microeconometric empirical analysis is required.

11.2 SOME EVIDENCE IN EUROPE AND THE US

There have been numerous studies of the impact of tax reforms on labor supply in the United States and the United Kingdom. In most of these studies male workers are found to respond very little to changes in tax rates, while the labor supply of married women and lone mothers are found to be far more responsive, Pencavel (1986); Blundell (1997); Blundell, Duncan and Meghir (1998); and Blundell and MaCurdy (1999). We can look at the labor supply decision as consisting of two steps: the 'participation' decision, that is to say, the decision whether to work (or look for work), and the hours decision, that is to say how much to work, conditional on participation. Of these two choices, participation tends to be the most responsive to changes in economic incentives.

Most of the males in the relevant age intervals are participating in the labor market, while in many countries the labor market participation among married women has been rather low. For married women the reasons are twofold. In the first place, to take care of small children implies that less time can be devoted to working outside the home. How difficult it is to combine the raising of children and participation in labor market activities, depends on the availability of childcare centers, maternity leave programs and the wage level of child carers in private markets. In the United States and the United Kingdom there are fewer childcare centers and the maternity leave is less generous than in the Scandinavian countries. Thus, as we should expect, the labor market participation of married women in the United States and the United Kingdom has been less than in the Scandinavian countries, but higher than in countries like Italy and France. The reasons for the latter could be cultural, or the fact that the wage structure is less even in the United States and the United Kingdom. The latter may imply that the wage level of a nanny is so low compared to the wage that the married women can get that she can afford to hire a nanny and participate in the labor market. It should be noted that the change in fertility in Europe would make the female labor force more like the male labor force in Europe. Thus in the coming years the whole labor force in Europe will most likely become less responsive to changes in tax rates.

The second reason why the married female labor market participation is lower than among males is the role of the husband as the main breadwinner with a higher potential income than the female. The higher the income that the married female can enjoy without working, the less the probability that she will work. This is due to the income effect in labor supply.

Lone mothers' labor market participation is negatively affected by having small children to look after. Moreover, the government benefit paid to lone mothers may have a strong negative impact on labor supply, at least in Europe, and including the United Kingdom. For many people, a reduction in government benefit if they are working, comes at the top of a marginal tax on wage income. Thus the effective marginal tax is much higher than the ordinary marginal tax rate, and the disincentive to participate in labor market activities is rather strong, Walker (1990).

Although there are strong disincentives to participate in the labor market activities among married women and lone mothers, there is of course room for increasing labor supply in these groups provided that the improvement in the economic incentives are strong enough. It should be noted that males and females approaching the retirement age also are facing a discrete labor market choice, namely to continue working or to retire. Hence, we should expect individuals in these age groups to be more responsive to changes in economic incentives than younger individuals.

Devanzo et al. (1973) was one of the first studies to point out that most of the wage- and income-responsiveness in labor supply was concentrated at, or near, zero hours of work. Later studies on the labor supply of married women both in the United States and the United Kingdom gave strong support to this finding, Borjas and Heckman, (1978); Cogan (1981); Hausman and Ruud (1984); Blundell et al. (1988); Ilmakunnas and Pudney (1990); and Dickens and Lundberg (1993).

The tax policy reforms in the United Kingdom in the 1980s raised the marginal tax rate for some individuals, reduced it for others, while some were not exposed to any change at all. These reforms provide the researchers with good opportunities for studying the impact of tax reforms on labor supply. On repeated cross-sections set covering the period 1978–1992, with a focus on married women and with employed husbands, Blundell et al. (1998) estimated the impact of these tax reforms on female labor supply. Results are reported in the form of 'after-tax-wage' elasticities. The authors conclude that although the uncompensated wage elasticities are smaller than the wage elasticities reported for US women, they are moderately sized and clearly significantly different from zero. Income elasticities are estimated to be negative, and the compensated elasticities are thus positive and high enough to lead to the following conclusion: 'Our conclusion is that major tax reform should take into account behavioral effects since our compensated elasticities suggest that the welfare effects are not eligible.'

An important issue to consider is how changes in economic incentives affect labor supply for individuals with different potential income. The higher the wage rate, the higher one would expect that the potential income would be, and/or is. One of the first to study this problem was Break (1957). Based on interviews with a group of lawyers and accountants in the United Kingdom he found that the majority of these affluent men were not affected in their labor supply by the strong disincentives embedded in the British tax system at the time. Across the Atlantic, Moffit and Wilhelm (1998) found similar weak effects of a tax reform in 1986 on the labor supply of the affluent American men. The authors found no evidence of change in hours of work in response to the marginal tax rate cuts in the 1986 reform. On US data, Dickens and Lundberg (1993) report that labor supply responds more strongly to changes in economic incentives in households with low income than in households with high income. For the households with the highest income, they report that the labor supply curve is even backward bending.

Notwithstanding the above reservations on lowering the marginal tax rates on high incomes, this choice has prevailed in the United States, the United Kingdom and most of Europe. Besides the (dubious) efficiency motivations, there might of course be other good reasons for flattening the marginal rates profile, such as simplifications, reducing incentives to evade taxes, coping with mobility of highly skilled labor and fiscal competition. In the last decade, policy and research focus has shifted towards more finely tuned issues such as redesigning the mechanisms for low-income support, strengthening the incentives to work for the poor, and reconciling work and childbearing (e.g. Duncan and McCrae1999; Keane 1995; Eissa and Liebman 1996; Blundel 2000). Overall, the results of these studies confirm that behavioral responses—and particularly those from married women—are strong enough to get some efficiency and/or equality return from the effort spent in redesigning incentives and institutions. Some representative studies and their results are summarized in Table 11.1.

11.3 FISCAL AND SOCIAL POLICIES: MODELING THE BEHAVIORAL RESPONSES

Most of the empirical and policy analysis of labor supply and taxes up until the beginning of the nineties are very close to the textbook presentation of the labor supply decision. The consumer commands a fixed wage rate on the labor market, which reflects her marginal productivity. She is free to choose any number of hours of work at that wage. She satisfies her needs by combining earned income (plus eventually other incomes from different sources, e.g. transfers) with 'leisure' time (i.e. the time not sold on the market). She chooses the allocation of time that best meets her needs or preferences. The empirical model at this point consists in specifying a functional relationship between the

Table 11.1. *Empirical evidence regarding the relationship between labor supply elasticities and income or wages*

Authors	Coverage	Methodological approach/type of data	Results
Devanzo et al. (1973)	United States. Men.	Labor supply model, estimated on micro data, including information about participation/ non-participation and hours.	Virtually all of the labor supply wage- and income responsiveness is found at or near the zero-hours point.
Borjas and Heckman (1978)	United States. Men.	Labor supply model, estimated on micro data, including information about participation/non-participation and hours.	Labor supply estimates are more responsive to wages and incomes when participation decisions are accounted for than when only hours of work, given participation, gare used in estimating labor supply.
Arrufat and Zabalza (1986)	United Kingdom, 1974. Married women.	Micro data based on the General Household Survey. Labor supply model, with husbands' labor supply treated as exogenous.	The estimated total labor supply elasticity for married women is 2.03, out of which 1.41 is driven by participation decisions.
Dagsvik et al. (1988)	France, 1979. Women.	Labor supply model, estimated on micro data collected from the INSEE survey 'Budgets des Familles 1978–1979'. The data include information about participation/non-participation and hours.	The estimated total labor supply elasticity is on average around 3, out of which approximately 1.4 is driven by participation decisions.
Juhn et al. (1991)	United States, 1970–89. Men.	Current population survey (CPS) data. Fraction of year spent working regressed on individual wage rates (or estimated wage rates).	The participation decision is more elastic for workers with low wages (or low potential wages). For example, the estimated partial labor supply elasticities are approximately five times higher for workers in the 1–10 percentile than for workers in the 61–100 percentile of the wage distribution.

Aaberge et al. (1995)	Norway, 1979. Married couples.	Labor supply matching model, estimated on micro data collected from the Level of Living Sample Survey.	Both participation and hours elasticities are higher the lower is household income. For example, for all men (women) the estimated uncompensated labor supply elasticity is 0.45 (1.82) out of which 0.29(0.83) is due to participation. For the 10 per cent poorest, the corresponding numbers are 2.23(3.09) and 1.89 (1.85).
Aaberge et al. (2000)	Married couples in Italy (1987), Norway (1986) and Sweden (1981)	Participation decisions as well as hours of work (for Sweden only working couples). Accounts for non-convex budget sets and restrictions on hours offered in the market.	For Italy see next entry. For Norway the simulated direct uncompensated labor supply elasticities for all men (women) are 0.28 (0.91) out of which 0.17 (0.37) is due to participation. For working couples in Sweden in 1981 the simulated direct labor supply elasticities are -0.02 for men and 0.07 for women.
Aaberge et al. (1999)	Italy, 1987. Married couples.	Labor supply matching model estimated on data from the Survey of Household Income and Wealth.	The simulated uncompensated direct elasticities for men (women) are 0.05 (0.74) out of which 0.04(0.65) is due to participation. For the 10 per cent poorest the corresponding numbers are 0.08 (3.44) and 0.05 (2.84).
Moffit and Wilhelm (1998)	United States, 1983–1989. Affluent men.	Data is collected from the Survey of Consumer Finances (SFC) and used to evaluate hours of work responses to the 1986 Tax Reform Act.	The labor supply of high-income men is inelastic with respect to the marginal tax rate. There is no evidence of changes in hours of work in response to the marginal tax rate reductions legislated in the 1986 Tax Reform Act.

Source: Røed and Strøm (2002).

labor supply decision on the one hand, and wage rate and other incomes on the other: $h = h(w, y)$. With observations on h, w and y, one can estimate this function and use it to simulate new decisions given new values of w and/or y. Taxes complicate the picture but the basic framework does not change. However the same framework imposes serious limitations. For example not all the tax rules can be easily represented. Simultaneous household decisions are cumbersome to model. The same holds for modeling constraints as for choice of hours.

During the last two decades, a different framework has become more popular, where the consumer is assumed to choose among jobs (i.e. 'packages' of hours requirements, wages and other characteristics), rather than along a continuum of hours for a fixed wage rate. Also, the empirical analysis consists in directly estimating the preferences as revealed by the observed choices, rather than going through the specification of a 'labor supply function'. This different approach accounts for the fundamental heterogeneity of the alternative job packages that form the consumer's opportunity set, and simplifies enormously the representation of complex tax rules, of simultaneous household decisions and of constraints on hour choices.[1] In most of this chapter we rely on a modeling framework that belongs to this approach. In particular it is a simultaneous model of household labor supply of both spouses, it allows an exact representation of the budget sets independent of how complex they are, and it accounts for quantity constraints and limitations in the choice of hours of work. An outline of this modeling framework is provided in Appendix A.[2]

11.4 MEASURING SOCIAL WELFARE: EFFICIENCY AND EQUALITY

In order to choose between alternative tax policies, one needs a criterion for aggregating household incomes, or welfare, into social welfare. Using household welfare rather than income as the informational basis of the social welfare function means that not only income but also the value of leisure is taken into account. A social welfare function is essentially a weighted sum of individual households' incomes or welfare indexes, where the weights reflect the social (e.g. the planner's) attitude towards inequality. For example, if the planner cares at all about inequality, she/he should give more weight to the poor than to the rich. The particular form of social welfare

---

[1] The foundations of this new approach reside in McFadden's work on discrete choice (e.g. Manski and McFadden 1981). Important extensions are Ben-Akiva and Watanatada (1981) and Dagsvik (1994).

[2] An interesting recent development consists in representing the household as a set of agents that bargains or plays some sort of game, rather than acting as a unit of decision. The empirical implementation of these models is more problematic. Among others, examples are provided by Hearnes *et al.* (2003) and Chiuri and Longobardi (2002).

function that we use is such that it can be expressed as the product of an efficiency index (namely the simple average of individual incomes or welfare levels), times an index of equality (closely related to the well-known Gini inequality index):

$$Social\ Welfare = Efficiency \times Equality$$

As a consequence, the effect of a given policy upon social welfare can be approximately expressed as:

$$\%\ Variation\ in\ Social\ Welfare = \%\ Variation\ in\ Efficiency \\ + \%\ Variation\ in\ Equality$$

Instead of using the total (or average) amount of income or welfare as a measure of efficiency, one might want to use different criteria. Recently, criteria inspired by the 'equality-of-opportunity' philosophy have been developed. The idea is that in weighting individual incomes or welfare levels one should care only about that part of inequality that is due to different exogenous opportunities, and not to the residual part due to, say, different effort. According to the approach proposed by J. Roemer (1993, 1998), for example, it turns out that the equality-of-opportunity criterion essentially amounts to using the average income or welfare among the least favored (opportunity-wise, e.g. those with lowest parental income or education) as the efficiency index: the implications being using the standard concept of efficiency versus the equality-of-opportunity concept as developed by J. Roemer. In what follows, we will present simulation exercises where alternative policies are ranked according to their effects on efficiency and on equality. More details on the computation and use of efficiency and equality indexes can be found in Appendix B.

11.5 THINKING ABOUT TAX SYSTEM REFORMS: AN EXERCISE FOR ITALY

At least since the end of the 1960s two basic ideas have informed the debate on tax-transfer systems reforms. The first idea is concerned with *efficiency* (the size of the pie). Since the late seventies, the progressive tax systems prevailing in most advanced economies have been criticized for giving bad incentives and paying too high a price for income equalization. Suppose, now, that I live in a country with a very progressive tax system and my marginal tax is 50 per cent. Suppose I am offered 5000 euros (gross) to write a report, so that I could earn 2500 euros net of taxes. To keep things simple, let us assume I am the only one endowed with the skills to do the job. Say I decided not to do it. But suppose now there is a change in taxes, and from my current income level, my marginal tax is lowered to 20 per cent. I would now earn €4000. So this time I might decide to do it. I would be better off. Even more importantly, the government would now collect €1000 more from me in additional taxes, which means that someone else down the line could also be made better off through larger transfers or lower taxes or better public services. If policy makers believe that such opportunities for being more productive concern mostly high-income people, the implication is that tax rates should be made less progressive. This basic scheme embodying the idea of improving efficiency by reducing progressivity—together with other appealing features such as simplicity—is the so-called 'Flat Tax', namely, a proportional tax. Every one pays, let us say, 20 per cent of gross income. As said above, the advocates of this reform more or less explicitly assume that the rich are more responsive than the poor. It is expected that the FT would lower marginal taxes for the rich and increase them for the poor, and possibly also for average income people. To promote this as a good reform efficiency-wise, most FT supporters tend to think that the good incentives given to the rich outweigh the bad incentives given to the poor. During the 1980s and 1990s, in particular, the United States, and most European countries, made significant moves towards the FT by reducing the number of brackets and/or the progressivity of the bracket marginal rates, besides, in some cases, reducing the average tax rate (Røed and Strøm 2002). Analyses by Hausman and associates (Hausman 1980, 1981; Burtless and Hausman 1978; Hausman and Ruud 1984) have been very influential both from the point of view of the political debate and from that of the evaluation methodology. It should be added that a pure FT is equivalent to an expenditure tax. What one says about the FT is therefore directly relevant in view of the debate on income taxation versus expenditure taxation.

The second idea is mainly concerned with *distribution*. The various policies implemented to help the poor and the needy (tax exemptions, subsidized prices, in-kind, benefits, etc.) have long been criticized for being costly, chaotic and possibly iniquitous. Maybe we can think up something more direct, simple and transparent? Suppose you define a minimum guaranteed income. If you happen to be above that level in your own right, that's all right. If not, you will receive a transfer just sufficient enough to push your income up to the guaranteed level. On any income above the guaranteed level you will need to pay taxes (according to some rule). This system is called 'Negative Income Tax' (NIT). In the most radical formulation, the NIT mechanism replaces any other redistributive policy. Between the end of the 1960s and the middle of the 1970s in the United States, many econometric analyses and social experiments were performed in order to evaluate NIT-like mechanisms.

Both ideas have a number of versions and variations. They can also be combined. For example, we can have the NIT combined with a FT above the guaranteed minimum income (we call this rule the NIT + FT). More recently, especially in the United States and the United Kingdom, other low-income support mechanisms have become more fashionable, where wage subsidies to the working poor are used to supplement their income, or where the transfer envisaged by the NIT is made conditional upon some minimum labor effort (or such like, e.g. participating in a training program). These alternative income support schemes are sometimes labeled as 'Workfare' (WF).

The above ideas—together with some implementations—have been circulating for more than three decades as elements of the social and economic policy debate and of the empirical economic research. During this time, theorists were developing sophisticated models for characterizing optimal tax rules. The two strands of research have proceeded with very little interaction. In what follows, we will first discuss some simulation exercises based on a microeconometric model of household labor supply, aimed at comparing hypothetical reforms inspired by FT or NIT or WF schemes. Then we will discuss some further analysis where we establish an explicit connection between microeconometric research and inquiry into optimal taxation.

Before entering the details of these exercises, we draw attention to what is probably the easiest way to characterize the behavioral implications of the model that we are going to use, namely computing labor supply elasticities with respect to wages. They are computed through microsimulation, that is to say, the wage is increased, and the individual responses are simulated and then averaged. They are illustrated in Figures 11.6a and 11.6b (see p. 222), which show marked differences among spouses and a strong inverse relation between elasticity and household income. In a sense, they tells us that all responses come from among the poor and average-income households and in particular from among the women living in those households. Figures 11.6a, b must be kept in mind as a polar star, since they suggests that:

- the effects of any simulated reform will be driven by this pattern of elasticities
- the design of an optimal—in some sense—tax rule should properly exploit the same pattern of elasticities.

11.5.1 *Comparing three reform proposals*

In Italy, a consideration of the above ideas from the perspective of reforming the tax-transfer system has emerged with some delay compared to the United States or the United Kingdom. It is interesting to note that the fiscal platforms proposed by the two coalition parties running the 2001 Italian Parliamentary any elections contained reform proposals very close to the FT (Casa delle Libertà, right coalition), and to the NIT + FT or the WF + FT (Ulivo, left coalition) respectively.[3] We comment here on a simulation exercise that compares a FT, a NIT + FT and a WF + FT rule, as an alternative to the

---

[3] We are making a loose analogy between theoretical schemes and actual fiscal platforms. A more detailed and specific presentation and analysis of the platforms can be found in a CHILD working paper by Baldini and Bosi (CHILD WP 03/2001). See also CHILD WP 03/2002 by Chiuri and Longobardi.

current system. Figures 11.1a–1c provide an illustration of the three systems compared to a standard progressive rule qualitatively similar to the current Italian one.

In order to simulate the effects of the three hypothetical reforms we use a microeconometric model (see Appendix A) that we developed previously. The effects are estimated using a sample of about 2200 Italian households (extracted from the 1993 Survey of Household Income and Wealth by the Bank of Italy). The model takes into account the decisions of household members: whether to work or not, and how much. These decisions depend on various personal and family characteristics, on job and earning opportunities and on the tax-transfer rule. In other words, it represents, down to the micro-decisions level, the process by which the pie is being baked and sliced. More technical details can be found in Aaberge *et al.* (1998). Previous exercises applied to Italy have adopted non-behavioral simulations for evaluating reforms similar to the ones mentioned

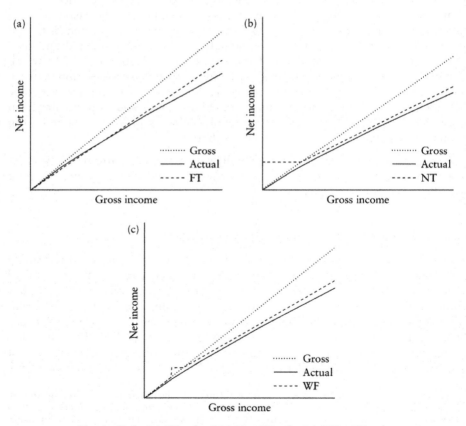

Figure 11.1. (a) *FT rule*; (b) *NT + FT rule*; (c) *WF + FT rule*

above.[4] When account is not taken of behavioral responses, the dimension of the (gross) 'cake' is obviously fixed. However, the crucial issue in efficiency–equality evaluation resides precisely in the possibility that the dimension (along with the distribution) of the cake *may* change. Less distortionary tax rates *may* generate a larger amount of resources available for redistribution; a better designed redistribution and income support system *may* not only foster equality but also improve the configuration of incentives and by this route contribute in its turn to efficiency. In this paper we use a model of household labor supply to evaluate stylized versions of the above reform ideas. A behavioral model might reveal the possibility of improving both efficiency and equality.

Our model accounts for quantity constraints and 'involuntary' unemployment: for example some individuals might have a choice set that does not contain any job opportunities, or maybe only very unattractive ones (see again Appendix A, and the background papers for more details). Therefore not every individual looking for a job with standard conditions will be able to find one. On the other hand, while running the simulations, we keep the opportunities fixed: gross wage rates and hours characterizing the various opportunities in the choice set. In principle this is certainly a drawback, since a different level and composition of labor supply might in turn induce a change in wages and hours available on the market. In practice—at least in a partial equilibrium perspective—the drawback might be minor, since the overall changes in labor supply obtained in the simulations are sufficiently small to assume that opportunities is constant likely to be a reasonable approximation.[5]

When we simulate the working of a particular tax-transfer rule, we adjust its parameters (for example the fixed tax rate in the case of the FT) so that the total net tax revenue collected by the government is equal to the current one. To simplify things, the guaranteed income level of the NIT + FT and of the WF + FT systems is set in advance equal to three-quarters of the poverty line (adjusted for household size). The minimum amount of hours worked in the year (by the household as a whole) to qualify for the transfer in the WF + FT system is set equal to 1000. It turns out that in order to generate the same total net tax revenue the three reforms require the marginal and average tax

----

[4] Baldini and Bosi (2001) use a static microsimulation model to evaluate the effects on income distribution and on net tax revenue of the two reforms contained in the electoral platforms of the two opposed coalitions, and conclude that they both are undesirable. The (almost) flat tax proposal—proposed by the centre-right coalition—would, according to the results of Baldini and Bosi, entail a major loss in revenue; to keep revenue constant, an unbearably high rate would be required. On the other hand, the 'social dividend + flat rate' reform, proposed by the centre-left coalition, would have positive effects on redistribution, but again would require an exceedingly high flat rate to keep the revenue constant. Another example of non-behavioral simulation analysis of this type of reforms is provided by Bourguignon *et al.* (1997).

[5] Of course one might want to account for General Equilibrium effects. We are currently working with Norwegian data on matching the microecoeconometric model with a Computable General Equilibrium model (Aaberge, Colombino, Holmøy and Wennemo 2003).

rates reported in Table 11.2. Note that all the reforms imply a lower average tax rate than the current system. Since the total tax revenue (the numerator) is kept constant, the total gross income (the denominator) must have increased and therefore household choices must have changed.

We stressed the ability of the model to represent behavior and choices, so what are the new choices once a new tax-transfer system is implemented? Figures 11.1–11.5 and Table 11.3 illustrate some of the results. We can summarize as follows:

(a) all three reforms bring about more (gross and net) income;
(b) the larger amount of income is due to a larger (and/or more productive) labor supply concentrated among the low- and average-income household;

Table 11.2. *Tax rates of various tax reforms*

Tax rule	Marginal tax rate	Average tax rate
Current (1993)	27.0 (*)	20.4
FT	18.4	18.4
NIT + FT	28.4 (**)	19.5
WF + FT	27.3 (**)	19.8

Key: (*) Marginal tax rate faced by the average income individual.
      (**) Marginal tax rate faced by individuals with income above the guaranteed level.

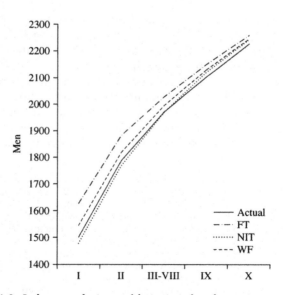

Figure 11.2. *Labor supply (annual hours) under alternative tax reforms, by income decile*

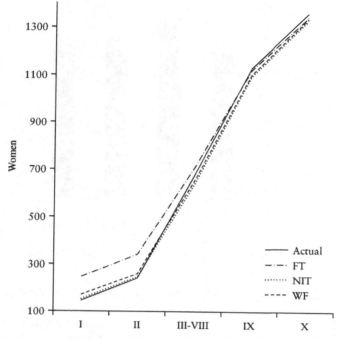

Figure 11.3. *Labor supply (annual hours) under alternative tax reforms,
by income decile*

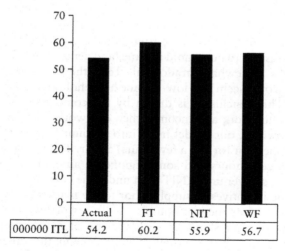

000000 ITL	Actual	FT	NIT	WF
	54.2	60.2	55.9	56.7

Figure 11.4. *Gross household income under alternative tax reforms, by income decile*

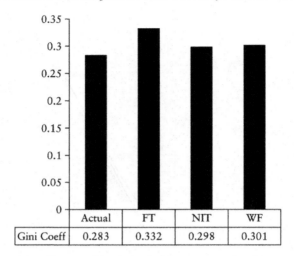

Figure 11.5. *Gini coefficient of net household income under alternative tax reforms*

(c) the increased labor supply is proportionally more significant among women;

(d) the NIT + FT and the WF + FT rules seem to escape the much feared risk of reducing labor supply among the low-income households;

(e) all three reforms imply a more unequal household income distribution, notably so for the FT rule.

Probably (b) and (d) are the most striking results. Result (a) supports the view that by flattening the marginal rates profile one can obtain efficiency gains. However (b) tells us that those gains come from an unexpected source: namely, not the high-income households but rather the low- and average-income households. This is clearly due to a pattern of labor supply elasticities that vary markedly with respect to household income (and gender)—see Figures 11.6a, b. Result (d) looks somewhat paradoxical. Take the NIT for example. From Figures 11.1 it would seem that low-income households have lower incentive to supply labor. This conclusion is driven by the comparison between income when one does not work and income when one works one hour (or maybe a few hours). However, our model takes into account that there are not many jobs requiring one hour (or just a few hours) a year. The relevant comparison is rather between zero hours and some significant amount of hours. Since the average tax rate is lower under NIT than under the current rule, it may well be the case that the incentives to supply labor to the market are reinforced, even for the (originally) low-income households. It is worthwhile noting that the above result would not show up with the use of a traditional model that assumes all type of jobs are equally available. On the other hand, if the opportunity set were more uniformly dense hours, then one should indeed

Table 11.3. *Participation rates, annual hours of work, gross income, disposable income and taxes for married couples under alternative tax regimes by deciles of disposable household income under 1993 taxes*

Tax regime	Decile	Participation rates, per cent		Annual hours of work				Households, 1000 ITL 1993		
				Given participation		In the total population		Gross income	Taxes	Disposable income
		M	F	M	F	M	F			
1993-tax rules	1	95.6	14.1	1571	1030	1501	145	15221	525	14695
	2	97.5	19.9	1832	1209	1787	241	24372	2109	22263
	3–8	98.9	43.8	1991	1546	1970	677	48187	8960	39227
	9	99.3	65.5	2117	1731	2103	1133	85135	19983	65152
	10	99.4	74.4	2237	1828	2225	1361	128396	34365	94032
	All	98.5	43.7	1972	1590	1943	694	54225	11074	43150
FT	1	95.4	19.6	1706	1264	1627	247	22933	4219	18714
	2	97.8	24.4	1924	1397	1882	342	31761	5845	25917
	3–8	99.0	44.7	2048	1585	2027	709	54142	9961	44181
	9	99.4	64.5	2162	1741	2150	1124	89459	16460	72999
	10	99.5	73.2	2267	1834	2257	1344	132888	24452	108435
	All	98.6	45.0	2036	1623	2008	731	60189	11074	49115
NIT	1	95.28	14.44	1551	1056	1478	152	16404	−1952	18356
	2	97.13	19.91	1820	1240	1768	247	26199	2537	23662
	3–8	98.63	41.42	1996	1540	1969	638	49801	9538	40263
	9	99.21	63.29	2138	1733	2121	1097	86985	20218	66767
	10	99.49	72.59	2252	1832	2241	1331	130581	32714	97867
	All	98.29	41.87	1976	1589	1942	665	55897	11074	44823
WF	1	95.32	15.19	1621	1117	1545	170	17655	−247	17902
	2	97.45	20.28	1866	1285	1818	260	27280	2956	24324
	3–8	98.82	42.20	2018	1548	1994	653	50669	9487	41182
	9	99.31	63.56	2145	1738	2130	1105	87455	19569	67885
	10	99.49	72.96	2256	1833	2244	1338	131013	31538	99476
	All	98.45	42.52	2001	1597	1970	679	56742	11074	45668

expect a significant negative effect on participation from NIT-like mechanisms. It must be added, however, that even in the last case, the effect could be mitigated by lowering the marginal tax rate that phases out the transfer (which is equal to 100% in the version we simulate).

A more sophisticated step consists in using welfare instead of income for evaluating the reforms. Essentially this operation amounts to taking into account not only income but also the value of leisure as reflected by the utility function. Since through the model we get estimates of household utility functions, we can derive the money equivalent of utility levels. Such a measure can be used in various ways depending on whether we are willing to make inter-household comparisons or not. If we prefer to avoid such comparisons, an

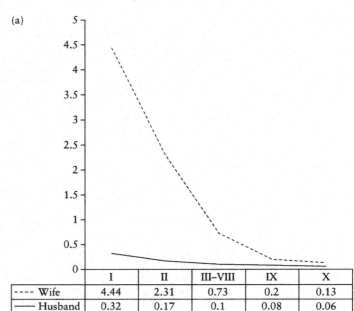

(a)

	I	II	III–VIII	IX	X
---- Wife	4.44	2.31	0.73	0.2	0.13
—— Husband	0.32	0.17	0.1	0.08	0.06

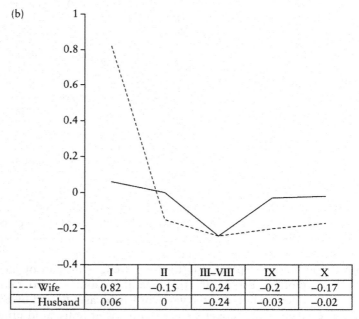

(b)

	I	II	III–VIII	IX	X
---- Wife	0.82	−0.15	−0.24	−0.2	−0.17
—— Husband	0.06	0	−0.24	−0.03	−0.02

Figure 11.6. *(a) Labor supply elasticity with respect to own wage by household income decile and (b) Labor supply elasticity with respect to partner's wage by household income decile*

interesting application consists in identifying the households who are better off (winners) or worse off (losers) after a reform. Figure 11.7 reports the percentage of winners for each reform. All three reforms bring about a majority of winners. A tentative implication is that any of them would win against the current system in a referendum; also, WF + FT does better than NIT + FT, which in turn does better than FT. The aggregate percentage of winners, however, masks large differences between income deciles, as illustrated in Figure 11.8. It seems that the reforms have very different distributional implications.

Can we put together efficiency effects and distributional effects into a synthetic index? Section 11.4 and Appendix B explain how to obtain measures of individual welfare, make them comparable, aggregate them into a social welfare measure and disentangle efficiency and equality effects. A particularly useful result is that the index of social welfare can be expressed as the product of the average individual welfare (a measure of efficiency, the average size of the 'cake') times an index of equality of the welfare distribution, which depends on the inequality aversion parameter. For a particular value of the inequality aversion parameter ($k = 2$) the index of equality turns out to be equal to 1 minus the familiar Gini index of the welfare distribution. Figure 11.9 uses the above criterion to illustrate the percentage variation of social welfare and of its components under the three reforms. All reforms are *more efficient* than the current system. The FT implies *less equal* slices. But the NIT + FT and WF + FT

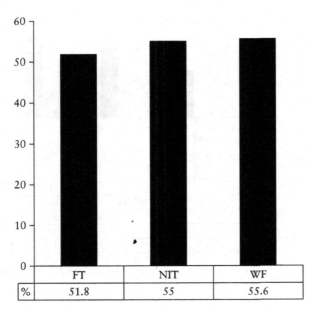

%	FT	NIT	WF
	51.8	55	55.6

Figure 11.7. *Percentage of welfare winners*

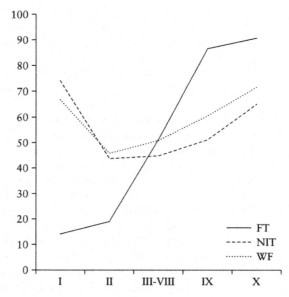

Figure 11.8. *Percentage of welfare winners by household income decile*

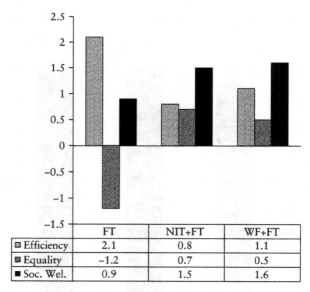

	FT	NIT+FT	WF+FT
Efficiency	2.1	0.8	1.1
Equality	−1.2	0.7	0.5
Soc. Wel.	0.9	1.5	1.6

Figure 11.9. *Reform effects on social welfare and its components*

imply *more equal* slices. So we did find tax-transfer rules that bring about a bigger pie *and* more equal slices too.

11.5.2   *Looking for the best*

Are there better ideas than those considered above? More generally, what's the best tax-transfer rule? This is the object of inquiry of a very sophisticated branch of economic analysis, called 'Optimal Taxation.' This literature, however, is mainly theoretical. Here we present a rather uncommon type of inquiry, whereby an estimated empirical model (the same used in the previous subsection) is applied to real data in order to find an optimal tax-transfer rule according to some social welfare criterion. We limit ourselves to the class of tax-transfer rule defined by a lump-sum transfer plus two marginal tax rates, namely:

$$x = \begin{cases} c + (1 - t_1)y & \text{if } y \le \bar{y} \\ c + (1 - t_1)\bar{y} + (1 - t_2)(y - \bar{y}) & \text{if } y > \bar{y} \end{cases}$$

where

$c = $ lump-sum transfer
$t_1, t_2 = $ marginal tax rates
$x = $ disposable income
$y = $ gross income
$\bar{y} = $ average individual gross income

We run the model (simulating the new household choices) until the social welfare criterion also used in the previous section is maximized with respect to c, t_1 and t_2 under the constraint that total net tax revenue is kept equal to the current one. The exercise is repeated for many different values of the inequality aversion parameter. Some results (EO) are summarized in Table 11.4 and 11.5. Here we exclude negative values of c, namely, lump-sum taxes. We just mention that by allowing lump-sum taxes the optimal tax rule turns out to be the pure lump sum for any value of $k > 0.3$. At first sight the results look rather surprising, since they imply lower marginal tax rates on higher incomes. However notice that the rules are still progressive: the progressivity is introduced through the lump-sum subsidy rather than through progressive marginal rates. In fact, the optimal tax rules turn out to be close to NIT-like rules, where the starting marginal rate is not necessarily 100 per cent but still significantly lower than the next one. It is interesting to observe that this shape of the tax rule is close enough to the ones recently computed by Saez (2001) by feeding optimal taxation formulae into a calibrated model. The resulting rule envisages a lump-sum transfer, high initial marginal tax rates, which then rapidly decrease. The only important difference is, that for higher incomes, Saez obtains marginal tax rates that increase again.

Of course, we must remember that in the simulation exercise previously mentioned, we constrained the tax rule to contain only two marginal rates. This was done in order to ease the computational burden. It might well be the case that if we search within a more general class of tax rule we get a profile even closer to Saez's. Indeed the pattern of labor supply elasticities illustrated in Figures 11.2 and 11.3 supports such a conjecture. The elasticity in the highest deciles is essentially zero. Recall the argument used above to motivate the desirability—efficiency-wise—of the FT (which also apply to NIT + FT and to WF + FT). Is it true that the rich are more responsive, and by working more and exploiting better opportunities, they contribute to a bigger pie? Well, the answer is no. Our model says that the rich hardly move: they simply collect a larger slice thanks to lower taxes. A large part of the contribution to the bigger pie comes instead from lower- and middle-income households (and especially from their female members). Even though most of them face a higher marginal tax rate, by supplying more labor they can access jobs that are better paid than before, since the average tax rate is lower than before. The efficiency gain attached to the FT mechanism (whether associated or not with the NIT or the WF) apparently comes from an unexpected direction. The reforms perform better than the current system not because they lower the marginal tax rate for the rich, but because they lower the average tax rate, and this may also open better opportunities for the not-so-rich and the poor. Our simulations suggest that by flattening the tax rates profile, we do indeed have an efficiency gain. However, the behavioral responses that generate the gains are very different from those commonly assumed and suggest that the proposed reforms might be improved upon by reducing progressivity, not so much in favor of the very high-income deciles but rather in favor of the low- and average-income deciles. Higher marginal taxes imposed on high-income brackets would simply extract a rent and would hardly imply any loss in efficiency.[6]

In Appendix B, we also present an alternative social welfare function that takes into account the so-called 'Equality of Opportunity' criterion. In Table 11.4 we report the results of some simulations using the EOp criterion. Income instead of welfare was used in this case. However we are able to compare these results with others that also are based on income but with the standard EO criterion. Since (comparing Table 11.4 with Table 11.5) it turns out that the EO results are rather close, either using income or welfare, we can speculate that the same might happen under the EOp criterion. The most striking result is that EOp implies optimal tax-transfer rules that are much more progressive than those

---

[6] This conjecture might turn out to need some qualification. For example it might happen that very high marginal tax rates imposed on high incomes discourage current average income people to jump to higher income levels. We are currently exploring the performance of more complex tax rules. Optimizing with respect to general tax rules with the use of a behavioral microeconometric model—instead of representative agents or simple assumptions on the distribution of types as in the theoretical literature on optimal taxation—although logically straightforward, imposes a high computational burden.

Table 11.4. *EO-optimal and EOp-optimal tax rules (income based)*

k	EO			EOp		
	c	t_1	t_2	c	t_1	t_2
∞	0	0.31	0	0	0.31	0
3	0	0.31	0	0	0.11	0.35
2	0	0.31	0	2500	0.25	0.53
1	2000	0.30	0.18	12500	0.86	0.78

Table 11.5. *EO-optimal tax rules (welfare based)*

k	c	t_1	t_2
∞	1000	0.37	0.00
1	1000	0.37	0.00
0.5	2740	0.37	0.13
0.4	10000	0.76	0.56

implied by EO[7]. The result is somewhat surprising since EOp is commonly thought to be a less interventionist philosophy with respect to EO.

11.5.3 *The reforms and female participation and fertility*

There is a long tradition of evaluating reforms on the basis of their effects on labor supply. A sharp departure from this tradition is done by Hausman (1981), who notes that the welfare effects of taxes might be (and actually are in his exercise) fairly large, notwithstanding minor behavioral effects. He recommends that policy makers should not worry so much about labor supply effects, and instead should focus on welfare effects. The message is important but it should be received with some caution and flexibility. In this contribution we use a social welfare function to scale reforms since it is a theoretically well-founded way to summarize the reform effects (actually a sort of 'compressing' utility). However it is still useful to complement the information compressed into a social welfare function with other details. Both the utility function adopted in the model and the social welfare function used in the evaluation provide only an approximation to what might be important to the households and the policy makers. For example, the policy maker might judge that female labor market participation per se is important for dynamic

---

[7] To be more precise, what we call here EOp is in fact a combination of the (pure) EOp criterion with the EO criterion, which is applied to the distribution within the least favored group. When $k = \infty$, the criterion collapses to the pure EOp.

efficiency considerations that are not fully taken into account by the model (e.g. more participation today might imply a higher productivity tomorrow). Fertility might also be important per se if one thinks that the number of children is not a pure private good but rather something with public good and externality components. What happens then to female participation and fertility, under the above reforms? We have already seen the general picture of labor supply effects of FT, NIT and WF in Figures 11.2 and 11.3. Table 11.3 shows some more details. Overall female labor supply does not move much. We observe a modest increase under FT and modest reductions under NIT and WF. However, important changes are going on below this calm surface:

- first, all the reforms induce a larger supply from the poorest deciles, and a smaller supply from the richest deciles. Recall that all the reforms imply an increase in the average net wage. Therefore the result can be interpreted as due to a substitution effect prevailing among the low deciles and a wealth effect prevailing among the high deciles. A role is probably played also by cross-elasticities (see Fig. 11.6b). We find that labor supply from women living in poor households increases rather elastically, not only with respect to their own wage but also with respect to their partner's wage. That is to say, at low levels of household income, partners' incomes are complements rather than substitutes. Since as a consequence of the reforms the average net wage increases for both partners, this reinforces incentives to participate for women living in low-income households;
- secondly, under all reforms, household income increases much more than (female and male) labor supply. Besides the modest increase in the average net wage due to less progressive rates, the increase in income must therefore be due to a change in the composition of participants. More productive individuals move in and less productive ones move out. The process might have some interesting implications in terms of intra-household time allocation, matching of partners and so on, that we cannot fully pursue here.

As to fertility, in principle, one could argue that child 'production' and care are components of leisure and therefore induce the effects of changes in the budget sets on fertility from basic estimates of labor supply responses. However, the model used above for reform evaluation is estimated under the assumption that the number of children is exogenous. We can make some suggestive speculations based on another modeling exercise where labor supply and number of children are both treated as simultaneous choice variables (Colombino 2000).[8] This model does not allow a detailed representation of the

---

[8] This other model is not completely comparable to the previous one, not only because it treats fertility as endogenous but—among other things—because it uses an 'average tax rate' linear approximation to the true budget constraint. Moreover it is a model of wife's decisions (labor supply and number of children), given husband's supply decision (exogenous). However, the dataset used and the basic methodology are similar.

tax-transfer regime. We can only infer some implications of the reforms if we approximate them as changes in the average tax-rate and in exogenous income. It turns out that essentially all the three reforms can be approximated as a lowering of the average tax rate and an increase in exogenous income. When we feed the model with these changes, we get a slight positive effect on the number of children, that is to say, a prevalence of the income effect (not only the exogenous income effect, but also the income effect embodied into the wage effect).[9]

APPENDIX 11.A

Modeling household labor supply

To give a brief outline of the modeling framework we will, for expository reasons, focus on the labor supply of single individuals. The extension to the labor supply of married couples is however straightforward. The individuals are assumed to choose among jobs. Each job is characterized by a wage rate w, hours of work h and other characteristics j. Examples of these other characteristics are commuting time to work, fringe benefits in terms of free parking, hygiene, etc. The individuals are assumed to choose the job that maximizes his or her utility, given a budget constraint that transforms gross income into net income, and given the opportunity set of the individual. Formally, the labor supply model looks like the following:

$$\text{Max } U(C, h, j; Z)$$
$$\text{with respect to } \{h, w, j\}$$
$$\text{given,} \tag{1}$$
$$C = f(wh, I)$$
$$\{h, w, j\} \in S$$

Here U is the (ordinal) utility level, C is net income equal to after-tax income, $f(\cdot)$ is a function that transforms gross income into net disposable income (i.e. the tax-transfer rule), I is non-wage income and S is the opportunity set that the individual faces. Z is a vector that contains variables that affect preferences, like age, number of small children etc. Some of these variables are unobserved by the analysts. Non-working is of course an alternative. In that case $h = w = 0$. The opportunity set also covers non-market opportunities.

To the analyst both preferences and opportunity sets are random. At best the analyst can derive the probability for the observed and assumed optimal choice

[9] In Colombino and Di Tommaso (1996), the own wage effect upon fertility is negative. However, that effect is measured keeping constant the intertemporal wealth. On the other hand, increase in intertemporal wealth (as reflected in cohort effects) due for example to increasing wages, would have a positive effect on fertility. Therefore the results in Colombino and Di Tommaso (1996) can be reconciled with those derived from Colombino (2000).

of the individual, that is, a job of type {h, w}. To obtain an expression for that probability, one has to assume how the random element enters the utility function and how this random variable, a taste-shifter, is distributed across jobs for a given individual, and across individuals, given the job. Moreover we also have to deal with how opportunities should be specified and how the random elements here are distributed.

In the first place, we assume that the utility function can be factorised as:

$$U(C, h, j; Z) = \nu(C, h, z_1)\varepsilon(h, w, j) \qquad (2)$$

where $\nu(\cdot)$ is the deterministic part of the utility function, z_1 is the vector of observed characteristics and $\varepsilon(\cdot)$ is the random variable measuring job or household characteristics unknown to the analyst. $\varepsilon(\cdot)$ is assumed to be identical and independent, distributed across jobs and individuals. The distribution function is assumed to be the extreme value distribution function of type III. If the variance of ε is infinitely large, to the analysts the choices of the individuals seem to have been made at pure random. The economic variables entering the deterministic part of the utility function will then explain nothing of what we observe. At the other extreme, if the variance ε is close to zero, then to the analyst all choices made by the individuals can be explained entirely by the deterministic part of the utility function. The individuals then make their labor supply choice according to what maximises their deterministic utility function. This latter extreme case is actually the approach taken in the so-called Hausman tradition, Burtless and Hausman (1978); Hausman (1980, 1981, 1985); Blomquist (1983, 1992); Hausman and Ruud (1984); Arrufat and Zabalza (1986). In this literature the functional form of the utility function is specified so that hours supplied becomes a convenient function of the marginal wage rate and of an income variable. To get a stochastic relationship, a parameter in the corresponding deterministic utility function is assumed to be random, with the justification that there is some unobserved heterogeneity in the individual labor supply responses.

Next, we represent the opportunity sets by a probability density function. One can interpret this as follows. Imagine that an individual has access to jobs that can be given a three-dimensional description—like a box. Inside the box there are many cells, each of them characterized by three sides, which reflect offered hours, the wage rate and 'other' attributes of a job. We assume that the individual knows his or her 'box' containing job opportunities. But as analysts we do not. The probability density representation of the opportunity set is then like folding a wet blanket over the 'box'. Now, there are many individuals, each with a different number of available jobs and of different types. The best skilled may have a much bigger 'opportunity box' to choose from than the less skilled. To capture this, we represent the choice set S by imposing a probability density on the choice set S. Let $p(h, w; q)$ denote the probability density of jobs of type (h, w). q is a vector of observed variables, like education and working experience, which reflects that the opportunities of individuals differ. The q-variables affect the moments in the probability distribution.

Our representation of opportunities allows for the fact that jobs with offered hours in a certain range are more likely to be found than other jobs. The clustering of offered hours in certain intervals may be due to the production technology of firms (in car production the workers have to be together at the same time, they cannot come and go as the wish), or due to the outcome of negotiations between employers and employee organizations. Many individuals are observed to rush to and from work at the same time. It would be strange to assume that this is due to preferences.

Moreover, our representation of opportunities also allows for wages to vary across jobs for the same individual. In the 'Hausman approach', and also in studies closer to ours such as Dickens and Lundberg (1993) and van Soest (1995), the individual has a fixed wage rate. Thus in these studies human capital endowments of the individual determine entirely his or her wage rate. This does not accord with more recent labor market theories, in which job-specific wage rates are due to efficient wages and wages determined in negotiations between the employers and employee associations. Wage dispersion among observationally identical workers seems also to be empirically supported (Krueger and Summers 1988; Edin and Zetterberg 1992).

We observe the chosen h and w. From the assumptions made above, we can derive the probability of the chosen job with these characteristics, (h, w).

Let $\varphi(h, w; I, z_1, q)$ denote this probability and let us use the definition $\nu(C, h; z_1) = \nu(f(wh, I), h; z_1) = \psi(h, w; I, z_1)$. Then we obtain:

$$\varphi(h, w; I, z_1, q) = \frac{\psi(h, w; I, z_1) p(h, w; q)}{\sum_{x \geq 0} \sum_{y \geq 0} \psi(x, y; I, z_1) p(x, y; q)} \tag{3}$$

For the proof we refer to Aaberge, Colombino and Strøm (1999).

Expression (3) is analogous to a multinomial logit model with the exception that the deterministic part of the outcome function of a particular choice, $\nu(f(wh, I), h; z_1)$ is weighted by the probability density of jobs with the characteristics (h, w), i.e. by $p(h, w; q)$. The intuition behind expression (3) is that the probability of the optimal choice, $\varphi(h, w; I, z_1, q)$, can be expressed as the relative attractiveness of jobs of type (h, w), weighted by a measure of how available this type of job is, i.e. by $p(h, w; q)$. To proceed with estimation one has to specify the functional form of the deterministic part of the utility function, that is, the functional form of v, and hence ψ, and the probability density $p(h, w; q)$.

With regard to the functional form of the utility function we have employed a rather flexible functional form. Depending on the value of the parameters, the deterministic part of the utility function can be linear in consumption and leisure as well as log-linear in these two variables. Moreover, again depending on the parameters, it also allows for a labor supply that is backward bending. The latter means that the higher the wage rate is, the less the labor supply will be. If so, the income effects dominate over the substitution effects. In fact, the functional form specification allows for the responses on wage rate to vary a lot across individuals, depending on their economic situation (the magnitude of w and I) and the characteristics z_1. The functional form can also yield a linear labor supply curve. As mentioned above, this is the only form that the Hausman approach applies. The problem with a labor supply curve, which is linear in the wage rate is that by assumption the labor supply elasticity tends to increase with the wage rate. The linearity assumption thus implies that the more highly skilled, with high wage rates, are more responsive than those with lower skills, and hence lower wage rates (see Røed and Strøm (2002) for further discussion).

In the specification of the probability density of opportunities, we will assume that offered hours and offered wages are independently distributed. The justification for this is that offered hours, in particular normal working hours, are typically set in rather infrequent negotiations between employers and employee associations, while wage negotiations are far more frequent in which the hourly wage tends to be set independently of working hours. Offered hours are assumed to be uniformly distributed, except for hours related to full-time jobs. Thus, this opportunity density for offered hours implies that it is far more likely to find jobs with hours that accord with a full-time position than jobs with other working loads. To account for the fact that the availability of any job at all may vary across, say, regions, the proportion of market opportunities may depend on where the individual lives for example, in the north or the south of Italy. The wage rate is assumed to be lognormal distributed, with the expectation depending on individual characteristics.

It is beyond the scope of this chapter to go into detail about specifications of the model, estimation methods and estimation results. Instead we refer to Aaberge, Colombino and Strøm (1999) and Aaberge, Colombino, Strøm and Wennemo (2000), where the modeling and estimation method is explained and where empirical results for labor supply among married couples in Italy are given. In Aaberge, Colombino and Strøm (2000) similar estimation result for Norway, Sweden and Italy are also given and compared.

APPENDIX 11.B

Social welfare functions

The standard approach in evaluating tax systems is to employ a social evaluation or welfare function as the basic evaluating instrument. This function is commonly used to summarize the changes in (adult-equivalent) income/welfare resulting from introducing various alternatives to the actual tax system in a country. The simplest way to summarize the changes that take place is to add up the income/welfare differentials, implying that individuals are given equal weights in the social welfare function independently of whether they are poor or rich. However, if besides total welfare we also care about the distributional consequences of a tax system, then an alternative to the linear additive welfare function is required. In this study we rely on the rank-dependent social welfare functions that have their origin in Mehran (1976) and Yaari (1988),[10] and are defined by:

$$W_k = \sum_{i=1}^{n} p_k\left(\frac{i}{n}\right) X_{(i)} \quad k = 1, 2, \dots \tag{4}$$

where $X_{(1)} \leq X_{(2)} \leq \cdots \leq X_{(n)}$ are the ordered income (or—more generally—welfare) levels of a sample of size n of the population, and $p_k(i/n)$ is a positive decreasing weight function.[11] A preliminary problem to solve consists in computing income or welfare measures that can be compared across households. We use money-metric utility measures as explained in King (1983) and Aaberge, Colombino and Strøm (2001). The inequality aversion exhibited by W_k decreases with increasing k. As $k \to \infty$, W_k approaches inequality neutrality and coincides with the linear additive welfare function defined by:

$$W_\infty = \frac{1}{n} \sum_{i=1}^{n} X_{(i)} \tag{5}$$

It follows by straightforward calculation that $W_k \leq W_\infty$ for all k and that W_k is equal to the mean W_∞ for finite k if, and only if, the distribution function is the egalitarian distribution. Thus, W_k can be interpreted as the equally distributed level of income (or welfare). As recognized by Yaari (1988) this property suggests that I_k, defined by:

$$I_k = 1 - \frac{W_k}{W_\infty}, \quad k = 1, 2, \dots \tag{6}$$

---

[10] Several authors have discussed rationales for this approach, see e.g. Sen (1974), Hey and Lambert (1980), Donaldson and Weymark (1980, 1983), Weymark (1981), Ben Porath and Gilboa (1992) and Aaberge (2001).

[11]

$$p_k(t) = \begin{cases} -\log t, & k = 1 \\ \dfrac{k}{k-1}(1 - t^{k-1}), & k = 2, 3, \dots \end{cases}$$

can be used as a summary measure of inequality. Actually, I_1 is equivalent to a measure of inequality that was proposed by Bonferroni (1930), while I_2 is the Gini coefficient.[12]

Equality of opportunity as a benchmark for evaluation of social policy

For a given sum of income, the standard social welfare functions take their maximum value when everyone gets the same income and may thus be interpreted as equality of outcome (EO) criteria when employed as measures for judging between alternative policy regimes, for example tax systems. However, as indicated by Roemer (1998) the EO-criterion is controversial and suffers from the drawback of receiving little support among citizens in a nation.[13] This is simply due to the fact that differences in outcomes resulting from differences in efforts are in general considered ethically acceptable and thus should not be the target of a redistribution policy. An egalitarian redistribution policy should instead seek to equalize those income differentials for which the individuals should not be held responsible, because they were beyond their control. Problematic life conditions or events—whether concerning employment, health, housing etc.—typically originate from a mixture of bad opportunities, bad luck and 'wrong' decisions. Social policies can affect the number and the quality of opportunities, the probability of unlucky events, and also the appropriateness of decision-making by providing information upon available choices, and counseling on good procedures for learning and processing information. In order to design good social policies one has to disentangle as far as possible the contribution of opportunities, chance, preferences and decision-making ability to the individual labor market successes. Thus, not only the outcome, but its origin and how it was obtained, matters. This is the essential idea behind Roemer's (1998) theory of equality of opportunity where people are supposed to differ with respect to 'circumstances'. Circumstances are attributes of the environment of the individual that influence the earnings potential of the individual, and which are 'beyond his control'. Thus, as distinct from the standard utilitarian EO approach, Roemer's (1998) EOp approach is non-'welfarist'; one needs to know the efforts expended by the individuals, and not simply the outcomes they enjoy under them.

Assume that $X_t(i/n_t)$ is the income (or welfare) level of the individual with rank i in the income distribution of type t, where:

$$i = 1, 2, \ldots, n_t \quad and \quad t = 1, 2, \ldots, r,$$

i.e. $X_t\left(\dfrac{1}{n_t}\right) \leq X_t\left(\dfrac{2}{n_t}\right) \leq \cdots \leq X_t\left(\dfrac{n_{t-1}}{n_t}\right) \leq X(1) \quad$ for $\quad t = 1, 2, \ldots, r$

[12] For further discussion of the family $\{I_k : k = 1, 2, \ldots\}$ of inequality measures we refer to Mehran (1976), Donaldson and Weymark (1980, 1983), Bossert (1990) and Aaberge (2000, 2001).
[13] See also Dworkin (1981), Arneson (1989, 1990), Cohen (1989) and Roemer (1993).

The differences in incomes within each type are assumed to be due to different degrees of effort for which the individual is to be held responsible, whereas income differences that may be traced back to circumstances are considered to be beyond the control of the individual. As indicated by Roemer (1998) this suggests that we may measure a person's effort by the quantile or relative rank (i/n_t) of the income distribution where he is located. Next, Roemer declares that two individuals in different types have expended the same degree of effort if they have identical relative positions (relative rank) in the income distribution of their type. Thus, an EOp (Equality of Opportunity) tax policy should aim at designing a tax system such that is $\min_t X_t(q)$ maximised for each quantile q. However, since this criterion is rather demanding and in most cases will not produce a complete ordering of the tax systems, a weaker ranking criterion is required. To this end Roemer (1998) proposes to employ as the social evaluation function the average of the lowest income at each quantile,

$$\widetilde{W}_\infty = \frac{1}{\min_t n_t} \sum_q \min_t X_t(q) \qquad (7)$$

Thus, $\widetilde{W}_\infty$ ignores income differences *within* types and is solely concerned about differences that arise from differential circumstances. By contrast, the EO criteria defined by (4) does not distinguish between the different sources that contribute to income inequality. As an alternative to (4) and (7) we introduce the following extended family of EOp welfare functions,

$$\widetilde{W}_k = \sum_q p_k(q) \min_t X_t(q) \qquad (8)$$

where $p_k(q)$ is defined by (5).

The essential difference between $\widetilde{W}_k$ and $\widetilde{W}_\infty$ is that $\widetilde{W}_k$ gives increasing weight to the welfare of lower quantiles in the type-distributions. Thus, in this respect $\widetilde{W}_k$ captures also an aspect of inequality within types. As explained above, the concern for *within* type inequality is greatest for the most disadvantaged type, that is, for the type that forms the largest segment(s) of $\{\min_t X_t(q) : q \in [0, 1]\}$.

We may decompose the EOp welfare functions, $\widetilde{W}_k$, as we did with the EO welfare functions W_k. Accordingly, we have that

$$\widetilde{W}_k = \widetilde{W}_\infty(1 - \tilde{I}_k), \quad k = 1, 2, \ldots \qquad (9)$$

where $\tilde{I}_k$ defined by

$$\tilde{I}_k = 1 - \frac{\widetilde{W}_k}{\widetilde{W}_\infty}, \quad k = 1, 2, \ldots \qquad (10)$$

is a summary measure of inequality for the mixture distribution $\tilde{F}$. Expression (9) demonstrates that the EOp welfare functions $\widetilde{W}_k$ for $k < \infty$ take into account value judgments about the trade-off between the mean income and the inequality in the distribution of income for the most EOp disadvantaged people.

Note that the EOp criterion was originally interpreted as more acceptable from the point of view of individualistic conservative societies. Our extended EOp welfare functions can be considered as a mixture of the EO welfare functions and the pure EOp welfare function; they are concerned about inequality between types as well as inequality within the worst-off distribution. EOp looks at what happens to the distribution formed by the most disadvantaged segments of the intersecting type-specific distributions. Moreover, the pure version of the criterion only looks at the mean of the worst-off distribution. By contrast, EO takes into account the whole income distribution. For a given sum of incomes, EO will consider equality of income (everyone receives the same income) as the most desirable income distribution. The pure EOp will instead consider equality in mean incomes across types as the ultimate goal. Since the extended EOp combines these two criteria, transfers that reduce the differences in the mean incomes between types as well as the income differentials between the individuals within the worst-off distribution are considered equalizing by the extended EOp. Thus, in the case of a fixed total income also the extended EOp will consider equality of income as the most desirable distribution. However, by transferring money from the most advantaged type to the most disadvantaged type, EOp inequality may be reduced. Whether it is more 'efficient' to reduce inequality between or within types, depends on the specific situation. When labor supply responses to taxation are taken into account, the composition of types in the worst-off distribution will change and depend on the chosen welfare function ($\widetilde{W}_k$) as well as on the considered tax rule. Thus, the large heterogeneity in labor supply responses to tax changes that is captured by our model(s) makes it impossible to state anything on EOp- or EO-optimality before the simulation exercises have been completed.

12

What Policy Should Do

In this part of the book we have analysed the important links between the growth of female labor participation, motherhood, and household welfare. We have focused more closely on countries in the south of Europe, where reconciling labor market activities and childrearing appears to be more problematic in several dimensions. In this section we summarize the most important policy implications that are derived from our results.

The results of the empirical analyses on the joint decision of having a child and participating in the labor market, based on the data from several European countries, indicate how different combinations of social and labor market policies (e.g. part-time employment opportunities, larger supply of childcare provision, parental leave) designed to reconcile work and childrearing simultaneously impact on work and fertility decisions.

Our results show that the 'best option' seems to be a combination of part-time employment, childcare, and parental leave immediately following the birth of the child (a combination offered in Denmark, Sweden and Norway, where in fact both fertility and female employment are high). In this way, women can continue working during their childbearing years, enabling them to maintain an attachment to the labor market while directly taking care of their children at least part-time. This 'convex combination' of work and motherhood may have some negative, but apparently limited, impact on career perspectives and wages.

An alternative might be a long optional maternal leave period that allows women to take care of their children full-time for several months post-birth (an option which is available in Germany and France for example). This solution would permit women to keep their jobs, but the costs in terms of career and human capital loss may be significant, sometimes more relevant than those associated with spells of unemployment. This empirical evidence emerges especially in countries where benefits are very low (such as in Germany) and therefore encourage mainly less-educated women to take the leave option.

With other options it appears to be more difficult to combine work and childrearing. When full-time jobs are the only ones available in the labor market, for example, there are positive implications for wage differentials (which are lower), but a greater burden is shifted to the entire family in the absence of available and affordable childcare (such as in Italy and Spain). Here cultural attitudes need to be considered, given that informal childcare (mainly provided by the grandparents) is preferred by a significant proportion of households, even when formal childcare is available. In these contexts, fertility and participation rates as a consequence are lower.

The importance of a father's contribution implies that a more equal share of the care of children could be achieved, thereby encouraging paternity leave, which implies raising the parental leave benefit (given the higher wages of men relative to women).

Our research also points to some undesired results of mothers' employment. Mothers' employment during periods of childhood care appears to have both short-term and long-term consequences on children's wellbeing. The short-term effects of increased early maternal employment are lower levels of socio-emotional adjustment and cognitive outcomes among younger children. The long-term effects have their strongest manifestation in lower educational attainment for children in their late teens and early twenties. The effects of paternal employment seem to be less marked.

Thus, growing up in a family in which the mother is employed outside the home appears to have some adverse consequences on children's welfare, suggesting a negative effect of the loss of the mother's childcare time. Social policies aimed at increasing the supply of adequate childcare for dual-earning families should, therefore, not neglect the goal of increasing quality of services to help compensate for this loss of mother's childcare time.

On the other hand, there is evidence that growing up in a low-income household tends to have some adverse consequences on children's educational and labor market outcomes as compared to children growing up in more affluent households. Therefore, if women's work is characterized by strong labor market attachment and continuity, this may imply higher family income, and children's life chances may be unaffected or even positively affected by the decision of both parents to work.

The analysis of the implications of the changes in women's and men's labor participation on family income distribution shows that at a more micro-level, the shift in the wife's role in the household from caregiver to income producer tends to make the spouses more 'symmetric', with potentially heavy effects on the level of resources within the household, and both the inter-household and intra-household distribution of consumption and welfare. For example, in countries where the proportion of dual-earner households is high (in all income and education groups), inequality in household income is lower.

Our analysis of household taxation policies in different social welfare systems has demonstrated that women living in low and average-income households are much more responsive to economic incentives than women or men in other income groups. The implication is that a profitable direction for reform might consist in lowering marginal tax rates specifically on low and middle incomes. Given that the structure of own and cross-elasticities do not produce any significant reduction in labor supply at low-income levels when introducing universal support mechanisms, there is scope for redesigning the tax-transfer regime in order to have more efficiency and more equality at the same time. Social and fiscal policies can be combined to improve the labor market participation of low-income mothers who, especially in Mediterranean countries, are facing greater constraints in their labor supply decisions.

Given that an important factor in the reduced levels of fertility in southern European countries is the postponement of first births, tax reduction policies for the young may also contribute to forming families earlier in life, thus reducing the negative impact of postponement of births on total fertility levels.

The empirical evidence presented here indicates that the employment goals established by the European Union—the so-called Lisbon target—cannot be reached simply through the progressive, constant increase in the level of female education. This natural trend, in place in Italy for some years now, has, indeed, led to an increase in higher labor participation rates by women. Yet it is insufficient to meet the Lisbon target figures for Italy, which necessitate an increase in female employment rates of nearly twenty percentage points.

The results we have obtained show how a sizeable increase in participation could be obtained through family policies that reduce the burden on women of household and family responsibilities (i.e. greater flexibility in the employment arrangements, improvements in childcare availability and quality) as well as changes in tax transfer regimes that achieve more equality in income distribution without negative effect on participation and fertility.

Comments

GIOVANNI ANDREA CORNIA

Del Boca *et al.*'s study is a timely and interesting attempt to analyse the determinants of female labor supply in the European countries, to examine whether the Lisbon target of creating some 15 million new jobs for women by 2010 is likely to be achieved, and to evaluate the female labor supply and child welfare impact of policies in the field of childcare, parental leave, part-time employment and tax and transfers.

The authors also consider the indirect impact on fertility of policy changes in the field of parental leave, part-time employment and tax-and-transfers. The reason for this inclusion is that, at present, low female participation (particularly in southern Europe) is accompanied by extremely low fertility rates (well below the replacement rate) that affect the long-term sustainability of the existing pay-as-you go pension systems while—at the same time—representing a source of dissatisfaction for the families that, on average, indicate that the 'desired number of children' is consistently higher than the average number of children per family. In sum, the relation between labor force participation of women and the policies towards it is intrinsically intertwined with the issues of child wellbeing, and of fertility. A further interesting aspect of the report is the accent it places on the equity impact of changes in both policies (e.g. different tax rules) and outcomes (e.g. higher labor force participation by women). Clearly, the authors wish to move from the present equilibrium to another superior one without causing deteriorations in other key areas.

The report is articulated in four sections that conveniently overlap—if only in part—to create sufficient linkages between the various aspects of the problems being investigated. The first section (Ch. 8) analyses at length, including by means of cross-sectional econometric estimates, the determinants of female labor force participation and fertility, the complex relation between female labor supply, availability of part-time or temporary jobs, social policies (such as maternity and parental leave, availability of childcare services and child allowances), and fertility. The chapter concludes that the main factors responsible at the same time for low female participation and low fertility are a mismatch between job supply and demand, and lack of affordable childcare. It reaches this conclusion by arguing that greater availability of flexible part-time arrangements, subsidized childcare services and parental leave options would reconcile childrearing and female participation.

The second section (Ch. 9) discusses exhaustively the impact on child wellbeing of mother's employment during childhood, particularly during the initial

24–36 months of life, focusing on the trade-offs between her time spent in nurturing the child and the generation of greater incomes for the family and the child itself. The net result of these two mutually offsetting effects is found to vary across national environments, but it is probably less favorable for richer families/countries where the marginal income effect might be less pronounced. The third section (Ch. 10) in turn, examines the effects on the inter- and intra-household distribution of income of an increase in female employment and finds that such effects are—in most cases—both favorable, pointing in this way to the additional important benefits of policies encouraging higher work participation among women. Finally, Section 4 (Ch. 11) presents a fascinating discussion of how greater labor force participation, greater overall welfare and an improvement of both inter- and intra-household income distribution could be achieved by changes in policies on taxation and income support. One key empirical finding of this section is that female labor supply elasticities are much higher at low levels of income, a result that influences the findings of the microsimulations carried out in the study, which show that efficiency and equity would both be maximized by the adoption of a tax rule that reduces tax progressivity, not so much in favor of the very rich, but more of the middle-class and the poor.

It is a clearly written, well-documented report and argued in an analytical fashion. A number of new results are produced which, though obviously requiring further empirical validation, are highly relevant both analytically and policy-wise. It is therefore not too difficult to agree with most of the points and recommendations made in the overall study. The suggestions and comments for improvement that follow have therefore to be seen from this perspective.

The first comment concerns the far greater attention paid by the report to 'supply side' as opposed to the 'demand side' of female labor force participation. For instance, Chapter 8 assumes that the provision of a more generous parental leave (among other things) would increase the participation of women in the labor force. Likewise, Chapter 11 assumes that a change in tax-transfer rules would affect the labor supply, but does not say anything on whether this additional labor supply might affect the wage rate or the unemployment rate (both of which also depend on labor demand). While the supply side of female labor can be legitimately and usefully studied independently from an analysis of the demand side, an eventual use of the report for policy purposes would require paying greater attention to (a) demand factors: wage rate, capital accumulation, deregulation, credit cost, availability of small enterprises (i.e. areas in which the situation is not particularly favorable, e.g. in some regions, such as southern Italy, or in self-employment); or, (b) at least to the possible effects on the wage rate, unemployment rate and so on of an increase in supply.

A second related comment concerns the degree of realism to which the report, and the implicit or explicit models that underlie it, reproduce the economic and social reality being investigated. This becomes particularly important if the analysis is going to be used—as one would hope—to inspire public policy. In this regard, one wonders, for instance, whether there might be scope for paying greater attention to 'dual labor markets' comprising a formal market (in which taxation, transfers and childcare provisions apply), and an informal labor market (which is expanding rapidly in many countries) where the same rules do not apply. The introduction of dual labor markets in the analysis, could alter the conclusion of the study in some cases. One could argue, for instance, that the provision of more generous maternity leave might lead to the informalization of some formal sector jobs, especially if the cost of these new provisions is to be borne by the firms. Likewise, one could imagine that a favorable change in tax rule along the lines proposed in Chapter 11 could increase the transfers of labor from the informal to the formal sector, with uncertain net effects in terms of overall additional labor supply.

Thirdly, the analyses in the report could perhaps pay greater attention to social norms, or at least to their inertia over the short and medium term. Perhaps, the low participation rates among women with children of less than 3 years of age are the result of a cultural norm that increases the preference of mothers to raise their children up until, perhaps, 3 years of age. If this is true, then the effect of changes in the transfer, labor market and taxation policies analysed in the report may be at odds with those envisaged in by the authors in this study, at least in the short term.

Fourthly, the report presents implicit or explicit policy recommendations, chapter by chapter, but does not explore their overall consistency. The problem that could be caused by such an approach can be illustrated here with one example. Altogether, one could describe the problems raised by the chapters discussed above, and their proposed solutions, as a policy exercise in which the government has to reach two 'policy objectives' (to increase the labor force participation of women to the level foreseen by the Lisbon declaration while raising the fertility rate) through changes in three 'policy tools' ((i) transfers for parental leave and child allowances; (ii) incentives for the provision of part-time jobs; and (iii) tax and transfers), subject to two 'constraints' or caveats (do not worsen child outcomes such as child health, education and psychosocial scores later in life; and do not worsen the inequality of the distribution of household income).

Given this hypothesis, let us now suppose, for instance, that, as proposed in Chapter 11, the tax rates are lowered and that, as a result, the female labor supply increases. However, if such an increase in female labor supply is not accompanied by the introduction of complementary social policies, fertility could fall while child outcomes might deteriorate, though one would observe an improvement in inter-household income distribution, and in the bargaining position of women within the family. Obviously, this 'second best' result could be improved upon if provisions in the field of parental leave, part-time employment and subsidized care for children 18–36 months of age were to be adopted. Decisions along this line would lead to a 'first best' situation in which female labor supply would grow, child outcomes and fertility would not deteriorate (and may even improve), and income inequality would decline.

However, the introduction of the social policy measures just described would entail greater public expenditure, and/or a considerable lowering of the cost of childcare by private providers, and/or a redefinition of social norms (e.g. the allocation to childcare of a greater share of the leisure time of fathers). Yet, these changes might not be feasible or may generate other negative effects. Consider for instance, the fiscal cost of the additional social policies proposed. If the government concerned followed the Maastricht criterion strictly, greater expenditure would be feasible only if taxes were raised. But a decision to raise taxes would nullify the initial policy decision to lower taxes so as to increase female labor supply.

Obviously, if one were to relaxe the policy constraints under which the policy problem at hand needs to be solved, everything would be easier. For instance, if one relaxed the constraint 'do not worsen child outcomes', then the solution of the policy problem would be easier, and one could find a solution relatively easily satisfying all other criteria. But the decision to ignore the impact on child outcomes would entail a considerable and politically difficult-to-digest intra-generational redistribution of welfare from one social group (children) towards another (working-age women), with negative long-term effects on the welfare of children and—even more importantly—of the future generations as a whole. It is evident that, though more complex, the search for universal solutions is preferable to both equity and efficiency viewpoints.

This simple policy simulation suggests that further analyses should pay greater attention—to the interactions between the various positive and normative analyses carried out in the report. While this objective could be achieved through the development of a general equilibrium model, in the context of this study it would more likely be better achieved by a systematic examination of the compatibility of alternative packages of the three types of measures proposed (taxes, subsidies and labor policies) in relation to the objectives discussed above, given the constraints that the authors have explicitly adopted.

Finally, it might be useful to conclude these comments with a simple methodological warning. A good part of the analyses carried out in the study are mostly based on, aggregate (national) cross-sectional data. While this is a common approach in the social sciences, it is also one that does not always help in effectively capturing the short term effects of policy changes and other changes at the national level, due to the well-known problems posed by structural differences across countries that are only in part corrected by the econometric techniques. Greater use of time series analysis may therefore be advisable, if time and data constraint allow it.

VALÉRIE LECHENE

This study on the effect of social policies on labor market participation of women and fertility aims to bring evidence to bear on the question of how to 'allow women to work and have children'. To answer this question, the authors of the report present a very thorough critical review of the evidence and literature, as well as original results on women's labor force participation and fertility, children's welfare and the effect of tax reform. My discussion will have two parts. I will start by asking what is meant by the phrase 'allowing women to work and have children', as well as why it should be considered desirable that women work, that they have children and that they should do both. The next question to consider is why should policies be designed to promote this double aim rather than leaving individual choice and the markets to operate without intervention. I will then consider how we can answer the question of how would behavior change if social and fiscal policies were modified, in the light of the contribution of the different sections or chapters that make up the report.

Women labor force participation and fertility: Why incentives and which incentives?

The phrase 'allowing women to work and have children' implies that there is a tension between working and having children. Chapter 8 documents that this was infact the case in a number of countries until the mid-1980s, with a negative association between women's labor force participation and fertility. But the more recent period has seen a different type of situation emerging, with a group of countries—Italy, Spain and Greece—where both fertility and labor force participation are low.

The first question to ask is whether the tension between work and fertility, or the fact that in some countries both participation and fertility are low result from the demand side or the supply side of the labor market—or from both? In other words, are there economic constraints which prevent women from achieving optimal combinations of labor market participation and fertility, or are the observed situations the result of choice? The question is valid because the incentives are different in both cases, and Chapter 8 contributes to this debate by bringing together considerable amounts of evidence available on this aspect of the problem.

On the labor market, the demand side could generate just such a tension—for instance if employers were reluctant to hire women of child-bearing age, or mothers of young children. The case in which employers have a preference for hiring workers of one gender over the other when these workers' characteristics (and hence their productivity) are equivalent, is discriminatory. Discrimination, although illegal, is very difficult to establish, as it requires demonstrative proof that workers' characteristics are equivalent. Another possibility where tensions might arise between fertility and labor market participation, would be if the structures of the labor market were such that there were few or no contracts affording the flexibility mothers find desirable to be able to conduct an active life and raise young children. Indeed, Chapter 8 presents evidence of a positive association between prevalence of part-time work, and labor force participation of women and fertility. However, one needs to ask the question from which direction does the causality in this association come—a particularly difficult task on the basis of cross-country comparisons. Is it the case that societies in which fertility and women's labor force participation are high are societies that will promote labor market structures that will sustain this? Evidence presented by Florence Jaumotte shows that stated preferences reveal that women in Mediterranean countries have preferences for full-time work over part-time. However, it is not entirely clear whether to interpret this as a preference for full-time over part-time in general, or as a preference over the regimes of part-time work which exist in Mediterranean countries. Therefore, should governments in Italy, Greece and Spain create legal and economic incentives to promote part-time work? Would it be cost effective policy? To answer these questions, one needs to know whether tastes in northern countries (where prevalence of part-time work and labor force participation and fertility are high) are different from preferences in southern countries, or whether economic conditions are different, and if so why. Finding out whether tastes for work and children are different in different countries is not an easy task. Stated preference surveys (such as the recent survey described by Professor Boeri) are an important tool. Another way is to perform the type of structural analysis for which Chapters 8 and 11 of the report lay the foundations.

Still considering the labor market, but turning now to the supply side, it becomes obvious there exists a tension, because having children requires a commitment in terms of time, which is always at a premium. It is also because purchased childcare is an imperfect substitute for parents' own time spent with children that there is this tension: time spent with one's children reduces the amount of time available for all other activities, as documented in Chapter 9 of the report.

Finally, the report also mentions a role for labor market conditions in shaping outcomes in terms of participation and fertility. Greater labor market uncertainty and higher unemployment levels appear to be associated with both lower fertility and participation. The report paints a picture which makes it apparent that the situation is very complex and that a multitude of factors, some economic, some institutional, combine to generate the situation we witness. Therefore, we can understand the phrase 'allowing women to have children and work' as meaning designing a set of legal circumstances and entitlements, which ensure that women of childbearing age are not discriminated against in the labor market, but also promoting the supply of women's labor, that is to say, creating circumstances which are conducive to working at the same time as having children. Such circumstances include the availability of alternatives to mother's childcare time, which are as close substitutes as possible, as well as providing incentives to work.

As economists, we need to ask the question why intervention should be needed rather than letting individual interactions and markets operate? There are two types of reasons why intervention might be needed. One set of reasons is where individuals' preferences differ from the preferences of society. Here it could be that individuals' optimal number of children is less than society's optimum. Another reason could be that preferences of individuals and society coincide, but that, because of market imperfections, the outcomes in terms of fertility and labor force participation are inefficient. For instance, it could be that women might not be able to borrow to pay for childcare, and that if they stay at home, they lose their skills. In this case, there would be fewer children, and inefficient outcomes on the labor market besides. Evidence exists that the ability to borrow from family is associated with a greater probability of labor force participation, and greater fertility (Del Boca, 2002). This type of argument justifies the passing of laws on parental leave, childcare and part-time work. The answer to the question of why intervention should be needed also raises the question as to the form of intervention required. Indeed, as economists, we know that in order to increase welfare levels, most of the time it is considered superior to give money rather than goods or services, as the latter can be exchanged for goods and services, hence yielding higher levels of utility. However, in this case, intervention is generally designed to take the form of laws for parental leave and childcare subsidies, rather than giving parents money. The reasons for the latter can be that there are externalities to having 'bad' children in society, and that the level of expenditure on childcare without subsidies would be suboptimal from the point of view of society.

Finally, the question of the necessity for intervention can be considered from a different angle: Why is it desirable that women work and have children? There is one argument against women working when they have children. Indeed, as documented in Chapter 9, there is considerable evidence that mothers' labor force participation, at least during the first years of the life of their children, has detrimental effects on a number of child outcomes. On the other side, there is a variety of arguments why women should have the possibility to work. It is considered that work brings empowerment for women, together with a better society on the whole. Arguments pertaining to the fragility of marriage can also be put forward. It is sometimes also argued that it is better for growth if women work.

With regard to children, as argued in the introduction of the report, there is an issue with sustainability of pensions. But the pension issue can be settled through immigration. If we take the long view, we see that all our countries are peopled by individuals whose descendants immigrated in the not so distant past. Finally, we may ask whether fertility is not self-regulating, in the sense that if fertility falls below the optimal level in terms of sustainability of pensions, will it automatically increase? At any rate, if it is indeed because of constraints that women do not have children, then intervention is warranted.

There remains a question of timing. Should women work and have children at the same time? Or should society create a framework similar to that existing in Denmark, where women have children and then go back to work after the children have reached an age where it is considered that paid childcare constitutes an acceptable substitute to mother's care?

How to predict the effect of social and fiscal policies on behavior?

What would enable us to go beyond statistical associations in order to understand the behavioral mechanisms at play? In other words, when we observe different situations in different countries, or between different individuals, we want to know how, if the parameters of the environment were to change, individuals' behavior would change. In the present context, we want to know if, faced with the social and fiscal policies of the Danes, Italians will have the same fertility and labor force participation as the Danes. The problem is that the sole comparison between the Danish situation and the Italian situation does not tell us whether the Italians, faced with the same incentives, would respond in the same way as the Danes, because we do not know whether, in fact, they chose to have different social and fiscal policies in view of the fact they have different preferences concerning work and children. There are two ways in which to resolve such problems of endogeneity. When we observe that there is a negative association between work and children, we do not know whether women who have children do not work because they do not want to work, or because they cannot work when they have young children. What we would need to observe, in order to discern between the two possibilities, are changes (or differences) that are not chosen by individuals. An example can be put forward, strictly for the purpose of illustrating both the method and the difficulty of its implementation, in case of interest. Do individuals who lose their children work more? By the same logic, if jobs are destroyed exogenously, do individuals have more children? This question shows that it is difficult to come up with natural experiments that would allow for an answer. Thus we are left with the route of structural models and exclusion restrictions. Labor supply and fertility are determined jointly, which we can express in the following manner:

$$L = F_1(F, X, u_1)$$

$$F = F_2(L, Z, u_2)$$

where L is labor force participation, F is fertility, X and Z are sets of individual characteristics, u_1 is an unobserved taste for labor, conditional on X and F, and

u_2 is an unobserved taste for fertility, conditional on Z and L. To fix ideas, suppose a linear structure:

$$L = \alpha F + X'\beta + u_1 + \lambda u_2$$

$$F = \gamma L + Z'\delta + u_2 + \theta u_1$$

The question we would like to answer is the following: How would fertility and labor force participation change if the availability, for instance, of childcare were to increase? Increases in childcare availability can lead to increases in fertility, because the opportunity cost of children is lower. Increases in fertility in turn lead to lower labor force participation. But increases in childcare availability also lead to increases in labor force participation, because the opportunity cost of time for a given number of children is lower. Therefore, the net effect on labor force participation can be positive or negative, depending on the relative magnitudes of the various effects. Such a question is an empirical question; answering it can be tackled within a structural framework such as the one outlined above, where identification relies on the possibility of observing elements which lead to variation in labor force participation but not fertility, and in fertility but not labor force participation. This example using childcare is illustrative, but it is an example which applies to anything thought to affect labor force participation and fertility, as envisaged in Chapter 8.

Conclusion

This report brings together a lot of evidence on labor market participation and fertility in European countries. It amply demonstrates that the processes driving fertility and labor force participation are very complex. On the basis of the evidence presented, we can probably agree about the likely causes of low participation and low fertility in southern European countries: labor market rigidities and imperfections, high fixed costs of participation, institutional constraints. It is also clear that there are differences in taste. It appears that there is a political will to take legislative initiatives to try and correct for some of these imperfections and inefficiencies. The next task then is to establish which policies are more cost effective, so as to formulate recommendations in terms of social and fiscal policies. As the introduction of the report concludes, now it is possible to begin thinking about this.

References

Aaberge, R., Colombino, U., and Strøm, S. (1999): Labor Supply in Italy: An Empirical Analysis of Joint Household Decisions, with Taxes and Quantity Constraints, *Journal of Applied Econometrics*, 14, 403–422.

—— —— —— and Wennemo, T. (2000): Joint labour supply of married couples: efficiency and distribution effects of tax and labour market reforms, in: Mitton L., Sutherland H. and M. Weeks (Eds.) *Micro-simulation Modelling for Policy Analysis: Challenges and Innovations*, Cambridge University Press.

—— (2000), 'Characterizations of Lorenz Curves and Income Distributions', *Social Choice and Welfare*, 17, 639–653.

—— (2001), 'Axiomatic Characterization of the Gini Coefficient and Lorenz Curve Orderings', *Journal of Economic Theory*, 101, 115–132.

—— and Aslaksen, I. (2003), 'Decomposition of the Gini Coefficient Revised: the Effects of Wives' Earnings on Family Income Inequality', mimeo.

—— Aslaksen, I. and Wennemo, T. (2000), '"Birds of a Feather Flock Together": Married Women's Labour Income and Decomposition of Family Labour Income Inequality', mimeo, Research Department, *Statistics Norway*.

—— Colombino, U. and Strøm, S. (1999), 'Labor Supply in Italy: An Empirical Analysis of Joint Household Decisions with Taxes and Quantity Constraints', *Journal of Applied Econometrics*, 14, 403–422.

—— —— and —— (2000), 'Labour supply responses and welfare effects from replacing current tax rules by a flat tax: empirical evidence from Italy, Norway and Sweden', *Journal of Population Economics*, 13(4), 595–621.

—— —— and —— (2004), 'Do More Equal Slices Shrink the Cake? An Empirical Investigation of Tax-Transfer Reform Proposals in Italy', *Journal of Population Economics*, 17(4).

—— —— —— and Wennemo, T. (2000), 'Joint Labour Supply of Married Couples: Efficiency and Distribuitional Effects of Tax Reforms', in Sutherland, Mitton, Sutherland and Weeks (eds), *Microsimulation Modelling for Policy Analysis: Challenges and Innovations*, Cambridge: Cambridge University Press, UK.

—— —— Holmøy, S., Strøm, B. and Wennemo, T. (2004), 'Population ageing and fiscal sustainability: An integrated micro-macro analysis of required tax changes', *Working Paper CHILD* no. 6/2004, http://www.child-centre.it

—— Dagsvik, J. K. and Strøm, S. (1995), 'Labor Supply Responses and Welfare Effects of Tax Reforms', *Scandinavian Journal of Economics*, 106(4), 635–659.

Ahn, N. and Mira, P. (2001), 'Job bust baby bust? Evidence from Spain', *Journal of Population Economics*, 14(3), 505–522.

—— and —— (2002), 'A note of the relationship between fertility and female employment rates in developed countries', *Journal of Population Economics*, 667–682.

Albrecht, J. W., Edin, P. A., Sundström, M. and Vroman, S. B. (1999), 'Career Interruption and Subsequent Earnings: a Re-examination Using Swedish Data', *Journal of Human Resources*, 2, 294–311.

Amato, Paul P. and Gilbreth, J. G. (1999), 'Nonresident Fathers and Children's Well-Being: A Meta Analysis', *Journal of Marriage and the Family*, 61, 557–573.

Antecol, Heather and Bedard, Kelly (2002), 'Does Single Parenthood Increase the Probability of Teenage Promiscuity, Drug Use and Crime?'. *Unpublished paper*, Claremont McKenna College.

Arneson, R. (1989), 'Equality and Equality of Opportunity for Welfare', *Philosophical Studies*, 56, 77–93.

——(1990), 'Liberalism, Distributive Subjectivism, and Equal Opportunity for Welfare', *Philosophy & Public Affairs*, 19, 159–194.

Arrufat, J. L. and Zabalza, A. (1986), 'Female Labor supply with Taxation, Random Preferences and Optimization Errors', *Econometrica*, 54, 47–63.

Baizan, P., Billari, F. and Michielin, F. (2002), 'Political Economy and Lifecourse Patterns: the Heterogeneity of Occupational, Family and Household Trajectories of Young Spaniards', *Demographic Research*, 6, art. 8, 189–240.

Baldini, M. and Bosi, P. (2001), 'An Evaluation of Tax Reforms With Focus on Children Welfare', *Working Paper CHILD* no. 3/2001, http://www.child-centre.it

Bardasi, E. and Gornick J. C. (2000), 'Women and Part-Time Employment: Workers' "Choices" and Wage Penalties in Five Industrialised Countries', ISER Working Paper 2000–11.

Barmby, T. and Cigno, A. (1990), 'A Sequential Probability Model of Fertility Patterns', *Journal of Population Economics*, 3(1), 31–51.

Baum, C. L. II (2003), 'Does Early Maternal Employment Harm Child Development? An Analysis of the Potential Benefits of Leave Taking', *Journal of Labor Economics*, 27(2), 408–448.

Baydar, N. and Brooks-Gunn, J. (1991), 'Effects of Maternal Employment and Child-care Arrangements on Preschoolers' Cognitive and Behavioural Outcomes: Evidence from the Children of the National Longitudinal Survey of Youth', *Developmental Psychology*, 27, 932–945.

Becker, G. (1960), 'An Economic Analysis of Fertility in Demographic and Economic Change in Developed Countries', NBER Conference Series 11, Princeton University Press.

——(1981), *A Treatise on the Family*, Cambridge, Mass.: Harvard University Press (enlarged edition, 1991).

—— and Lewis, H. G. (1973), 'On the Interaction between the Quantity and Quality of Children', *Journal of Political Economy*, 82, S279–S288.

Beets, G. and Dourleijn, E. (2001), 'Low and Late Fertility is Expected to Continue: Will New Population Policy Measures Interfere?', paper presented to the XXIVth IUSSP General Population Conference, 18–24 August, in Salvador, Bahia, Brazil.

Behrman, Jere R. (1997), 'Women's Schooling and Child Education: A Survey'. *Unpublished Paper*, University of Pennsylvania.

—— and Rosenzweig, M. R. (2002), 'Does Increasing Women's Schooling Raise the Schooling of the Next Generation?', *American Economic Review*, 92, 323–334.

——Foster, A., Rosenzweig, M. R. and Vashishtha, Prem (1999), 'Women's Schooling, Home Teaching, and Economic Growth', *Journal of Political Economy*, 107, 682–714.

Belsky, J. and Eggebeen, D. (1991), 'Early and Extensive Maternal Employment and Young Children's Socioemotional Development: Children of the National Longitudinal Survey of Youth', *Journal of Marriage and the Family*, 53, 1083–1110.

Ben-Akiva, M. and Watanatada, T. (1981), 'Application of a Continuous Spatial Choice Logit Model', in C. Manski and D. McFadden (eds), *Structural Analysis of Discrete Data with Econometric Applications*, MIT Press.

Benjamin, K. (2001), 'Men Women and Low Fertility', paper presented at annual meeting of PAA, Washington DC.

Ben Porath, E. and Gilboa, I. (1994), 'Linear Measures, the Gini Index, and the Income-Equality Trade-off', *Journal of Economic Theory*, 64, 443–467.

Bernal, R. (2002), 'Employment and Child Care Decisions of Mothers and the Well-being of their Children'. *Unpublished Paper*, New York University (November).

Bettio, F. and Villa, P. (1998), 'A Mediterranean Perspective on the Break-down of the Relationship between Participation and Fertility', *Cambridge Journal of Economics*, 22, 137–171.

Betson, D. and van der Gaag, J. (1984), 'Working Married Women and the Distribution of Income', *Journal of Human Resources*, 40, 295–301.

Biblarz, T. J. and Gottainer, G. (2000), 'Family Structure and Children's Success: A Comparison of Widowed and Divorced Single-Mother Families', *Journal of Marriage and the Family*, 62, 533–548.

Bien, W. (2000), 'Changing Values among the future parents of Europe'. Paper presented at the European Observatory on Family Matters, 15–16 (September).

Billari, F. (2002), 'The Patterns of Low Fertility', *Population and Development Review*, 28(4), 641–680.

——and Kohler, H. P. (2002), 'The Patterns of Low Fertility', *Population and Development Review*, 28(4), 641–680.

——Kohler, H. P. and Ortega, J. A. (2002), 'The Emergence of Lowest Low Fertility in Europe during the 1990', *Population and Development Review*, 28(4), 641–680.

Björklund, A. and Jäntti, M. (2000), 'Intergenerational Mobility of Socio-economic Status in Comparative Perspective', *Nordic Journal of Political Economy*, 26(1), 3–33.

——and Sundström, M. (2002), 'Parental Separation and Children's Educational Attainment'. *Unpublished Paper*, Swedish Institute for Social Research, Stockholm University.

Blanchet, D. and Ekert-Jaffe, O. (1994), 'The Demographic Impact of Family Benefits: Evidence from a Micro-Model and from Macro-Data', in J. Ermisch and N. Ogawa (eds), *The Family, the Market and the State in Ageing Societies: International Studies in Demography*, Oxford: Oxford University Press, 79–104.

Blau, D. M. (1999), 'The Effect of Income on Child Development', *Review of Economics and Statistics*, 81, 261–276.

Blau, D. and Robins, P. (1988), 'Childcare Costs and Family Labor Supply', *Review of Economics and Statistics*, 70(3), 374–381.

Blau, F. D. and Grossberg, A. J. (1992), 'Maternal Labor Supply and Children's Cognitive Development', *Review of Economics and Statistics*, 74, 474–481.

Blau, P. M. and Duncan, O. D. (1967), *The American Occupational Structure*, New York: Wiley.

Blomquist, S. (1983), 'The Effect of Income Taxation on the Labor Supply of Married Men in Sweden', *Journal of Public Economics*, 17, 169–197.

Blomquist, S. (1992), 'Estimation Methods for Male Labor Supply Functions. How to Take Account of Nonlinear Taxes', *Journal of Econometrics*, 70, 383–405.

Blundell, R. (1996), 'Labour Supply and Taxation', in M. Devereux (ed.), *The Economics of Tax Policy*, Oxford: Oxford University Press.

——(1997), 'The Impact of Taxation on Labour Force Participation and Labour Supply', *The OECD Jobs Study*, Working Paper Series no. 8.

——(2000), 'Work Incentives and "in Work"-Benefits-Reform: A Review, *Oxford Review of Economic Policy*, 16(1), 27–44.

——and MaCurdy, T. (1999), 'Labour Supply', in O. Ashenfelter and D. Card (eds), *Handbook of Labor Economics*, North-Holland.

——and Meghir, C. (1986), 'Selection Criteria for a Microeconometric Model of Labour Supply', *Journal of Applied Econometrics*, 1, 55–80.

Bonferroni, C. (1930), *Elementi di Statistica Generale*, Seeber, Firenze.

Bongaarts, J. (2001), 'Fertility and Reproductive Preferences in Post-Transitional Societies', in R. Bulatao and J. Casterline (eds), *Global Fertility Transition*, A Supplement to Volume 27, *Population and Development Review*, 260–281.

——and Feeney, G. (1998), 'On the Quantum and Tempo of Fertility', *Population and Development Review*, 24(2), 271–291.

Borjas, G. and Heckman, J. J. (1978), Labour Supply Estimates for Public Policy Evaluation, in Industrial Relations Institute, *Proceedings of the Thirty-First Annual Meeting*, Madison, WI: 320–331.

Bossert, W. (1990), 'An Approximation of the Single-series Ginis', *Journal of Economic Theory* 50, 82–92.

Bourgignon, F., Browning, M., Chiappori, P. A. and Lechene, V. (1994), 'Incomes and Outcomes: A Structural Model of Household Allocation', *Journal of Political Economy*, 102(6), 1066–1096.

——O'Donoghue, C., Sastre-Descals, J., Spadareo, A. and Utili, F. (1997), 'Eur3: a Prototype European Tax-Benefit Model', *DAE Working Paper #MU9703*, Micro-simulation Unit, Department of Applied Economics, Cambridge: University of Cambridge.

Bowlby, John (1969), *Attachment and Loss: Attachment*, New York: Basic Books.

Bradbury, B. and Jäntti, M. (2001), 'Child Poverty Across Twenty-Five Countries', in Bruce Bradbury, Stephen P. Jenkins, and John Micklewright (eds), *The Dynamics of Child Poverty in Industrialised Countries*, Cambridge: Cambridge University Press.

Break, G. (1957), 'Income Taxes and the Incentive to Work: An Empirical Study', *American Economic Review*, 47, 529–49.

Breen, R. and Goldthorpe, J. H. (2001), 'Class, Mobility and Merit: The Experience of Two British Birth Cohorts', *European Sociological Review*, 17, 81–101.

Brewster, K. and Rindfuss, L. (2000), 'Fertility and Women Employment in Indus-trialized Countries', *Annual Review of Sociology*, 26, 271–287.

Brewster, K. L. and Rindfuss, R. J. (1996), 'Childrearing and Fertility', *Population and Development Review*, 22(0), 258–289. Supplement

Brooks-Gunn, J., Han, Wen-Jui, and Waldfogel, J. (2002), 'Maternal Employment and Child Cognitive Outcomes in the First Three Years of Life: The NICHD Study of Early Child Care', *Child Development*, 73, 1052–1072.

Browning, M. and Meghir, C. (1991), 'The Effect of Male and Female Labor Supply on Commodity Demands', *Econometrica*, 59, 925–952.

Bumpass, L., Raley, R. K. and Sweet, J. A. (1995), 'The changing character of step-families: Implications of cohabitation and nonmarital childbearing', *Demography*, 32, 425–436.

Burtless, G. and Hausmann, J. A. (1978), 'The Effects of Taxation on Labor Supply', *Journal of Political Economy*, 86, 1103–1130.

Butz, W. P. and Ward, M. P. (1979), 'The Emergence of Countercyclical US Fertility', *American Economic Review*, 69(3), 318–328.

Callan, T. and Sutherland, H. (1997), 'The Impact of Comparable Policies in European Counties: Microsimulation Approaches', *European Economic Review, Papers and Proceedings*.

Cameron, S. V. and Heckman, J. J. (2001), 'The Dynamics of Educational Attainment for Black, Hispanic and White Males', *Journal of Political Economy*, 109, 455–499.

Cancian, M. and Reed, D. (1998), 'Assessing the Effects of Wives' Earnings on Family Income Inequality', *The Review of Economics and Statistics*, 80, 73–79.

——Danziger, S. and Gottschalk, P. (1992), 'Working Wives and Family Income Inequality among Married Couples', in S. Danziger and P. Gottschalk (eds), *Uneven Tides–Rising Inequality in America*, NY: Russell Sage Foundation.

Card, D. and Robbins, P. K. (1998), 'Do Financial Incentives Encourage Welfare Recipients to Work?', *Research in Labor Economics*, 17, 1–56.

Carlin, P. (1991), 'Intra-family and Time Allocation', in T. P. Schultz (ed.), *Research in Population Economics*, 7, Greenwich: JAI Press.

Carneiro, P. and Heckman, J. J. (2002), 'The Evidence on Credit Constraints in Post-Secondary Schooling', *Economic Journal*, 112, 705–734.

Case, A., Lubotsky, D. and Paxson, C. (2002), 'Economic Status and Health in Childhood: The Origins of the Gradient', *American Economic Review*, 92, 1308–1334.

Chase-Lansdale, P. L., Brooks-Gunn, J. and Zamsky, E. S. (1994), 'Young African-American Multigenerational Families in Poverty: Quality of Mothering and Grand-mothering', *Child Development*, 65, 373–393.

Cherlin, A. J. and Furstenberg, F. F. (1986), *The New American Grandparent: A Place in the Family, A Life Apart.* New York: Basic Books.

——Kiernan, K. E. and Chase-Lansdale, P. L. (1995), 'Parental Divorce in Child-hood and Demographic Outcomes in Young Adulthood', *Demography*, 32, 299–318.

Chiuri, M. C. (2000), 'Quality and Demand of Childcare and Female Labour Supply in Italy', *Labour*, 14(1), 97–118.

——and Longobardi, E. (2002), 'Welfare Analysis of Fiscal Reforms in Europe. Does the Representation of Family Decision Matter?' *CHILD WP 03/2002* (http://www.child-centre.it).

Cigno, A. (1991), *Economics of the Family*, Oxford: Oxford University Press.

Cogan, J. (1981), 'Fixed Costs and Labour Supply', *Econometrica*, 49, 945–964.

Cohen, G. A. (1989), 'On the Currency of Egalitarian Justice', *Ethics*, 99, 906–944.

Coleman, James S. (1988), 'Social Capital in the Creation of Human Capital', *American Journal of Sociology*, 94, 95–120.

Colombino, U. (1985), 'A Model of Married Women Labor Supply with Systematic and Random Disequilibrium Components', *Ricerche Economiche*, 39, 165–179.

——and Del Boca, D. (1990), 'The Effect of Taxes on Labor Supply in Italy', *The Journal of Human Resources*, 25, 390–414.

——and Di Tommaso, M. L. (1996), 'Is the Preference for Children so Low, or is the Price of Time so High? A simultaneous Model of Fertility and Participation in Italy with Cohort Effects', *Labour*, 10(3), 475–493.

——(2000), 'The Cost of Children When Children Are a Choice', *Labour*, 14, 79–95.

Commissione di Indagine sulla Povertà (1985), *La povertà in Italia*, Presidenza del Consiglio dei Ministri, Roma.

Connelly, R. (1992), 'The Effect of Childcare Costs on Married Women's Labor Force Participation', *The Review of Economics and Statistics*, 74, 83–90.

Corak, Miles (2001), 'Death and Divorce: The Long-Term Consequences of Parental Loss on Adolescents', *Journal of Labor Economics*, 19, 682–715.

Currie, J. and Cole, N. (1993), 'Welfare and Child Health: The Link Between AFDC Participation and Birth Weight', *American Economic Review*, 83, 971–985.

——and Thomas, D. (2001), 'Early Tests Scores, School Quality and SES: Longrun Effects on Wage and Employment Outcomes', *Research in Labor Economics*, 20, 103–132.

Dagsvik, J. (1994), 'Discrete and Continuous Choice, Max-stable Processes and Independence from Irrelevant Attribute', *Econometrica*, 4, 1179–1205.

Dalla Zuanna, G. and Michele, G. (eds) (2004), 'Strong family and low fertility', Springer, 179.

Datta Gupta, N. and Smith, N. (2000), 'Children and Career Interruptions: The Family Gap in Denmark', WP 00-03, Centre of Labour Market and Social Research, Aarhus.

Davies, R., Elias, P. and Penn, R. (1992), 'The Relationship between a Husband Unemployment and his Wife Participation', *Oxford Bulletin of Economics and Statistics*, 54(2), 145–171.

De la Rica, S. and Iza, A. (2003), 'The Role of Temporary Contracts in the Postponement of Maternity in Spain: A Life-Cycle Stochastic Mode', Paper presented at the ESPE 2003 Conference.

Dearden, L. Machin, S. and Reed, H. (1997), 'Intergenerational Mobility in Britain', *Economic Journal*, 107, 47–66.

Del Boca, D. (1997), 'Intra-household Distribution of Resources and Labor Market Participation Decisions' in I. Persson and C. Jonung (eds), *Economics of the Family and Family Policies*, London: Routledge.

——(2002), 'The Effect of Childcare and Part-Time on Participation and Fertility of Italian Women', *Journal of Population Economics*, 15(3), 549–73.

——(2003), 'Do Childcare Costs affect Labor Supply?', CHILD WP (http://www. childcentre.it).

——and Lusardi, A. (2003), 'Credit Market Constraints and Labor Market Decisions', *Labour Economics*, 10(b), 687–703.

——and Pasqua, S. (2003), 'Employment Patterns of Husbands and Wives and Family Income Distribution in Italy (1977–1998)', *Review of Income and Wealth*, 49(2), 221–245.

——Locatelli, M. and Pasqua, S. (2000), 'Employment Decision of Married Women: Evidence and Explanations', *Labour*, 14, 35–52.

——Locatelli, M. and Vuri, D. (2003), 'What Child Care Works Best? Evidence from Italy', CHILD WP 30/2003 (http://www.child-centre.it).

——Pasqua, S. and Pronzato, C. (2003), 'Analyzing participation and fertility in Europe', Paper presented at the European Conferences on ECHP and Report for the European Union of the Project MOCHO (The Rationale of Motherhood Choices: Influence of Employment Conditions and of Public Policies).

Del Bono, E. (2001), 'Estimating Fertility', Working Paper 2001, University of Oxford, Pembroke College.

Deleire, T. and Kalil, Ariel (2002), 'Good Things Come in Three: Single-Parent Multigenerational Family Structure and Adolescent Adjustment', *Demography*, 39, 393–413.

Desai, Sonalde, Chase-Lansdale, P. L. and Michael, R. T. (1989), 'Mother or Market? Effects of Maternal Employment on the Intellectual Ability of 4-Year Old Children', *Demography*, 26, 545–561.

Devanzo, J., Detray, D., and Greenberg, D. (1973), *Estimating Labour Supply Response: A Sensitivity Analysis*, Rand report R-1372-OEO, Santa Monica, The Rand Corporation.

Dickens, W. and Lundberg, S. (1993), 'Hours Restrictions and Labour Supply', *International Economic Review*, 34, 169–191.

Donaldson, D. and Weymark, J. A. (1980), 'A Single Parameter Generalization of the Gini Indices of Inequality', *Journal of Economic Theory*, 22, 67–86.

——and——(1983), 'Ethically flexible Indices for Income Distributions in the Continuum', *Journal of Economic Theory*, 29, 353–358.

Duncan, A. and Giles, C. (1998), 'The Labour Market Impact of the Working Families Tax Credit in the UK', Institute for Fiscal Studies, London.

——and McCrae, J. (1999), Household Labour Supply, Child Care Costs and In-Work Benefits: modelling the Impact of the Working Families Tax Credit, mimeo (http://www.ifs.org.UK/staff/alan_d.shtml).

Duncan, Greg J. and Brooks-Gunn, J. (1997(a)), 'Income Effects Across the Life Span: Integration and Interpretation', in Greg J. Duncan and Jeanne Brooks-Gunn (eds), *Consequences of Growing Up Poor*, New York: Russell Sage Foundation.

——and——(1997b) (eds), *Consequences of Growing Up Poor*, New York: Russell Sage Foundation.

————and Klebanov, P. (1994), 'Economic Deprivation and Early Childhood Development', *Child Development*, 62, 296–318.

——Teachman, J. and Yeung, Wei-Jun J. (1997), 'Childhood Family Income and Completed Schooling: Results from Sibling Models'. *Unpublished Paper*, Northwestern University (July).

Dustmann, C., Rajah, N. and van Soest, A. (2003), 'Class Size, Education and Wages', *Economic Journal*, 113, F99–F120.

Dworkin, R. (1981), 'What is Equality?' *Philosophy & Public Affairs*, 10, 185–246.

Edin, P.-A. and Zetterberg, J. (1992), 'Inter-Industry Wage Differentials: Evidence from Sweden and a Comparison with the United States', *American Economic Review*, 82(5), 1341–1349.

Eissa, N. and Liebman, J. (1996), 'Labor Supply Response to the Earned Income Tax Credit', *Quarterly Journal of Economics*, CXL, 605–637.

Engelhardt, H. and Prskawetz, A. (2002), 'On the Changing Correlation Between Fertility and Female Unemployment Over Space and Time', MPIDR Working Paper WP 2002-052, Max Planck Institute for Demographic Research.

—— Kogel, T. and Prskawetz, A. (2001), 'Fertility and Female Employment reconsidered', MPIDR Working Paper WP 2001-021, Max Planck Institute for Demographic Research.

Ercolani, M. and Jenkins, S. (1999), 'The Labour Force Participation of Women Married to Unemployed Men: Is There an Added Worker Effect?', mimeo.

Erikson, R. and Goldthorpe, J. H. (1992), *The constant flux: A study of class mobility in industrial societies*, Oxford: Clarendon Press.

Ermisch, J. (1989), 'Purchased Childcare, Optimal Family Size and Mother's Employment: Theory and Econometric Analysis', *Journal of Population Economics*, 2(2), 79–102.

—— and Francesconi, M. (2000), 'The Increasing Complexity of Family Relationships: Lifetime Experience of Lone Motherhood and Stepfamilies in Great Britain', *European Journal of Population*, 16, 235–249.

—— and —— (2001a), 'Family Matters: Impacts of Family Background on Educational Attainments', *Economica*, 68, 137–156.

—— and —— (2001b), 'Family Structure and Children's Achievements', *Journal of Population Economics*, 14, 249–270.

—— and —— (2001c), *The Effects of Parents' Employment on Children's Lives*, London: Family Policy Study Centre for the Joseph Rowntree Foundation.

—— and —— (2002), 'The Effect of Parents' Employment on Children's Educational Attainment', ISER Working Paper No. 2002-21, University of Essex, October.

—— and Wright, R. (1993), 'Wage Offers and Full-Time and Part-Time Employment by British Women', *Journal of Human Resources*, 28(1), 111–133.

—— Francesconi, M. and Pevalin, D. J. (2003), 'Parental partnership and joblessness in childhood and their influence on young people's outcomes', *Journal of the Royal Statistical Society*, Series A.

Esping-Andersen, G. (1999), *Social Foundations of Post Industrial Economies*, Oxford: Oxford University Press.

—— (2005), 'Unequal opportunities and the mechanisms of social inheritence'. in M. Corak (ed.), *Income Mobility between Generations*, Cambridge: Cambridge University Press.

European Commission (2002), *Employment in Europe 2002. Recent Trends and Prospects*, Luxembourg: Office for Official Publications of the European Communities, Employment and European Social Fund.

European Economy (1995), 'Performance of the EU Labor Market: Results of an ad hoc Labor Market Survey', European Commission B-1049, Brussels.

Eurostat (1999), *Demographic Statistics*.

Eurostat (2001), *Statistics in Focus*.

Euwals, R. and van Soest, A. (1999), 'Desired and Actual Labor Supply of Unmarried Men and Women in the Netherlands', *Labor Economics*, 6, 95–118.

Featherman, David L. and Hauser, Robert M. (1978), *Opportunity and Change*, New York: Academic Press.

Francesconi, M. (2002), 'A Joint Dynamic Model of Fertility and Work of Married Women', *Journal of Labour Economics*, 20, 336–380.

Gauthier, A. H. and Hatzius, J. (1997), 'Family Benefits and Fertility: An Econometric Analysis', *Population Studies*, 51(3), 295–306.

Ginsberg, Morris (1929), 'Interchange Between Social Classes', *Economic Journal*, 29, 554–565.

Ginther, Donna K. and Pollak, Robert A. (2000), 'Does Family Structure Affect Children's Educational Outcomes?' Working Paper 2000-13a, Atlanta: Federal Reserve Bank of Altanta.

Glass, David V. (ed.) (1963), *Social Mobility in Britain*, London: Routledge.

Goldhaber, Dan D. and Brewer, Dominic J. (1997), 'Why Don't Schools and Teachers Seem to Matter? Assessing the Impact of Unobservables on Educational Productivity', *Journal of Human Resources*, 32, 505–523.

Goldthorpe, John H. (1980), *Social Mobility and Class Structure in Modern Britain*, Oxford: Oxford University Press.

Gornick, J. C., Meyers, M. K. and Ross, K. E. (1998), 'Public Policies and Employment of Mothers: A Cross-National Study', *Social Science Quarterly*, 79, 35–54.

―― and ―― (1997), 'Supporting the Employment of Mothers: Policy Variation across Fourteen Welfare States', *Journal of European Social Policy*, 7, 45–70.

Graham, J., Beller, A. H. and Hernandez, Pedro (1994), 'The effects of child support on educational attainment', in Irwin Garfinkel, Sarah McLanahan and Philip Robins (eds), *Child support and child well-being*, Washington DC: Urban Institute Press, 317–354.

Gregg, P. and Machin, S. (1999), 'Childhood Disadvantage and Success or Failure in the Labour Market', in David Blanchflower and Richard Freeman (eds), *Youth Employment and Joblessness in Advanced Countries*, Cambridge, MA: National Bureau of Economic Research.

―― and Wadsworth, J. (1996), 'It Takes Two: Concentration of Employment in Families in OECD Countries', CEPR W.P., 304.

Greenstein, Theodore N. (1995), 'Are the "Most Advantaged" Children Truly Disadvantaged by Early Maternal Employment? Effects on Child Cognitive Outcomes', *Journal of Family Issues*, 16, 149–169.

Grogger, J., Karoly, L. A., Klerman, J. A. (2002), *Consequences of Welfare Reform: A Research Synthesis*, Report prepared for the Administration for Children and Families, US Department of Health and Human Services, Santa Monica, CA: RAND.

Grossman, Michael and Joyce, Theodore J. (1990), 'Unobservables, Pregnancy Resolutions, and Birth Weight Production Functions', *Journal of Political Economy*, 98, 983–1007.

Gustafsson, S. and Stafford, F. (1992), 'Daycare Subsidies and Labor Supply in Sweden', *Journal of Human Resources*, 27(1), 204–230.

―― and Wetzels, C. (2000), 'Optimal age at first birth: Germany, Great Britain, the Netherlands and Sweden' in S. Gustafsson and D. Meulders (eds), *Gender and the Labour Market*, Macmillan, London.

Gutiérrez-Domènech, M. (2002), 'Job Penalty after Motherhood: A Spanish Case in a European Context', Family Friendly Policies Conference IZA Conference, May, Bonn.

Hakim, K. (1997), *Key Issues in Women's Work*, London: Athlone.

Halsey, A. H., Heath, A. F. and Ridge, J. M. (1980), *Origins and Destinations*, Oxford: Oxford University Press.

Hammond, P. (1990), 'Theoretical Progress in Public Economics: A Provocative Assessment', *Oxford Economic Papers*, 42: 6–33.

Han, Wen-Jui, Waldfogel, J. and Brooks-Gunn, J. (2001), 'The Effects of Early Maternal Employment on Children's Later Cognitive and Behavioral Outcomes', *Journal of Marriage and the Family*, 63: 336–354.

Hanushek, Eric A. (2002), 'Publicly Provided Education', in Alan J. Auerbach and Martin Feldstein (eds), *Handbook of Public Economics*, Amsterdam: Elsevier Science. vol 4, chapter 30.

Harris, P. L. (1983), 'Infant Cognition', in P. H. Mussen (ed.), *Handbook of Child Psychology, Socialization, Personality, and Social Development*, New York: Wiley.

Harvey, Elizabeth (1999), 'Short-Term and Long-Term Effects of Early Parental Employment on Children of the National Longitudinal Survey of Youth', *Developmental Psychology*, 35, 445–459.

Hauser, R. M. and Featherman, D. L. (1977), *The Process of Stratification: Trends and Analyses*, New York: Academic Press.

Hausman, J. A. (1980), 'The Effects of Wages, Taxes and Fixed Costs on Women's Labor Force Participation', *Journal of Public Economics*, 14, 161–192.

—— (1981), 'Labor Supply', in H. Aaron and J. Pechman, (eds), *How Taxes Affect Behavior*, Washington DC: Brookings Institution.

—— (1985), 'The Econometrics of Non-Linear Budget Sets', *Econometrica*, 53, 1255–1282.

—— and Ruud, P. (1984), 'Family Labor Supply with Taxes', *American Economic Review*, 74, 242–253.

Haveman, R. and Wolfe, Barbara (1995), 'The Determinants of Children's Attainments: A Review of Methods and Findings', *Journal of Economic Literature*, 33, 1829–1878.

—— —— and Spaulding, J. (1991), 'Childhood events and circumstances influencing high school completion', *Demography*, 28(1), 133–157.

Hearnes, E., Jia, Z. and Strøm, S. (2003), 'Retirement in Non-Cooperative and Cooperative Families', *CHILD WP* 04/2003 (http://www.child-centre.it).

Hey, J. D. and Lambert, P. J. (1980), 'Relative Deprivation and the Gini Coefficient: Comment', *Quarterly Journal of Economics*, 94, 567–573.

Hill, M. A. and O'Neill, June (1994), 'Family Endowments and the Achievement of Young Children with Special Reference to the Underclass', *Journal of Human Resources*, 29, 1064–1100.

Hill, M. S. and Duncan, Greg J. (1987), 'Parental Family Income and the Socioeconomic Attainment of Children', *Social Science Research*, 16, 39–73.

—— —— Yeung, Wei-Jun H. and Duncan, Greg J. (2001), 'Childhood Family Structure and Young Adult Behaviour', *Journal of Population Economics*, 14, 271–299.

Horwood, L. J. and Fergusson, D. M. (1999), 'A Longitudinal Study of Maternal Labour Force Participation and Child Academic Achievement', *Journal of Child Psychology and Psychiatry*, 40, 1013–1024.

Hotz, V. J. and Miller, R. A. (1988), 'An Empirical Analysis of Life Cycle Fertility and Female Labor Supply', *Econometrica*, 56(1), 91–118.

Ilmakunnas, S. and Pudney, S. (1990), 'A Model of Female Labour Supply in the Presence of Hours Restrictions', *Journal of Public Economics*, 41, 183–210.

ISFOL (2001), *Rapporto trimestrale*.

Jacobsen, J. P. and Rayak, W. L. (1996), 'Do Men Whose Wives Work Really Earn Less?', *American Economic Review*, 86(2), 268–273.

Joshi, H. and Verropoulou, G. (2000), *Maternal Employment and Child Outcomes: Analysis of Two Birth Cohort Studies*, London: The Smith Institute.

Juhn, C. and Murphy, K. (1997), 'Wage Inequality and Family Labor Supply', *Journal of Labor Economics*, 15, 72–97.

Karoly, L. and Burtless, G. (1995), 'The Effects of Rising Earnings Inequality on the Distribution of U.S. Income', *Demography*, 32, 379–406.

Keane, M. (1995), 'A New Idea For Welfare Reform', *Federal Reserve Bank of Minnesota Quarterly Review*, Spring, 2–28.

Kelly, E. and Dobbin, F. (1999), 'Civil Rights Law at Work: Sex Discrimination and the Rise of Maternity Leave Policies', *American Journal of Sociology*, 105(2), 455–492.

Kiernan, Kathleen E. (1992), 'The Impact of Family Disruption in Childhood on Transitions Made in Young Adult Life', *Population Studies*, 46, 213–234.

——(1996), 'Lone Motherhood, Employment and Outcomes for Children', *International Journal of Law, Policy and the Family*, 10, 233–249.

——(1997), 'The Legacy of Parental Divorce: Social, Economic and Demographic Experiences in Adulthood', Centre for Analysis of Social Exclusion, London School of Economics, CASE paper 1.

Kimmel, J. (1998), 'Childcare Cost as Barrier to Employment for Single and Married Mothers', *The Review of Economics and Statistics*, 3, 287–299.

King, M. (1983), 'Welfare Analysis of Tax Reforms Using Household Data', *Journal of Public Economics*, 21, 183–214.

Klerman, J. A. and Leibowitz, A. (1994), 'Labor Supply Effects of State Maternity Leave Legislation', in F. D. Blau and G. Ronald (eds), *Gender and Family Issues in the Workplace*, New York: Russell Sage Foundation.

——and——(1999), 'Job Continuity Among New Mothers', *Demography*, 36(2), 145–155.

Knight, F. H. (1935), *The Ethics of Competition*, New York: Allen & Unwin.

Kravdal, Ø. (1996), 'How the Local Supply of Day-Care Centers Influences Fertility in Norway: A Parity-Specific Approach', *Population Research and Policy Review*, 15, 201–218.

Krueger, A. B. and Summers, L. H. (1988), 'Efficiency Wages and the Inter-Industry Wage Structure', *Econometrica*, 56(2), 259–293.

Kunze, A. (2001), 'Timing of Birth and Wages', paper presented *Family Friendly Policies* Conference, IZA Bonn.

Laitner, John (1997), 'Intergenerational and Interhousehold Economic Links', in Mark R. Rozenzweig and Oded Stark (eds), *Handbook of Population and Family Economics*, Amsterdam: Elsevier.

Lamb, Michael E (ed.) (1997), *The Role of the Father in Child Development* (3rd edn), New York: Wiley.

Lang, K. and Zagorsky, J. L. (2001), 'Does Growing Up with a Parent Absent Really Hurt?', *Journal of Human Resources*, 36, 253–273.

Laroque, G. and Salanie, B. (2003), 'Fertility and Financial Incentives in France', mimeo. CESIFO Economic Studies (2004), 50, 423–450.

Lefebvre, Pierre and Merrigan, Phillip (1998), 'Work Schedules, Job Characteristics, Parenting Practices and Children's Outcomes', Working Paper 77, Center for Research on Economic Fluctuations and Employment, Université du Québec à Montréal.

——Brouillette, L. and Felteau, C. (1994), 'Comportements de fecondité des Québecoises, allocations familiales et impots: Résultats et simulations d'un modèle de choix discrets portant sur les années 1975–1987' (Fertility Behaviour in Quebec, Family Allowances and Taxes: Results and Simulations with a Discrete Choice Model for the Years 1975–1987), L'Actualité-Economique, 70(4), 399–451.

Lehrer, E. (2000), 'The Impact of Women's Employment on the Distribution of Earnings Among Married-Couples Households: a Comparison between 1973 and 1992–1994', The Quarterly Review of Economics and Finance, 40, 295–301.

Lesthaeghe, R. and Willems, P. (1999), 'Is Low Fertility a Temporary Phenomenon in the European Union?', Population and Development Review, 25(2), 211–228.

Liu, H., Mroz, T. and Van der Klaauw, W. (2002), 'Maternal Employment, Migration, and Child Development'. Unpublished paper, University of North Carolina Chapel Hill (October).

Livi Bacci (2001), 'Too few children, too much family', in Daedalus, 130, Issue 3 (Summer).

Ludwig, J. (1999), 'School Spending and Student Achievement: New Evidence from Longitudinal Data'. Unpublished paper, Georgetown University.

Lumsdaine, Robin L. and Mitchell, Olivia S. (1999), 'New Developments in the Economic Analysis of Retirement' in Ashenfelter, Orley and Card, David (eds), 'Handbook of Labor Economics', 3, Elsevier Science.

Lumsdaine, R., Stock, J. and Wise, D. (1992), 'Three Models of Retirement: Computational Complexity versus Predictive Validity', in D. Wise (ed.), 'Topics in the Economics of Ageing', 19–57, Chicago: University of Chicago Press.

Lundberg, S. (1985), 'The Added Worker Effect', Journal of Labor Economics, 3, 11–37.

——(1988), 'Labour Supply of Husbands and Wives: A Simultaneous Equation Approach', The Review of Economics and Statistics, 70, 224–235.

Lutz, W., O'Neill, B. and Scherbor, S. (2003), 'Europe's population at a turning point', Science, 299, 1991–1992.

McCulloch, A. and Joshi, H. (2002), 'Child Development and Family Resources: Evidence from the Second Generation of the 1958 British Birth Cohort', Journal of Population Economics, 15, 283–304.

McElroy, M. and Horney, M. J. (1981), 'Nash-Bargaining Household Decision: Toward A Generalization of the Theory of Demand', International Economic Review, 22, 333–349.

McLanahan, Sara S. (1997), 'Parent Absence or Poverty: Which Matters More?' in Greg J. Duncan and Jeanne Brooks-Gunn (eds), Consequences of Growing Up Poor, New York: Russell Sage Foundation.

——and Sandefur, G. (1994), Growing Up with a Single Parent: What Hurts, What Helps, Cambridge, Mass.: Harvard University Press.

McLoyd, V. C. (1989), 'Socialization and Development in a Changing Economy: The Effects of Paternal Job and Income Loss on Children', *American Psychologist*, 44, 293–302.

Manski, C. and McFadden, D. (eds) (1981), *Structural Analysis of Discrete Data with Econometric Applications*, MIT Press.

Marenzi, A. and Pagani, L. (2003), 'The labor market participation of sandwich generation italian women', mimeo.

Martinez-Granado, M. and Ruiz-Castillo, J. (2002), 'The Decisions of Spanish Youth: A Cross-Section Study', *Journal of Population Economics*, 15(2), 305–330.

Mayer, Susan E. (2002), *The Influence of Parental Income on Children's Outcomes*, Wellington: Ministry of Social Development.

Mehran, F. (1976), 'Linear Measures of Inequality', *Econometrica*, 44, 805–809.

Messina, Julián (2003), 'Sectoral Structure and Entry Regulations', IZA Discussion Papers, 747.

Mincer, J. (1985), 'Trends in Women, Work, and Education', *Journal of Labour Economics*, Special Issue.

Missoc (2001) Social Protection in the member states in the EU: http://europa.eu.int/comm/employment/social/missoc.

Moffitt, R. A. and Wilhelm, M. (1998), 'Taxation and the Labour Supply Decisions of the Affluent', NBER Working Paper 6621.

Moore, Kristin A. and Driscoll, Anne K. (1997), 'Low-Wage Maternal Employment and Outcomes for Children: A Study', *Future of Children*, 7, 122–127.

Neumark, D. and Postlewhite, A. (1995), 'Relative Income Concern and the Rise in Married Women's Employment', National Bureau of Economic Research Working Paper N. 5044.

Ní Bhrolcháin, M. Chappel, R. and Diamond, Ian (1994), 'Scolarité et autres caracteristiques socio-demographiques des enfants de mariages rumpus' [Educational and socio-demographic outcomes among children of disrupted marriages.] *Population*, 49, 1585–1612.

NICHD Early Child Care Research Network (1997), 'The Effects of Infant Child Care on Infant-Mother Attachment Security: Results of the NICHD Study of Early Child Care', *Child Development*, 68, 860–879.

O'Brien, Margaret and Jones, Deborah (1999), 'Children, Parental Employment and Educational Attainment: An English Case Study', *Cambridge Journal of Economics*, 23, 599–621.

O'Reilly, J. and Fagan, C. (eds) (1998), *Part-time Prospects: An International Comparison of Part-time Work in Europe, North America and the Pacific Rim*, London: New York: Routledge.

OECD (1999, 2000, 2001), *Employment Outlook*.

Oláh, S. L. (1996), 'The impact of Public Policies on the Second-Birth Rates in Sweden: a Gender Perspective', *Stockholm Research Reports in Demography*, No. 98.

Organisation for Economic Cooperation and Development (2002), *OECD Employment Outlook*, Paris: OECD.

Parcel, Toby L. and Menaghan, Elizabeth G. (1994), 'Early Parental Work, Family Social Capital, and Early Childhood Outcomes', *American Journal of Sociology*, 99, 972–1009.

Parsons, D. O. (1975), 'Intergenerational wealth transfers and the educational decisions of male youth', *Quarterly Journal of Economics*, 89, 603–617.

Pasqua, S. (2001), 'A Bargaining Model for Gender Bias in Education in Poor Countries', *Quaderni del Dipartimento di Scienze Economiche e Finanziarie "G. Prato"*, N. 50 and CHILD WP 17/2001 (http://www.child-centre.it).

——(2001), 'The Added Worker Effect: a Comparison Between European Countries', mimeo.

——(2002), 'Wives' Work and Income Distribution in European Countries', CHILD WP 1/2002 (http://www.child-centre.it).

Pencavel, J. (1986), 'Labor Supply of Men: A Survey', in O. Ashenfelter and R. Layard (eds), *Handbook of Labor Economics*, 1, North-Holland, Amsterdam.

Périvier, H. and O'Dorchai, S. (2003), 'Women's Employment and Public Policies', in *The Rationale of Motherhood Choices: Influence of Employment Conditions and of Public Policies–State of the Art*, European Commission.

Phipps, S. and Burton, P. (1992), 'What is Mine is Yours? The Influence of Male and Female Incomes on Patterns of Household Expenditure', WP 92–12 Department of Economics, Dalhousie University.

Pollak, Robert (1971), 'Conditional Demand Functions and the Implications of Separable Utility', *Southern Economic Journal*, 37, 423–433.

Powell, L. M. (2002), 'Joint Labor Supply and Childcare Choice Decisions of Married Mothers', *The Journal of Human Resources*, 37(1), 106–128.

Ribar, D. C. (1992), 'Childcare and Labor Supply of Married Women: Reduced Form Evidence', *The Journal of Human Resources*, 27(1), 134–165.

Rizzi, D. (1996), *TBM: Un Modello Statico di Microsimulazione*, Dipartimento di Scienze Economiche, Università CaFoscari, Venezia.

——and Rossi, N. (1997), 'Minimo vitale e imposta sul reddito proporzionale', in da Empoli and G. Muraro (eds), *Verso un nuovo stato sociale*, Milano, Franco Angeli.

Roemer, J. (1993), 'A Pragmatic Theory of Responsibility for the Egalitarian Planner', *Philosophy & Public Affairs*, 10, 146–166.

——(1998), *Equality of Opportunity*, Harvard: Harvard University Press.

Røed, K. and Strøm, S. (2002), 'Progressive Taxes and the Labour Market: Is the Trade-Off Between Equality and Efficiency Inevitable?' *Journal of Economic Survey*, 16(1), 77–110.

Rønsen, M. (1998), 'Fertility and Public Policies—Evidence from Norway and Finland', Documents 98/12, *Statistics Norway*, Oslo.

——(2001), 'Market Work, Childcare and the Division of Household Labour. Adaptations of Norwegian Mothers Before and After the Cash-for-care Reform', Reports 2001/13, *Statistics Norway*.

——and Sundström, M. (1999), 'Public Policies and the Employment Dynamics Among New Mothers–A Comparison of Finland, Norway and Sweden', Discussion Papers no. 263, *Statistics Norway*.

Rosen, S. (1996), 'Public employment and the Welfare State in Sweden', *Journal of Economic Literature*, 34, 729–40.

Rosenzweig, Mark R. and Schultz, Paul T. (1983), 'Estimating a Household Production Function: Heterogeneity, the Demand for Health Inputs, and Their Effects of Birth Weight', *Journal of Political Economy*, 91, 723–746.

Rosenzweig, Mark R., and Wolpin, Kenneth I. (1980), 'Life-Cycle Labor Supply and Fertility: Casual Inferences From Household Models', *Journal of Political Economy*, 88(2), 328–348.

—— and —— (1995), 'Sisters, Siblings, and Mothers: The Effects of Teen-age Childbearing on Birth Outcomes in a Dynamic Family Context', *Econometrica*, 63, 303–326.

Ruhm, Christopher J. (1998), 'The Economic Consequences of Parental Leave Mandates: Lessons From Europe', *Quarterly Journal of Economics*, 113(1), 285–317.

—— (2000), 'Parental Employment and Child Cognitive Development', NBER Working Paper, no. 7666, April.

—— (2002), 'Parental Employment and Children' Welfare', Paper presented at the *Family Friendly Policies Conference*, IZA, Bonn.

—— and Teague, J. L. (1997), 'Parental Leave Policies in Europe and North America', in F. D. Blau and G. Ronald (eds), *Gender and Family Issues in the Workplace*, New York: Russell Sage Foundation.

Saez, E. (2001), 'Using Elasticities to Derive Optimal Income Tax Rates', *Review of Economic Studies*, 68, 205–229.

Schultz, P. T. (1990), 'Testing the Neoclassical Model of Family Labor Supply and Fertility', *The Journal of Human Resources*, 25, 599–634.

—— (1998), 'Eroding the Economic Foundations of Marriage and Fertility in the United States' in *Structural Change and Economic Dynamics*, Special issue on 'The Economics of the Family', D. Del Boca (ed.), 9, North-Holland, Amsterdam.

Sen, A. (1974), 'Informational Bases of Alternative Welfare Approaches', *Journal of Public Economics*, 3, 387–403.

Smith, J. P. and Ward, M. P. (1985) 'Time-Series Growth in the Female Labor Force.' *Journal of Labor Economics*, 3, 59–90.

Sleebos, J. (2002), 'Low fertility rates in OECD Countries: facts and policy responses', OECD Social, Employment and Migration Working Paper, 15–02 OECD, Paris.

Solon, Gary R. (1999), 'Intergenerational Mobility in the Labor Market', in Orley C. Ashenfelter and David Card (eds), *Handbook of Labor Economics*, vol. 3A, Amsterdam: North-Holland.

Stiglitz, J. (1986), *Economics of the Public Sector* (2nd edn), New York: W. W. Norton.

Strauss, J. (1990), 'Households, Communities and Preschool Children's Nutrition Outcomes: Evidence from Rural Côte d'Ivoire'. *Economic Development and Cultural Change*, 38, 231–261.

Sundström, M. (1994), 'More Children and More Paid Work: Birth-Leave-Work Strategies of Swedish Women in the 1980s', *Stockholm Research Reports in Demography*, no. 82, Stockholm University.

Thomas, D. (1990), 'Intra-Household Resources Allocation: An Inferential Approach', *The Journal of Human Resources*, 25, 635–664.

Todd, Petra E. and Wolpin, Kenneth I. (2003) 'On the Specification and Estimation of the Production Function for Cognitive Achievement', *Economic Journal*, 113, F3–F33.

United Nations (1995, 2000), 'Human Development Report', New York: United Nations.

Van de Kaa, D. (1998), 'Postmodern fertility preferences: from changing value orientation to new behaviour'. *Working Papers in Demography*, no. 74, Australian National University.

van Soest, A. (1995), 'Discrete Choice Models of Family Labor Supply', *Journal of Human Resources*, 30, 63–88.

Vandell, D. and Ramanan, J. (1992), 'Effects of Early and Recent Maternal Employment on Children from Low Income Families', *Child Development*, 63, 938–949.

Vuri, D. (2001) Fertility and Divorce European University Working Papers, 2001–5.

Waldfogel, J. (1998), 'The Family Gap for Young Women in the United States and Britain: Can Maternity Leave Make a Difference?', *Journal of Labor Economics*, 16(3), 505–545.

——(2002), 'Childcare, women's employment, and child outcomes', *Journal of Population Economics*, 15, 527–48.

——Han, Wen-Jui and Brooks-Gunn, J. (2002), 'The Effects of Early Maternal Employment on Child Development', *Demography*, 39, 369–392.

Walker, I. (1990), 'The Effects of Income Support Measures on the Labour Market Behaviour of Lone Mothers', *Fiscal Studies*, 11(2), 55–75.

Wenk, D. A. and Garret, P. (1992), 'Having a Baby: Some Prediction of Maternal Employment Around Childbirth', *Gender and Society*, 6(1): 49–65.

Wetzels, C. (2002), 'Does Motherhood Really Make Women Less Productive? The Case of the Netherlands', Paper presented at the Bilbao ESPE Conference.

Weymark, J. (1981), 'Generalized Gini Inequality Indices', Mathematical Social Sciences, 1, 409–430.

Willis, R. J. (1973), 'A New Approach to the Economic Theory of Fertility Behavior', *Journal of Political Economy*, 81(2), 3–18.

Winkler, A. (1998), 'Earnings of Husbands and Wives in Dual-earner Families', *Monthly Labor Review*, 121(4), 42–48.

Wolfe, B., Wilson, K. and Haveman, Robert (2001), 'The Role of Economic Incentives in Teenage Nonmarital Childbearing Choices', *Journal of Public Economics*, 81, 473–511.

Yaari, M. E. (1988), 'A Controversial Proposal Concerning Inequality Measurement', *Journal of Economic Theory*, 44, 381–397.

Final Remarks

GIUSEPPE BERTOLA

Women in the labor market and in the Lisbon strategy

Even before attending the conference I knew that economics offers important explanations for patterns followed by the occupational and productive situation of the female gender, but I did learn a lot from both the two interesting reports and from the discussion.

Whether, and where, women work depends on familiar demand and supply forces. On the labor demand side, structural and technological features determine the productivity of women, and men, in various market and non-market activities. Clearly, the relevant features are different over time and across countries, and are not homogeneous within groups of workers of either gender. The availability of washing machines at home and of computers at the office makes a lot of different to the relative productivity of working in either place, and the first report offers important insights as to the role of education in affecting productivity within and across gender groups.

But labor supply is also important: producing is useful and earning a living is necessary, but working is not a pleasure. Hence female (and male) employment outcomes depend on features that make labor market participation possible and pleasurable for workers, and many such features are importantly affected by institutions and policies. State provision of day-care services, and availability of public employment opportunities, are particularly relevant to women's employment outcomes. All institutional features of the labor market, however, also matter for participation and employment: labor–income taxation tends to privilege informal employment, and collective wage-setting practices pursued by unions can increase female unemployment, and so on.

The interplay of demand and supply forces may result in more or less formal female employment. Like everything in economics, a higher female employment rate is not an unambiguously good (or bad) thing: its costs and benefits depend on whether it is determined by technological or policy influences, on the demand or the supply side. I did learn a lot from the second report as regards its positive implications for fertility, and its negative (on average) implications for the quality of care provided to children, an under-represented group in even very democratic countries' political interactions. Better childcare is on average provided by mothers who do not participate in the labor market than by paid strangers—whether the private nannies of rich families, or public employees, or publicly subsidized providers, as in the case of UK in-work benefits paid to single mothers who start their own day-care facilities.

Of course, taking mothers and childcare out of the family has many benefits alongside such costs. The balance of costs and benefits entailed by collective interventions depends on structural features, as well as on one's viewpoint, and at the end of the conference it is not easy to tell whether reforms are advisable.

One thing is clear: it would be pointless to advocate implementation in, say, Afghanistan or in Sweden's current policy framework. But less pointless, in fact, than to wish that such a framework had been adopted by Sweden or any other western country 150 years ago. And since the pros and cons of female employment depend on specific features, it is equally clear that it need not be optimal to increase female employment rates to the 60 per cent advocated by the Lisbon guidelines in every country, or every region, every city, every family.

In fact, the Lisbon documents do not emphasize female employment as much as other issues, and are far from specific as regards policy action that might increase it. Someone once joked that to see the Lisbon target implementation problems clearly, economists and policy makers should be encouraged to become acquainted with the particular forty-something Andalusian or Sicilian lady who would need to be employed should the 60 per cent target need to be implemented immediately in Spain or Italy. The cohort analysis of the first report in Part I actually offers a more hopeful message, indicating that as generations age, the female employment target may actually be achieved by those countries, so the lack of focus by the Lisbon process on that target may be justified. (Economists and policy makers should definitely worry more about the fifty-something blue collar workers who would need to be prevented from retiring in order to meet the mature worker employment target.)

But many aspects of Lisbon and earlier EU policies bear on European female employment rates. Gender equality of wages has actually been enshrined since the Treaty of Rome, and parental leave is (at least in theory) also legislated at the EU level. Of course, forcing wage equality may well hamper employability of female workers, and mandatory parental leave may also backfire, making women of child-bearing age *ex ante* less desirable employees, even as it tries to offer high quality motherly care. Empirical cross-country panel studies confirm that female employment rates tend to be lower, and unemployment rates higher, in countries with more heavily regulated labor markets (Bertola, Blau, Kahn, 2002, and references therein). It is also empirically clear and theoretically sensible (Messina, 2003) that employment, and especially female employment, is lower in countries where the services component of GDP is smaller, whether because of lower economic development or institutional features affecting public employment and private service firm creation. To the extent that both at-home childcare and formal employment in later life are desirable components of a woman's life cycle, the kind of 'activation' policies advocated by the Lisbon and Amsterdam EU policy process might perhaps fruitfully be applied to mothers whose children are grown and need to become *ex post* suitable employees in a difficult formal labor market.

However, in the long run and when we have reached the end of this book, can we tell whether policies meant to increase female employment are desirable in countries where it is low? I am afraid not: to answer that question, we would need to have figured out whether, and how, institutional interference with *laissez faire* outcomes needs to be reformed in the light of changing structural/technological circumstances. This is a hard interaction to assess, and the largely cross-sectional perspective of the two reports can only offer partial glimpses of relevant phenomena. And, of course, the world changes all the time, but institutions are hard to design and harder to change, because they would not be institutions if they changed over time.

To see how difficult it would be to come up with definite reform recommendations in this delicate area, consider labor taxes and contributions, which have a relatively prominent role in both parts of the report in this volume. The first part points out that formal female employment would enlarge the tax base. The second argues that marginal tax rates on low wages would have beneficial effects on both efficiency and distribution. They are both right, but they do not offer a complete assessment of *all* the pros and cons of tax reforms.

Of course a smaller wedge between employers' costs and workers' take-home pay could only increase employment. However, removing the stay-at-home subsidies built into the tax system of all countries is clearly an anti-family policy action. It may be inefficient, if working at home with small children is still a very productive activity, to imply that childcare should be subsidiarily left to families by the state. Tax revenue is needed, and it is unlikely that increasing female employment by reducing its taxation would increase it. More or less relevant distortions are generated by all taxes, not only labor taxes. To assess whether recent structural and technological changes call for reducing taxes on low-paid female work, one would need to study how the availability of, for example, washing machines and computers affects the shape (not just the level) of women's relative productivity at home and in the office.

Finally, in a stable institutional setting, current contributions entitle workers to future pension benefits. To the extent that this is the case, payroll taxes need not discourage labor supply: but to the extent that in a pay-as-you-go system current contributions are used to pay current pensions, promising actuarially fair benefits to lure women into formal employment does not solve the system's sustainability problem. Increasing current payroll taxes along with future pension liabilities can, at most, delay the crash of a demographically unsustainable pension system.

GØSTA ESPING-ANDERSEN

A jobless and childless Europe?

At the macro-level, European nations must raise female employment levels without this resulting in a childless future. And, at the micro-level, Europe's citizens face major welfare disequilibria due to the difficulties of reconciling children and paid employment. On both counts we seem locked into a Paretian sub-optimality and, hence, our chief goal must be to identify a strategy towards a superior welfare–efficiency mix. The key to ensure better macro-level performance lies, in my view, less in labor market reform than in resolving incompatabilities and perverse incentive effects at the household level.

The Macro Story

A quantum leap in women's employment is *sine qua non* for long-term sustainability, in particular among the rapidly ageing Continental and, especially, southern European countries. Italy and Spain, for example, must raise female employment by 20 percentage points in order to adhere to the Lisbon target for 2010. As Pissaridis *et al.* argue, this is not necessarily an impossible task *if* member countries succeed in de-regulating often very rigid labor markets, and *if* policy can help reduce the incompatabilities that working mothers often confront. Their study concludes on a fairly optimistic note, pointing to the surge in participation among young female cohorts in countries like Italy and Spain. Indeed, the goal of 60 per cent female employment may, at least theoretically, be realistic for even the laggard countries. But this, I would imagine, will occur on the backdrop of very low fertility levels.

A resurgence of births now will not correct the demographic imbalance that will culminate around 2030–2050. But if the current low-fertility equilibrium (with constant immigration) were to persist, demographic projections tell us that the Spanish population by the end of the century will have shrunk to 10 million, and the Italian to little more (Lutz *et al.*, 2003). Macro-economically this must be bad news indeed and, besides, few people would want to live in a society without children. Put differently, I think it would be a good idea to endogenize fertility rates in macro-economic analyses of female employment.

Pissaridis *et al.*'s emphasis on labor market deregulation and mother friendly policy as the means to stimulate female employment is, at first glance, quite convincing. Restrictions regarding part-time employment and flexible work schedules are no doubt major obstacles for women seeking to reconcile motherhood and careers. Very rigid labor and product markets, as well as high fixed labor costs, all contribute to the sluggish rate of job growth—especially in services—that besets the EU countries and, worse, they raise the walls that the outsiders must climb in order to gain employment in the first place. Likewise, most EU member states offer little or no day care or elderly care services, and some maternity leave schemes implicitly encourage women to interrupt their careers, with adverse consequences for their life-long employment and earnings prospects. It is surely uncontroversial that we need to improve upon our employment and family policies if we seriously aspire to maximize women's employment. But these are, in my view, only necessary, and not sufficient, preconditions—in particular if we simultaneously insist on fertility levels that actually correspond to what citizens truly desire (and what society needs).

Untangling the Fertility Puzzle

The trade-off between motherhood and employment has undergone several re-definitions in the past century. In the 1930s, Gunnar and Alva Myrdal's famous study, *Kris i Befolkningsfraagan*, defined the challenge as 'how to ensure that women who work will be able to have the number of children they desire'. They took it for granted that women had to work. Moving forward to the 1960s and 1970s, the nascent women's movement posed the issue as to 'how to ensure that mothers will be able to work'. The backdrop for their reading of the issue was the postwar housewife norm and the belief that women *had to have children*. In latter-day society the challenge is being re-defined once again, now as 'how can we ensure that women can realize their joint preference for children and employment?'

Falling birth rates and radically delayed first births may, to many observers, be interpreted as revealed preferences. Some demographers now cite post-modern values as the driving force (Van de Kaa 1998); others assume that modern women simply give higher priority to careers. There are, however, two key factors that must be understood well. One, as Hakim (1997) has emphasized, we should not forget the pervasive heterogeneity of women's life preferences. The share of women that put careers first remains everywhere quite modest—as also does the proportion of traditional women who are single-mindedly family oriented now. The majority fall in between, meaning that they insist on family formation but also want to remain employed. Of course, the profile of preferences is correlated with education—but only up to a point.

Considering such a distribution of life preferences, it would be tempting to believe that birth rates are negatively correlated with women's educational attainment. Such a linear relationship does emerge in countries like Italy and Spain. It does not exist in others, such as the Nordic countries. Indeed, Danish and Swedish fertility is substantially lower among the less educated and culminates among women with some university education. In Spain, one can identify one source of non-linearity: women with precarious fixed-term work contracts have, across-the-board, far lower fertility rates than any other group.

The non-linearity in Scandinavia is best explained by one variable: type of employment. Women differ only little in terms of having one child. The really important variance, has to do with having 2 + children. In southern Europe, the few women who do accomplish the latter are predominantly the less educated and non-employed. In Scandinavia they are predominantly university educated women working in the 'soft economy,' namely, mainly welfare state jobs.[1]

All this brings me back to Pissaridis *et al.*'s labor market arguments. I do not see any clear relationship between labor market deregulation and the joint maximization of women's employment and births. Deregulation may possibly stimulate job growth, but if there is one lesson that fertility correlations tell us, it is that labor market precariousness is anathema to family formation. In all countries, unemployment is associated with low fertility. The exceptionally low birth rates we find among fixed-term employed women in Spain reflect their extraordinary degree of precariousness. Indeed, Spain represents a troublesome example of partial labor market deregulation that has resulted in strong dualisms between protected insiders and precarious outsiders—the latter being overwhelmingly young workers.

The single best interpretation is that women simply cannot risk having children until they (and their partners) attain some modicum of security. Vice versa, being employed in secure and 'mother-friendly' soft economy jobs in Denmark implies that women can have the number of children they actually desire. So, if we accept that employment and fertility must be regarded as joint objectives, a simple strategy of deregulating labor markets may easily be counterproductive unless it is coupled to measures that create economic and job security.

We come now to the other key factor that we must understand well. It is unlikely that actual birth rates mirror real preferences. We have substantial survey evidence that shows that women (as well as men) in childbearing ages expressedly desire, on average, 2.2–2.3 children (Bien 2000). With few national exceptions, this target is surprisingly convergent, from Finland to Portugal. And, equally important, one finds little variation by level of men's or women's educational status. If, then, we register fertility rates hovering around 1.1–1.2 in many EU countries—and in some regions even far below 1.0—we might very well interpret this as a sign of major welfare deficiencies that citizens confront.

---

[1] Preparing for the Alghero conference, I ran a series of Kaplan—Mayer survivor functions to estimate the probability of a woman having a second and third child within 6 years of the previous child. In Denmark, the probability of having a second child was 0.82; in Italy, 0.59, and in Germany, only 0.51. As to the third child (following the second), the probability in Denmark is 0.35 but only 0.19 in Italy and 0.17 in Germany. In other words, the 2 + child scenario is roughly twice as likely in Denmark as in Italy or Germany.

The Micro Story

The joint analysis of fertility and employment that would be desirable in macro-economic analyses is, as Del Boca *et al.*'s study exemplifies, now standard in micro-economic research. Indeed, if we also consider heterogeneous preferences we quickly realize that we are dealing with a hugely complex endogeneity. High and persistent levels of marital homogamy imply that partners select themselves according to educational attainment, social status, and life projects. Following Becker, choices regarding labor supply and fertility are jointly made. And women's life course priorities are no doubt pre-empted already by their choice of education and of partner.

The new dilemmas that Del Boca *et al.* examine have their roots in the changing role of women. Indeed, a pretty good argument can be made that this is the core revolutionary impulse behind ongoing social change. When one studies life-course behavior over the past, say, 50 years one is struck by a massive gender-assymetry: all the while that women have adopted a new life course, men have barely changed at all. We see a masculinization of female biographies, in terms of educational attainment, postponed marriage and family formation, and life-long attachment to employment. This, in turn, underpins the changing household structure, more fragile families, and declining birth rates. It also underpins the changing employment structure, as the disappearance of the housewife leads to externalization of personal and social service activities. Possibly, women are reaching the limits of life-course masculinization and, possibly, a new positive equilibrium will require that men embark upon a parallel feminization of their life course.

So far, the policy debate has shunned such radical change and has, instead, focused on remedies that help reconcile women's double role. This is also the approach taken by Del Boca *et al.* Their analysis centers on mother-friendly social policy, like leave schemes and day care, and on making motherhood compatible with employment. The issue, in essence, lies in the rising cost of having children and the question we confront is, who should pay?

Most EU member states adhere to the traditional view that children are a private good and that the cost should, accordingly, be internalized in the family itself. Although maternity and parental leave legislation has become more generous almost everywhere, the key component, namely access to affordable childcare, has been largely ignored in all but a handful of countries. The lacuna of childcare, combined with too long leave entitlements, is likely to either reduce fertility or to induce mothers to interrupt employment—in either case easily sub-optimal in welfare terms.

The cost of day care must be regarded as a regressive tax on women's labor supply. If, as in most EU countries, access to affordable quality public care is almost non-existent, the alternative is either a grandmother or private care. The former is likely to disappear, and the latter is priced out of the market for most families. But, it is exactly among less educated and lower income couples that women's added labor supply is most urgent. This is the reservoir of female labor supply that needs to be mobilized to achieve the Lisbon targets. And when we consider the rising risk of low incomes in young households, it is evident that this is where women's employment is key to family wellbeing. We know that mothers' employment is the single most effective measure against child poverty. In other words, we witness an epochal change in terms of the true value of children. Societal ageing implies that children are increasingly a collective good; it also implies that the quality of tomorrow's children is increasingly a collective concern.

It follows that the cost of children needs to be redistributed. There is, first of all, a ready-made argument that the childless should subsidize parents. There is, secondly, a strong case in favour of redistribution towards lower income families. A brief glance across the EU informs us that most governments do exactly the opposite. Instead of direct (and progressive) childcare subsidies, the standard approach is tax deductions to child families—a policy that redistributes towards the upper-end of the income scale.

A Nordic-style universal day care subsidy is clearly the most equitable *and* efficient option. It is equitable because it ensures that basically all families will have access and, hence, it neutralizes the regressive tax on women's labor supply. It yields substantial efficiency dividends because it helps minimize mothers' employment interruptions, implying superior career-long earnings. Indirectly, this also means more revenue to the Exchequer over the long haul and, indeed, it is likely that most of the original day care subsidies will, later, be recuperated as a result of mothers' improved life long earnings. The case in favor of redistribution and subsidizing mothers is certainly not consensual. In a controversial article, Rosen (1996) argued that Sweden's generous subsidies to working mothers are unwarranted considering their negative productivity while children are small: the cost of keeping the mothers attached to the labor market, according to Rosen, exceeds, by far their economic product. I believe this is a fundamentally flawed analysis because it adopts a purely static cost–benefit calculus, comparing the relative cost of public outlays against the mothers' productivity, here and now. A more convincing analysis would incorporate the dynamic, long-term effects of any subsidy on the same mothers' cumulative career earnings (and, of course, on added tax revenues in the future).

The externalization of care for small children is a controversial issue since mothers' employment may have negative consequences for children's cognitive and motivational stimulus (for an overview, see Waldfogel, 2002). Although the question is far from resolved, the real issue has mainly to do with the quality of childcare institutions. Indeed, there is one clear positive result of universal high quality care, namely that it helps equalize children's cognitive abilities and, thus, secures more equality of educational attainment (Esping-Andersen, forthcoming). If day care helps reduce school failure and raises our human capital stock, there is clearly an added efficiency and welfare gain both to individuals and to society.

Rethinking the Policy Challenge

A comprehensive mother-friendly package of paid leave and affordable day care is, once again, a necessary but, alas, insufficient condition for a new positive equilibrium. It certainly may help substantially in moving the Pareto frontier into rosier territory. But if we truly aim to further women's joint preference for careers and kids in order to advance household and societal welfare, there remain two pending dilemmas. The first has to do with the quality of employment. It is evident that lack of part-time jobs is an important impediment for mothers with small children. Deregulation here is a must. But as I mentioned above, women's career preferences may jeopardize their fertility preferences if they find themselves locked into precariousness. Worse, in those countries where precariousness is widespread, job insecurity is likely to bundle in couples. There is little doubt that the resurgence of Scandinavian fertility is closely associated with an ample stock of protected 'soft economy' jobs, mainly in the public sector.[2] The first dilemma that we therefore need to resolve is how to harmonize labor market deregulation with employment security.

The second dilemma stems from the inherent trade-off that exists between gender equalization of wages, on the one hand, and gender desegregation of jobs, on the other hand. The massive concentration of women in Nordic welfare state jobs is driven both by supply and demand factors. Women self-select themselves into the soft economy so as to better reconcile high fertility with careers. But thanks to wage equality, generous leave schemes and expected fertility behavior, employers in the hard economy will rationally discriminate against women in their employment decisions. Hence, it comes as no suprise that the Nordic countries score very high on international job segregation indicies. The policies needed to jointly maximize fertility and employment will, in other words, easily harden the gender discrimination dilemma. Is there a way out? The answer seems to me quite straightforward: if we have reached a de facto limit to the masculinization of the female life cycle we are left with the only other option, namely to encourage men to embrace a more female life cycle. This would entail that the probability of male career interruptions converges with those of females. On the demand side, this should neutralize employers' gender-assymetric expectations and, accordingly, gender discrim-ination. On the supply side, it should weaken gender-specific self-selection in the labor market.

Can men be made to feminize their biographies? The economist's answer would be that it all depends on incentives. One source of such incentives may, paradoxically, come from rising gender wage equality. If expected cumu-lative life-time earnings begin to converge between men and women, so will the relative cost of interruptions. This may explain why Swedish men have

[2] Although cost-containment measures in the Nordic welfare states are visibly 'hardening' employment conditions in public employment.

gone further than anywhere else in taking up parental leave entitlements. But even strong incentives may clash against obstacles. If it is true that the competitive pressures on exposed firms are rising, it is doubtful whether employment—let alone careers—in the hard economy can be made compatible with a feminized male approach to work and family. Herein lies a great new analytical challenge to the social sciences.

Index

Printed in the United States
By Bookmasters